From Principles of Learning to Strategies for Instruction

Empirically Based Ingredients to
Guide Instructional Development

Robert J. Seidel
Kathy C. Perencevich
Allyson L. Kett
Authors

From Principles of Learning to Strategies for Instruction

Empirically Based Ingredients to
Guide Instructional Development

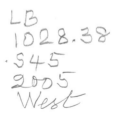
 Springer

Robert J. Seidel
Kathy C. Perencevich
Allyson L. Kett

Library of Congress Cataloging-in-Publication Data

A C.I.P. Catalogue record for this book is available
from the Library of Congress.

ISBN 0-387-23476-4   Printed on acid-free paper.
e-ISBN 0-387-23481-0

Printed in the United States of America.

9 8 7 6 5 4 3 2 1   SPIN 11310532

springeronline.com

DEDICATION

This book is dedicated to my mentor at the University of Pennsylvania, Professor William A. Shaw, Ph.D., who taught me never to accept conventional wisdom as the solution to a vexing problem; but to explore it from a multi-dimensional perspective, and arrive at my own solution --- which may or may not correspond to the conventional, but always will be wise.

RJS

TABLE OF CONTENTS

PREFACE xiii

ACKNOWLEDGEMENTS xvii

INTRODUCTION: OVERVIEW: PRINCIPLES OF LEARNING AND
STRATEGIES FOR INSTRUCTION xix

CHAPTER 1: HEURISTICS AND TAXONOMY............................. 1

   1.   FACTORS INFLUENCING ACQUISITION 2
   2.   FACTORS AFFECTING TRANSFER OF TRAINING...... 4
   3.   DIMENSIONS AFFECTING RETENTION 6
   4.   PRESCRIPTIVE ILLUSTRATION 6
   5.   THE INTERRELATEDNESS OF DOMAINS OF LEARNING......... 8
   6.   A POTENTIAL TAXONOMY 10
   7.   SCHEMA CONSTRUCTION 15

CHAPTER 2: A COGNITIVE DOMAIN EXAMPLE: READING................. 23

   1.   INTRODUCTION 24
      o   *Acquisition* 26
      o   *Automaticity* 26
      o   *Transfer: Near Term* 26
      o   *Transfer: Far Term* 27
   2.   SECTION I: INSTRUCTIONAL GUIDANCE............................ 27
      o   *Acquisition Process* 27
      o   *Exposure to storybook reading* 28
      o   *Practice sound and letter recognition* 29
      o   *Teach word-decoding skills* 29
      o   *Using examples and non-examples to reinforce decoding of words* 30
      o   *Automaticity Process* 31
      o   *Teach word recognition and vocabulary* 31
      o   *Use of context to facilitate word recognition* 32
      o   *Use oral and expressive reading to develop fluency* 33
      o   *Practice with appropriate levels of interesting texts and maximize time spent reading* 33
      o   *Transfer Process: Near Term* 34
      o   *Teach reading comprehension strategies* 34
      o   *Transfer Process: Far Term* 39
      o   *Metacognitive awareness* 40

        o *Comprehension monitoring* 40

        o *Reading with technology: Reducing cognitive load* 41

        o *Foster far term transfer through reading engagement* 43

        o *Concept instruction with text* 44

        o *Time spent in multiple contexts* 45

        o *Classroom environment* 46

  3.   SECTION II: SUPPORTING RESEARCH 47

        o *Research Supporting Acquisition and Automaticity* 47

        o *Transitioning from Automaticity to Transfer: Reading*

           Comprehension 49

        o *Strategic Reading* 51

        o *Near Term Transfer Process* 53

        o *Using prior knowledge* 55

        o *Questioning* 55

        o *Searching for information* 56

        o *Summarizing* 57

        o *Using graphic and semantic organizers* 57

        o *Elaborative interrogation* 58

        o *Far Term Transfer Process* 58

        o *Metaphorical reasoning* 59

        o *Multiple text environments* 60

        o *Reading engagement and motivation* .... .60

        o *Amount and breadth of reading* 63

        o *Reducing cognitive load* 65

        o *Implications of cognitive load theory for instructional*

           design 66

CHAPTER 3: PSYCHOMOTOR DOMAIN 75

  1.   INTRODUCTION 76

  2.   SECTION I: POSSIBLE INSTRUCTIONAL GUIDANCE 78

        o *Acquisition Process* 79

        o *Task and part-task analysis* 70

        o *Observation and mental rehearsal* 80

        o *Automaticity Process* 84

        o *Types of practice* 84

        o *Knowledge of results* 86

        o *Transfer Process: Near Term* 87

        o *Cognitive process model* 89

        o *Transfer Process: Far Term* 91

  3.   SECTION II: SUPPORTING RESEARCH 92

- o   *Psychomotor Learning: Distinction between Skill and Ability*..... 93
- o   *Taxonomies of Motor Skills* 95
- o   *Acquisition Process of Psychomotor Skills*................................. 98
- o   *Psychological factors* 98
- o   *Automaticity Process* 100
- o   *Types of practice*.. 103
- o   *Knowledge of results* 104
- o   *Transfer (Near Term and Far Term) Process*............................ 105
- o   *Transfer and functional context*... 106
- o   *A Conceptual Framework*.. 108

CHAPTER 4: AFFECTIVE DOMAIN... 115

1. INTRODUCTION... 114
2. SECTION I: INSTRUCTIONAL GUIDANCE.. 116
   - o   *Introduction*... 116
   - o   *Guidance Caveats*.. 116
   - o   *Acquisition Process* 117
   - o   *Resources for the parents* 118
   - o   *Establishing the mastery environment in the classroom*............ 119
   - o   *Automaticity Process* 123
   - o   *Reinforcing positive attitudes and habits*................................. 123
   - o   *Transfer Process: Near Term* 125
   - o   *Encouraging development of self-regulatory skills* 125
   - o   *Transfer Process: Far Term* 126
   - o   *Possible Strategies to use across Processes* 128
   - o   *Remediational Guidance* 128
3. SECTION II: SUPPORTING RESEARCH 129
   - o   *Introduction*... 129
   - o   *Acquisition Process* 130
   - o   *Development of trust*.. 130
   - o   *Learning of affect through associations* 131
   - o   *Automaticity Process* 132
   - o   *Near Term Transfer Process* 133
   - o   *Far Term Transfer Process* 133
   - o   *Motivation*... 134
   - o   *Self-regulatory skills*.. 137
   - o   *Help-seeking behaviors* 137
   - o   *An Organizing Framework*.. 139

CHAPTER 5: INTERPERSONAL DOMAIN 151

1. INTRODUCTION 152
2. SECTION I: POSSIBLE INSTRUCTIONAL GUIDANCE 154
    o   *Acquisition Process* 154
    o   *Promoting active and interactive learning* 155
    o   *Learning to care* 156
    o   *Project ACHIEVE* 159
    o   *Automaticity Process* 159
    o   *Transfer Process: Near Term* 161
    o   *Transfer Process: Far Term* 163
    o   *Adult interpersonal skill development* 165
    o   *Masterful coaching* 166
    o   *Coaching sequence at the National Leadership Institute* 167
    o   *Military leadership development* 168
3. SECTION II: SUPPORTING RESEARCH 168
    o   *Acquisition Process* 171
    o   *Automaticity Process* 173
    o   *Near Term Transfer Process* 174
    o   *Far Term Transfer Process* 177
    o   *Adult interpersonal skill development* 178
    o   *Conclusion* 179

CHAPTER 6: SUGGESTIONS FOR THE INTEGRATION OF
TECHNOLOGY 185

1. TECHNOLOGICAL ACCOMPLISHMENTS ....
    188
2. SECTION I: INSTRUCTIONAL GUIDANCE 189
    o   *Acquisition Process* 189
    o   *Automaticity Process* 190
    o   *Near and Far Term Transfer Process* 192
    o   *An Example of Instructional Technology Across
        Phases and   Domains* 194
    o   *Developer Guidance for Technology Integration* 196
3. SECTION II: SUPPORTING RESEARCH 198
4. HUMAN CONCERNS: CULTURE, ORGANIZATION, AND INDIVIDUAL 200
    o   *Learner Motivation* 200

CHAPTER 7: SUMMARY 211

1. COGNITIVE DOMAIN 213

2. PSYCHOMOTOR DOMAIN 213
3. AFFECTIVE DOMAIN 214
4. INTERPERSONAL DOMAIN 215
5. SUGGESTIONS FOR THE INTEGRATION OF TECHNOLOGY ... 216
6. CONCLUSION 217

ABOUT THE AUTHORS 219

INDEX 221

PREFACE

The primary goal of instructional design is improving the quality of learning and instruction. Instructional designers have focused on a number of areas of critical concern and developed a variety of techniques to achieve this goal (Reigeluth, 1983, 1999). Critical areas of concern for those who plan, implement and manage instruction include (a) needs assessment (identifying gaps or deficiencies in knowledge and performance to be addressed in instruction); (b) task analysis (identifying the types of knowledge, skills and attitudes to be developed during instruction); (c) learner analysis (determining who the learners are, what they know, relevant differences, etc.); (d) instructional strategies (developing strategies appropriate for the task and learners involved); and (e) assessment and evaluation (determining how to assess individual progress and evaluate programs). There are many books already in print that treat the general domain of instructional design, as well as texts that target each of these areas of concerns. Why then another book on these issues?

There are several answers to this question. Many of the available books treat instruction as a formal process that proceeds according to specific and detailed instructional systems development models (see, for example, Dick, Carey & Carey, 2005). Indeed, the US military has created a series of handbooks specifying details of the various instructional development processes (see Department of Defense, 1999). While these models are helpful to those new to the world of instructional design and can be used to ensure basic quality control of large-scale instructional development efforts, they do not provide practical instructional development guidance that is grounded in research and theory and derived from the underlying principles of learning and instruction.

Moreover, those books that do focus on very practical instructional development guidance generally do not provide the theoretical foundation and empirical support behind the guidance, which proves useful when designers and developers need to modify or elaborate design heuristics instructional strategies. Likewise, those books and articles that focus on theory and research findings often ignore practical implications for instructional design.

In short, there are not very many books that develop a practical approach to instructional development from a psychological perspective. One exception to this is van Merriënboer's (1997) *Training Complex Cognitive Skills*, which provides a very solid psychology foundation for an instructional design model appropriate for complex domains. While van Merriënboer's *Training Complex Cognitive Skills* provides an excellent model of theoretically and empirically grounded instructional design principles, it is now somewhat dated and it lacks sufficient emphasis on the practical aspects of applying the model and does not carry the breadth of domain coverage of this volume.

The current volume strikes a nice balance between theory and practice and provides a straightforward model of instruction that is easily connected with relevant research but equally easy to apply to instructional development projects. The model is developed in Chapter 1 and is based on a combination of product or outcome characteristics (e.g., types of knowledge to be acquired) and process considerations (e.g., acquisition processes as well as automaticity and transfer concerns). The middle chapters of the volume correspond to the four knowledge domains: cognitive, psychomotor, affective and interpersonal. There is a chapter dedicated to the integration of technology and a final chapter that summarizes the main points developed along the way.

The initial discussion of descriptive principles derived from learning theory and cognitive science research intertwined with prescriptive instructional strategies resonates with well-established instructional design thinking (Reigeluth, 1983). The organization framework around traditional types of knowledge provides familiar categories to help readers orient their thinking (Dick, Carey, & Carey, 2005). The detailed treatment of the interpersonal domain and the emphasis on technology integration clearly distinguish the book as a modern treatment of instructional development that goes well beyond traditional instructional system development models.

The pervasive insistence in this volume on connecting practice with theory establishes a standard of evidence-based practice that makes this book well worth reading. Indeed, in order for instructional design to continue to progress and contribute to the improvement of learning and instruction, such evidence-based practice will be critical. Providing guidelines for instructional development that are not grounded in theory and empirical research does not help individual designers and developers develop an understanding for when and why different instructional strategies are appropriate or how they might be modified to be more effective. Likewise, simply publishing empirical research on learning outcomes to be read and discussed among educational researchers and academics will not contribute much to improved practice. Therefore, this volume should provide a well-grounded and useful tool for instructional developers.

When Robert M. Gagné was asked why he became an instructional researcher, he answered without hesitation that it was to improve learning (see the *Tribute to Gagné* DVD available from the Association for Educational Communications and Technology – http://www.aect.org). Instructional designers are in the business of helping to improve learning. This book will help them accomplish this important goal.

Professor J. Michael Spector [1]
Learning Systems Institute, Associate Director
C4600 University Center
Florida State University
Tallahassee, FL 32306

ENDNOTES

[1] Dr. Spector's recent research is in the areas of intelligent performance support for instructional design and in system dynamics based learning environments. He helped found and is the President of the International Consortium for Courseware Engineering (ICCE). He also serves on the International Board of Standards for Training, Performance and Instruction (IBSTPI). Dr. Spector's core area of competencies include the following: Automated Instructional Design Systems, Courseware Engineering, Evaluation of Instructional Design and Development Systems, Instructional Systems Design and Development, Intelligent Performance Support Systems, Multimedia and Web-Based Design and Development, Open and Distance Learning and Implications for Universities, System Dynamics Applications in Education and Training.

REFERENCES

Anderson, J. R. (1981). A theory of language acquisition based on general learning principles. In *Proceedings of IJCAI-81*, 165-170.

Department of Defense (1999). *Department of defense handbook: Instructional systems development/Systems approach to training and education.* MIL-HDBK-29612. Washington, DC: Department of Defense. Available online at http://www.au.af.mil/au/awc/awcgate/edref/hbk2.pdf

Dick, W., Carey, L., & Carey, J. O. (2005). *The systematic design of instruction (5th ed.).* New York: Allyn & Bacon.

Reigeluth, C. M. (1983). Meaningfulness and instruction: Relating what is being learned to what a student knows. *Instructional Science, 12*(3), 197-218.

Reigeluth, C. M. (Ed.). (1999). *Instructional-design theories and models, Volume II: A new paradigm of instructional theory*, Mahwah, NJ: Lawrence Erlbaum Associates, Publishers.

Van Merriëboer, J. J. G. (1997). Training complex cognitive skills: A four-component instructional design model for technical training. Hillsdale, NJ: Educational Technology Publications.

ACKNOWLEDGMENTS

Even such a modest volume as this one cannot succeed without the help of family, colleagues, and friends. We wish to express our appreciation to a number of people, who have provided motivational support, insightful help, comments, and reviews of our chapters in various stages of development. First of all, we are grateful to the U.S. Army Research Institute for providing us access to resources, and in particular, the encouragement provided by the Directors of ARI, Drs. Edgar Johnson and Zita Simutis. Next, we want to express our appreciation to Dr. Robert Ruskin, Director of the Consortium Research Fellows Program of the Consortium of Universities of the Washington Metropolitan Area, for the vision in seeing the value accruing to the Consortium's graduate fellows for participating in this effort.

A number of colleagues and friends from academia, industry, and government gave freely of their time for review and provided a broad perspective on topics of learning and instruction. They made many helpful suggestions regarding the various chapters and without the benefit of their insights, the volume would not have achieved completion. An initial thanks is owed to Dr. Marshall Farr for engaging the senior author in long, productive, and often pun-filled discussions on the concept of transfer. Certainly, his influence is felt in our four-stage model. Drs. Dexter Fletcher, Jack Hiller, Harold Wagner, and Capt. Paul Chatelier (USN, Ret.) provided initial reactions to, and encouragement for, the concept. Dr. Harry O'Neill, Professor of Learning and Instruction at the University of Southern California, added to that and provided perceptive reviews of some early drafts. Dr. Ok-Choon Park, U.S. Department of Education, contributed his unique perspective to the evolution of our taxonomy, and later helped by reviewing Chapter 6, Suggestions for the Integration of Technology. Dr. Rich Rosenfield, a practicing clinical psychologist, was particularly helpful in the revision of Chapter 4, the Affective Domain. Dr. Michelle Sams was influential in the revision of Chapter 3, the Psychomotor Domain. Tony Carrell, M.A., gave useful commentary from the perspective of a coach and potential implementer (K-12) of the suggestions in Chapter 3. Mrs. Tara K. Carrell, M.A., as a potential K-6 instructional developer, made very useful suggestions for the revision of Chapter 5, the Interpersonal Domain.

A particular, heartfelt thanks and gratitude is owed to Dr. Greg Kearsley, visiting Professor of the College of Engineering at the University of Wisconsin, Madison and adjunct professor in UMUC Graduate School of Management and Technology, University of Maryland. His specialty these days is distance education. Greg read and reviewed virtually the entire book and made many discerning suggestions for improvements.

Finally, a never-ending appreciation is extended to our significant others for their patience, cooperation, and unbelievable support throughout the process of creating this book: Sylvia Seidel and Stephen Perencevich.

RJS, KCP, & AK

INTRODUCTION

OVERVIEW: FROM PRINCIPLES OF LEARNING TO STRATEGIES FOR INSTRUCTION

The purpose of this book is to help educators and training developers to improve the quality of their courseware. We hope to do this by providing a useful approach for suggested instructional prescriptions that will be firmly based upon empirically derived, descriptive psychological principles of learning. This book has extended rather than replaced earlier behavioral models while building on the contributions of many scientists. Our view is that education and training provide prescriptive rules, whether intuitive or explicit, by which their instruction to students is ordered. There have been many attempts at organizing these prescriptions (e.g., Merrill, M. D., 1973, 1999; Merrill, P., 1971; Reigeluth, 1983, 1999). Montague's attempt (1987) entitled *What Works* has been the one with most empirical bases. However, all have been taken from the instructional literature with at most an intuitive allusion to the psychological literature on learning and cognitive development. A welcomed exception to this has been the recent work of Sweller and his associates (1989, 1998). Their research efforts have attempted an empirical approach to instructional design organized from their particular, theoretical position, two-component, and cognitive overload theory. Our approach is intended to draw from a broad coverage of the psychological literature, and not from a particular learning or cognitive theory.

PRESCRIPTIVE STRATEGIES

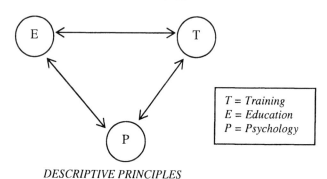

DESCRIPTIVE PRINCIPLES

Figure 1. Relationships among disciplines.

In general, the approach can be described in the figure shown above. As noted, prescriptive strategies exist in training (T) and in education (E); and both the methods and content of these prescriptions can be shared, thus the bi-directional relationship indicated by the arrows. What needs to be made explicit is the relationship that both of these prescriptions share with the descriptive laws and principles of psychology (P). Note also the bi-directional relationship established between training and psychology, and education and psychology.

The figure is intended to indicate that the descriptive laws of psychology provide the basis for how cognitive development, learning, meta-cognition, and other psychological organizing principles can provide the basis for prescriptions of instructional strategies. Both training and education can inform new psychological research possibilities based upon evidence from their applications. Ideally, there should be an ongoing cybernetic relationship amongst all three disciplines.

Too often, one or the other of these disciplines has proceeded as if the others did not exist and could not provide any fruitful advice. For example, in recent years such terms as "situated learning" and "authentic learning," among others, have been held as new constructs for education. Yet both terms have roots earlier in the training literature and in the psychology of learning literature. In the training research back in 1957 to early 1960's, Shoemaker and other researchers at HumRRO (1967; Shoemaker et al., 1958) discovered and published the principle of "functional context." This research resulted in the Army's adopting new methods for training. It included introducing training material only in the context of the tasks to be performed ultimately on the job. This meant, for example, introducing nomenclature for weapons' parts or other system components only in the context of, and at the appropriate time (i.e. during the training of how to operate those weapons) as the course of instruction proceeds from simple to complex. There's no doubt that this research and principle has led to the Army's current motto "train as you fight." Yet both training and education have ignored the fact that the antecedents for both of these relativistic principles were rooted in the perceptual research of Brunswik (1944).

Brunswik (1944), while studying the horizontal-vertical illusion ["an overestimation of the upright as contrasted to the horizontal" (p. 17)] in the laboratory, decided to investigate its universality by examining its efficacy in the natural environment. His findings showed reversal of the effect outside the laboratory. From the results of this study and others, which he conducted, Brunswick coined the term "ecological validity." This concept has shown to be extremely important in Ericsson's work on the study of expert performance in representative verses contrived tasks (e.g., Ericsson, Patel, & Kintsch, 2000). Clearly, more than two generations ago, he showed the value of contextual relevance for both perception and learning. Do Brunswik's ecological findings mean, however, that the entire foundation of psychological principles must be reduced to relativism? We think not. Despite Bruner's (1990) assertions in his book *Acts of Meaning* to the contrary, relativistic applications of psychological principles can be seen as instantiations of, and not the denial of, generic principles. For example, the important principle of contiguity for association of events is not denied by the fact that in society where values play a strong role, certain content can be more readily associated than others. This could simply argue for the inclusion of "motivational intensity" as an additional factor in learning.

Similarly, the antecedents for "cognition" and "cognitive development" can be found in the learning research of E. C. Tolman (1932, 1948, 1951) and others (e.g., Shaw & Seidel, 1969). While this research was formally conducted with rats, the results clearly showed that both spatial and relational cognitions can be developed in these organisms and cannot be explained by simple behaviorism. Rather, they require some type of informational analysis in order to fully explain the data. Historically, these antecedents are rarely acknowledged; however, they foreshadowed the shifts in focus from stimulus-response (SR) units to cognitive units. Yet the units of focus; i.e., the structural units invoked to explain human understanding, appeared to be the major theoretical shift in psychology from pre-1960 to the present (Wasserman & Miller, 1997). The switch to information processing was heralded by Hebb's 1960 American Psychological Association (APA) address and was followed by the Miller, Galanter, and Pribram's invention (1960) of the test-operate-test-exit (TOTE) construct. Thereafter, the evolution continued with renewed interest in operationally defining schemas, initially conceived by Bartlett (1932), (e.g., Rumelhart & Norman, 1988) and with continual attempts to define cognition and cognitive development as replacements for stimulus-response learning and behaviorism. The process continues to the current day. Mayer (1999), for example, focuses on cognitive development through *constructivist learning*. According to Mayer, "constructivist learning is active learning in which the learner possesses and uses a variety of cognitive processes during the learning process" (1999, p. 146).[1]

To parse these proposed cognitive processes, the method of cognitive task analysis has been devised. It has its roots in traditional, behavioral task analysis started in the 1920's. The traditional task analysis typically overlooks cognitive processes involved in learning, whereas the cognitive task analysis explicitly includes them. A frequently used method for analyzing tasks in the learner's cognitive structure is called GOMS – involving goal setting, a set of operators, methods of achieving the goals, and a set of selection rules for choosing among competing achievement methods for goals (Park & Seidel, 1987; see also Ericcson & Smith, 1991).

To avoid confusion between fact and interpretation of fact, the need exists to examine separately the facts and principles of acquisition, retention, transfer, and use on the one hand, from the proposed theoretical structural makeup of cognition, understanding, schemata, etc. on the other. A theory, which fits a particularly unique category as a bridge between learning, memory, and instruction, is Sweller's (1989) two component theory of cognition (see also Sweller et al., 1998). He and his associates propose encouraging schema development and automaticity of schemata as well as lowering cognitive overload as central factors to influence the design of instruction.

While many different theories have evolved to explain instructional strategies, none has been able to take full advantage of all the principles of the psychology of learning, which are based upon sound experimental evidence. Learning theorists in psychology have been at fault, at least to some degree, for pursuing a particular pet theory and attempting to extend its application beyond the experimental paradigm in which the theory was created. In so doing they have created a confusing field from which educators and trainers have had difficulty drawing consistent rules for developing useful instructional strategies. The authors come from a more expanded background as training and education researchers in one of the nation's historically largest applied training R&D Organizations. Therefore, we have expanded the perspective of the psychology of learning into the practical areas of course development and evaluation for education and training. We feel that this background is extremely beneficial in our attempt to synthesize the descriptive principles of learning in a recipe format useful for the practitioner and developer. It is therefore the goal of the authors to organize this volume so that, irrespective of the particular theory, the descriptive principles established from literature on the psychology of learning can provide recipes for unique instructional strategies appropriate for different classes of tasks. We recognize that these are not really prescriptive recipes; therefore, what we are really talking about is guidance for the instructional chef. We will cite relevant theories and the supporting research as pertinent for heuristics to generate instructional strategies as appropriate to their respective instructional tasks. At a theoretical level, there is a problem of isolation between the various theories and research paradigms. Each theory and paradigm uses different constructs and terminology and hence it is hard to identify commonalities.

A meta-theoretic framework is needed that makes it possible to see the overlap among theories and research paradigms as well as their unique contributions. In order to make the job an easier one for the reader, we categorize the theories based upon whether they represent learning theories per se, a bridge between learning and instructional theory, a bridge between learning theory and memory, or a technology-based extension of earlier learning theories, such as those which have emanated from computer science. In the learning theory and category for example, we place such theorists as E. C. Tolman (1932, 1948), Clark Hull (1943) and the connectionism of Edward Thorndike (1931). We also place in this category those theories that deal with problem solving and thinking, such as E. de Bono's (1969) theory of lateral thinking and Csikszentmilhayi's (Csikszentmilhayi & Csikszentmilhayi, 1988; Csikszentmilhayi, Rathunde, & Whalen, 1993) theories concerning problem finding as well as problem solving. In the bridging category between learning theory and instructional theory we would include John Anderson's Act theory (1981, 1982), Bruner's constructivist theory (1990), Gagne's conditions of learning theory (1977), Bandura's social learning theory (1977, 1986), Csikszentmilhayi's theory (1988) of emergent motivation, Sweller's two-component theory (1989), and Vygotsky 's theory about the development of higher psychological processes (1978). As theories bridging the gap between learning and memory we would cite mathematical learning theory (e.g., Atkinson, 1964) and information-processing theory (Miller, 1956).

As prominent examples of the last group of theories we would include the general problem solver (GPS) theory of Newell and Simon (1972), repair theory of Van Lehn (1996), script theory of Schank (1977), and artificial intelligence problem solver (SOAR) of Newell and his associates (Rosenbloom, Laird, & Newell, 1993). GPS and SOAR have more of a descriptive focus, whereas repair theory and script theory take on a prescriptive focus. The tri-archic theory of Sternberg (1988) is unique in that it represents a bridge among learning theory, memory, and instructional theory. It therefore represents both a descriptive and a prescriptive focus. Piaget's theory (1957) will be discussed strictly in terms of the relevance to Bruner's theoretical components, active, iconic, and symbolic (1990).

Theories that are included meet the criterion of relevance to some aspect of adult learning and instruction. Theories that focus on animal learning and learning disabilities are not included. Discussions of theories, including neurological research and activity system perspectives that may be of interest to academicians are not included because they are outside the scope and purpose of this volume. In cases where there are a number of researchers associated with a particular theoretical framework, the version associated with the originator or most prominent researcher is presented.

To help the reader in a practical way see the relationships between learning principles, task domains, and instructional strategies, we have arranged each of the chapters by classes of learning tasks from simple to complex. We have developed a four-stage model to organize this complexity. Moreover, the chapters are ordered according to knowledge domains: Cognitive, Psychomotor, Affective, and Interpersonal. The four chosen domains are particularly well-suited for practitioners and we provide elaborative examples that cover many instructional design situations commonly encountered. We have also included a chapter on the Integration of Technology to illustrate how the principles can be implemented with, and extended by, the use of computers in a real world context. While we present each domain in its own chapter, we do this as a convenient heuristic device; and do not intend that the reader see them as totally independent entities. In fact, we develop instances and frameworks, which show how they probably interact. The "recipes" (i.e. guidance) are provided within each chapter as recommended instructional strategies. They are given in the context of specific examples to help the learner and the instructor or training developer to maximize the benefits from the instructional process (whether for reading skill development or for psychomotor skill development like physical education).

The format within each chapter will present first a listing of the most relevant Descriptive Principles (from the psychological literature). Next, we follow with an Introduction, a discussion of the general instructional class of tasks for the domain in question; then, Section I, Recommended Instructional Strategies for the targeted, specific task (the guidance); and finally, Section II, the Supporting Research and the relevant theories.

ENDNOTES

[1] It should be noted that an interpretation of active and interactive relationships between the learner and the environment as the basis for learning was initially put forth by Dewey at the turn of the 20th century (1910; Dewey & Bentley, 1949).

REFERENCES

Anderson, J. R. (1981). A theory of language acquisition based on general learning principles. *Proceedings of IJCAI-81*, 165-170.
Anderson, J. R. (1982). Acquisition of cognitive skill. *Psychological Review, 89*(4), 369-406.
Atkinson, R. C. (1964). *Studies in mathematical learning theory.* Stanford, CA: Stanford University Press.
Bandura, A. (1977). *Social learning theory.* Oxford, England: Prentice-Hall.
Bandura, A. (1986). *Social foundations of thought and action: A social cognitive theory.* Englewood Cliffs, NJ: Prentice Hall.
Bartlett, F. C. (1932). *Remembering.* New York: Cambridge University Press.
Bruner, J. (1990). *Acts of Meaning.* Cambridge, MA: Harvard University Press.
Brunswik, E. (1944). Distal focusing of perception: Size-constancy in a representative sample of situations. *Psychological Monographs, 56*(1), 1-49.
Csikszentmilhayi, M. & Csikszentmilhayi., I. S. (1988). *Optimal experience.* New York: Cambridge University Press.
Csikszentmihalyi, M., Rathunde, K., & Whalen, S. (1993). *Talented teenagers.* New York: Cambridge University Press.
de Bono, E. (1969). *The mechanism of mind.* New York: Penguin Books, Inc.
Dewey, J. (1910). *How we think.* Boston: D.C. Heath.
Dewey, J. & Bentley, A. F. (1949). *Knowing and the known.* Boston: Beacon Press.
Ericsson, K. A., Patel, V., & Kintsch, W. (2000). How experts' adaptations to representative task demands account for the expertise effect in memory recall: Comment on Vicente and Wang. *Psychological Review, 107*(3), 578-592.
Ericsson, K. A. & Smith, J. (1991). Prospects and limits of the empirical study of expertise: An introduction. In K. A. Ericcson & J. Smith (Eds.), *Toward a general theory of expertise prospects and limits* (pp. 12-25). Cambridge: Cambridge University Press.
Gagne, R. M. (1977). *The conditions of learning.* New York: Holt, Rinehart, & Winston.
Hebb, D. O. (1960). The American revolution. *American Psychologist, 15*, 735-745.
Hull, C. L. (1943). *Principles of behavior.* New York: Appleton-Century-Crofts.
Mayer, R. H. (1999). Designing instruction for constructivist learning. In C. M. Reigeluth (Ed.), *Instructional-design theories and models, Volume II: A new paradigm of instructional theory* (pp. 141-159). Mahwah, NJ: Lawrence Erlbaum Associates, Publishers.
Merrill, M. D. (1973). Content and instructional analysis for cognitive transfer tasks. *AV Communication Review, 21*(1), 109-125.
Merrill, M. D. (1999). Instructional transaction theory (ITT): Instructional design based on knowledge based on knowledge objects. In C. M. Reigeluth (Ed.), *Instructional-design theories and models, Volume II: A new paradigm of instructional theory* (pp. 397-424). Mahwah, NJ: Lawrence Erlbaum Associates, Publishers.
Merrill, P. F. (1971, April 15). Task analysis – An information processing approach. Tech. Memo No. 27, Florida State University, Tallahassee, Florida.
Miller, G. A. (1956). The magical number seven, plus or minus two: Some limits on our capacity for processing information. *Psychological Review, 53*, 81-97.
Miller, G., Galanter, E., & Pribram, K. (1960). *Plans and structure of behavior.* New York: Holt.
Montague, W. (1987). *What works: Research findings about navy instruction and learning.* Washington, D.C.: Direction of Chief of Naval Education & Training.
Newell, A. & Simon, H. A. (1972). *Human problem solving.* Englewood Cliffs, NJ: Prentice-Hall, Inc.

Park, O. & Seidel, R. J. (1987). Instructional design principles and AI techniques for development of ICAI. *Computers in Human Behavior, 3*, 273-287.

Piaget, J. (1957). *Logic and psychology.* New York: Basic Books.

Reigeluth, C. M. (1983). Meaningfulness and instruction: Relating what is being learned to what a student knows. *Instructional Science, 12*(3), 197-218.

Reigeluth, C. M. (Ed.). (1999). *Instructional-design theories and models, Volume II: A new paradigm of instructional theory.* Mahwah, NJ: Lawrence Erlbaum Associates, Publishers.

Rosenbloom, P. S., Laird, J. E., & Newell, A. (Eds.). (1993). *The SOAR papers: Research on integrated intelligence, Vols. 1 & 2.* Boston, MA: MIT Press.

Rumelhart, D. E. & Norman, D. A. (1988). Representation in memory. In R. C. Atkinson, R. J. Herrnstein, G. Lindzey, & R. D. Luce (Eds.), *Stevens' handbook of experimental psychology (2nd Ed.), Volume 2: Learning and cognition* (pp. 511-587). New York: Wiley.

Schank, R. C. (1977). *Scripts, plans, goals, and understanding: An inquiry into human knowledge structures.* Hillsdale, NJ: Erlbaum Associates

Shaw, W. A. & Seidel, R. J. (1969). Informational context as a determinant of what can be learned. *Acta Psychologica, 31*(3), 232-260.

Shoemaker, H. A. (1967). The functional context method of instruction. HumRRO Professional Paper, 35-67.

Shoemaker, H. A., Brown, G, H., & Whittemore, J. M. (1958). Activities of field repair personnel with implications for training. HumRRO Technical Report, 48.

Sternberg, R. J. (1988). A triarchic view of intelligence in cross-cultural perspective. In: S. H. Irvine & J. W. Berry (Eds.), *Human abilities in cultural context* (pp. 60-85). New York: Cambridge University Press.

Sweller, J. (1989). Cognitive technology: Some procedures for facilitating learning and problem solving in mathematics and science. *Journal of Educational Psychology, 81*(4), 457-466.

Sweller, J., van Merrienboer, J. J. G., & Paas, F. G. W. C. (1998). Cognitive architecture and instructional design. *Educational Psychology Review, 10*(3), 251-296.

Thorndike, E. L. (1931). *Human learning.* New York: Century.

Tolman, E. C. (1932). *Purposive behavior in animals and men.* New York: Appleton-Century-Crofts.

Tolman, E. C. (1948). Cognitive maps in rats and men. *Psychological Review, 55,*189-208.

Tolman, E. C. (1951). *Collected papers in psychology.* Berkeley: University of California Press.

Van Lehn, K. (1996). Cognitive skill acquisition. *Annual Review of Psychology, 47,* 513-539.

Vygotsky, L. S. (1978). *Mind in society: The development of higher psychological processes* (M. Cole, V. John-Steiner, S. Scribner, & E. Souberman, Eds.). Cambridge, MA: Harvard University Press.

Wasserman, E. A. & Miller, R. R. (1997). What's elementary about associative learning? *Annual Review of Psychology, 45,* 573-607.

CHAPTER 1

HEURISTICS AND TAXONOMY

As indicated in the Introduction, in order to make sure that this is a practically useful book the authors wish to use the metaphor of preparing guidance for the instructional user.

As training or educational developers, we should start out with asking ourselves some questions: (a) what are the dishes we are trying to make? and (b) how big or ambitious a feast are we attempting to prepare? Translation: Can we identify what we expect the student to be able to do after he or she has digested my meal? We need to be specific. For example: is our goal to help the student acquire the ability to "appreciate a good piece of literature?" What does that mean in terms of measurement? How will we know that the student will be able to do this? How do we define the words operationally: appreciate, good, piece, and literature? The way in which we as developers answer these questions determine the content (and possibly the approach).

Similarly, if the goal is to help the student to acquire the ability to "change a flat tire," we should parse the goal words in the same way. We should specify what our expectations are for the student following the instruction. How we answer the detailed questions will determine the content of our course. We, therefore, need to be quite explicit about operationally defining our purpose and how we will measure achievement. This should translate into performance, however broad or specific, however near-term or far.

But the above represents only part of the ingredients for our meal. Now we must mix the content in such a way that we don't ask too much of the student at any given time. We need also to arrange the content ingredients in such a way that we can prevent distorting the meal. For these items, let's call them kitchen tools, we should turn to the factors affecting knowledge and skill acquisition (learning) as well as those affecting forgetting and transfer. For answers to the questions of specific goal setting and operationalizing our definitions, we can turn to the field of measurement. For sources to help us answer the latter questions, we can turn to the literature on the principles of learning from the field of psychology.

Let's start with the latter principles first. Over the years, definitions of learning have evolved from "a relatively permanent change in a behavioral tendency...[based on]...reinforced practice" (Kimble & Garmezy, 1963, p. 262) to "...the processing of information on a short time scale [by individuals during a lifetime, as opposed to species over centuries] defines the field of learning and cognitive psychology" (Estes, 1975, p. 1), and lately to "...learning as knowledge construction is based on the idea that ...a learner actively constructs a knowledge representation in working memory" (Mayer, 1999, p. 144). Incidentally, the latter is best described perhaps as an elaboration of an earlier view espoused by Dewey at the turn of the 20th century (1910, 1949). The authors maintain that regardless of the particular theory certain factors affecting acquisition have been found to be immutable as kitchen utensils.

Therefore, it is suggested that we consider an organization based upon the dimensions, which affect: (1) Acquisition of skill or learning, (2) Transfer of training, and (3) Retention (forgetting and extinction).

In that regard consider the following outline:

1. FACTORS INFLUENCING ACQUISITION

❑ **Contiguity of events** -- The general principle would seem to be that two events would best be associated with each other when they occurred in close proximity with one another temporally and spatially. To generalize to the cognitive level, it would seem that which event should occur first is really not as much of an issue as the new event should occur in the context temporally and spatially of the already existing knowledge.

❑ **Reinforcement** -- In the most generic sense, anything that occurs as a consequence of the desired response or achievement and strengthens its occurrence is called a reinforcer; or, in the opposite sense, anything that will weaken the occurrence of an undesirable response; e.g., good grades, praise, or on the other hand, some form of punishment like losing time off work or being given detention in school. Unfortunately, the use of punishment does not eliminate a behavior it merely suppresses it (see for example Skinner, 1953)

❑ **Knowledge of Results --** The more useful topic to consider is knowledge of results or informational feedback. Providing learner knowledge of the consequences of his or her actions results in the learner is establishing expectations. With information, the learner is able to correct errors and adapt to the requirements of the situation. Providing such feedback intermittently has been shown to be more valuable for learning than providing the information on every trial in a problem-solving environment (Druckman & Bjork, 1991; Seidel and Hunter, 1970).

❑ **Repetition** -- Other things being equal, the more frequently events occur together the greater is the probability that they will be associated. Also, with a problem-solving task, the greater the number of repetitions of trials, the more likely the student will be able to be successful. This should be accompanied by informational feedback, or what is sometimes called: knowledge of results.

- Distributed verses massed -- If a task is to be learned, it will be more readily accomplished by spreading the repetitions over time rather than trying to have the student accomplish it all at once. So if a given task is known to require ten hours to reach mastery, it will be learned better with the learning sessions spread out -- one hour per day over ten days -- rather than given all at once.
- Spaced review and practice -- This holds for spacing of reviews over time as well.

❑ **Amount of material**
- Chunking -- Independent of particular meaning of material group no more than five items or elements at a time to be learned; this is different from clustering. Clustering refers to presenting material together with similar meaning in order to aid long-term memory.

❑ **Amount of rehearsal** (includes reminiscence effect) -- Sometimes called time on task to be learned is clearest predictor of level of learning. The more time the learner spends practicing or rehearsing what is to be learned, then the more likely that individual will learn the target task. This factor is subject to diminishing returns, such that even though it takes two hours to learn ¾ of the task, it may take another two hours to reach mastery.
- Semantic material results in positive value (elaborated).
- Non-semantic material results in negative effect (maintenance).

❑ **Meaningfulness of units**
- Organization – A systematic ordering of materials; simple to complex, concrete to abstract, cueing with advanced organizers.
- Chunking vs. clustering -- As noted, clustering involves grouping by similarities of meaning to help long term memory; chunking covers the limits of capacity for holding items in working memory—more than five requires forming chunks or groups or else memory loss of some items occurs.
- Context effects -- Meaningfulness should involve the relationship between prior experiences of the learner, intrinsic links within the material to be learned, and the application to which the material is to be put. The latter has been variously called functional value (Dewey, 1910; Dewey & Bentley, 1949); functional context (Shoemaker, 1967); and most recently, authentic learning, by educational researchers (For an excellent discussion of the latter, see Chapter 6, pp. 93-113, in Meichenbaum & Biemiller, 1998.). Therefore, to be most effective and efficient, learning and instruction should be interactive, have real-world context, and accommodate to the individual learner uniqueness. Transfer is facilitated within a conceptual domain given a broad representation of positive and non-

examples.

- Prior knowledge/prerequisite skills -- On the learner side, this refers to the fact that prior experiences of the learner contribute unique associational networks of words, acts, and environments, which also influence the speed and quality of learning a target task. On the curriculum side, this refers to what skills the learner needs to possess prior to attempting to learn a target task in order to be successful at it. Whether the prior knowledge facilitates or hinders learning depends on the relationship between that knowledge and the domain task to be learned (Dochy, Segers, & Buehl, 1999).

When applying this factor to an entire course of instruction, the instructor should conduct the assessment continually with the introduction of each new task.

❑ **Part-task learning** -- Other things being equal, breaking up a large, complex task into smaller, more manageable units will aid learning (or processing information, or constructing meaning).

2. FACTORS AFFECTING TRANSFER OF TRAINING

❑ **Input** – Similarity of elements resulting in positive transfer effect from the old task to the new. The fundamental need is to identify those elements of the input (physical stimuli, cognitive abstractions, procedures, contexts, etc.) critical for positive transfer to take place (Druckman & Bjork, 1994).

❑ **Output** -- Similarity resulting in negative transfer effect. To accomplish positive transfer of abstract principles or strategies, multiple examples will facilitate transfer within a domain (near-term transfer); and multiple domain-contexts will aid transfer across domains (far term). A corollary to this principle is that the subject matter domain(s) should be made relevant to the experience base of the learner. Therefore, if the task is to instruct children for transfer, the material needs to be at a concrete level; e. g., ask them to distinguish animate from inanimate objects such as frogs vs. rocks, but not amoebas vs. airplanes (Wellman & Gelman, 1992). Another way of describing this is as follows:

- **Schema Formation:** To quote Rumelhart and Norman (1988, p. 537), "roughly, schemata are like models of the outside world. To process information with the use of a schema is to determine which model best fits the incoming information." Whatever the details of how our cognitive models are represented in memory, (and there are many different structures proposed; again see Rumelhart & Norman, 1988 for descriptions of alternative memory structures) they do provide for economy in processing, storage, and interpretation of information. Any procedure, which forces or encourages the abstraction of a principle or rule beyond the immediate concrete, context example aids in the development of schemas. Such a procedure enhances what we call when as noted above the examples are part of the domain of Near-term Transfer, focus.

Schemas operate at a meta-level either within a domain or can help across domains. Within a domain, their formation is helped by providing multiple examples and contexts, expanding the domain knowledge base for abstracting a principle (Seidel & Hunter, 1970). They are also helped, as Sweller and his associates note, by automaticity, with the resulting reduction of cognitive load (Sweller, 1989; Sweller et al., 1998).

Formation of schemas across the domains is also possible; and these principles operate at a higher order, meta-level, which we will call the meta-domain level. One example of this is the heuristic, meta-cognition, studied extensively by people like Tobias and Everson (2000). Other examples of meta-domain heuristics or principles would be any theories of learning, which may be offered as explanations for all kinds of learning. The four-stage model of learning, which we offer to the reader in Chapter 1, is such a meta-domain schema. Sweller's two component theory (1989) is another example. Some might call these context-free generalizations. The fact that we attempt to apply reading principles to help us learn various subject matters (or domains) means that reading principles are themselves examples of meta-domain schemas, or what we wish to label, Far Term Transfer. This is not to deny that learning and transfer are indeed situated in contexts (e.g., Lave & Wenger, 1991). We recognize as Lave and Wenger assert, that the focus of learning needs to encompass "...learning as participation in the social world..." (p. 43). However, we would assert that with sufficient attention given to variety of contexts, social included, and examples, meta-domain (if not context free, broadly context independent) cognitions, such as self-monitoring and symbol system abstractions like reading, Far Term Transfer can develop. Finally, cognitive flexibility theory (Spiro et al., 1995) emphasizes, in order to achieve advanced learning objectives, shifting an approach from simply "...the retrieval from memory of intact, pre-existing knowledge to an alternative constructivist stance that stresses the flexible reassembling of pre-existing knowledge to adaptively fit the needs of a new situation" (p. 87). This approach seems perfectly consistent with our position regarding the development of both Near-term as well as Far Term Transfer. As Spiro notes, "...we are concerned only with learning objectives important to advanced (post introductory) knowledge acquisition: to attain an understanding of important elements of conceptual complexity, to be able to use acquired concepts for reasoning and inference, and to be able to flexibly apply conceptual knowledge to novel situations" (Spiro et al.,

1995, p. 87). From our point of view, this is perfectly consistent with our focus on instructing for transfer from the beginning of a curriculum. Indeed, Far Term Transfer is maximized by helping the learner to develop a "flexible rule schema" by using a variety of examples (cases) and contexts during even the initial acquisition phase of learning. We illustrate this below in Table 1.1 and Figure 2.

3. DIMENSIONS AFFECTING RETENTION (FORGETTING/EXTINCTION)

❑ **Proactive interference** -- The detrimental effects on the recall of a set of associations is based on the learning of a prior set of similar associations. This effect gets stronger and retention gets poorer as the amount of prior materials increases and as time increases between original learning and testing for recall (Robinson, 1976).

❑ **Retroactive interference** -- Retention for material learned first gets poorer as the strength of learning a second set of similar materials increases prior to testing for recall of the first materials.

❑ **Withdrawal of reinforcement** -- The occurrence of the first event without the reinforcing event, which followed it during the acquisition of the association will decrease the expectation or association between the two events.

NOTE: If extinction is viewed as a form of further learning, it would explain why inconsistent reinforcement during acquisition generally yields greater resistance to extinction than consistent reinforcement during training. That is, inconsistency was the expectation built up during acquisition.

4. PRESCRIPTIVE ILLUSTRATION

A useful resource for showing the applications of these factors has been provided by Reigeluth's recent volume on instructional design (Reigeluth, 1999). In this edited volume, Reigeluth presents perspectives from some 24 varied instructional design theorists. For the most part the presentations are concerned with cognitive development. One very important exception, Romiszowski's views (1999) on psychomotor learning, will be dealt with later when we discuss a useful taxonomy for types of learning or skill acquisition. The presentations of the authors are made somewhat easier for the reader by the unique device of summarizing their chapters in the form of forewords at the beginning of each of the chapters.

The value of Reigeluth's tone for our handbook (1999) is that it assembles in a single volume the differing points of view of many leading instructional design theorists. The limitations of the book are that the views present a group of apparently unique perspectives within an academic tenor, which could be very confusing for a potential developer/practical user. We think it would be valuable to organize instructional perspectives by the kinds of underlying learning heuristics (call them micro-variables), which seem to be emphasized uniquely by each of the theorists. So for example, if we were to consider the heuristic of providing multiple contexts to aid conceptual learning, we note that in the chapter by Gardner (1999) and in the chapter by Perkins and Unger (1999) the authors clearly have this heuristic as a significant feature to their instructional design theory. Thus, they advocate connecting a few significant topics to powerful themes, diverse themes central to the domain. In fact, based upon adopting Gardner's approach to multiple intelligences, they advocate multiple approaches to take advantage of these.

Almost all of the theories note the value of knowledge of results or reinforcement for acquisition; however, this is most readily noted with Perkins and Unger (1999) in the form of the need for feedback and revisions, and in Schank et al.'s (1999) approach, where they emphasize situated feedback given as a consequence to an action, and time for student use. This is also specifically emphasized by Schwartz et al. (1999) in noting the value of feedback for checking understanding, providing motivation and in collaborative activities with other students.

If we consider the value of advanced organizers, we note that this is highlighted by Mayer (1999a), Perkins and Unger (1999), Schank et al. (1999), and Schwartz et al. (1999). Mayer, for example, interprets the value of advanced organizers in the structure of text in illustrations used with captions, animation, with narration, worked out examples, and elaborative questions all combining to integrate information. Since his theory focuses on the integration of information, providing these approaches of organizers facilitates the process.

Similarly, functional context is highlighted in the chapters by Schank et al. (1999) and by Schwartz et al. (1999). Schank and his associates describe need for example for making the context functionally relevant and meaningful and interesting while Schwartz et al. require that instruction be anchored in meaningful if not authentic tasks.

Repetition and rehearsal are given special attention by two of the instructional theorists. Perkins and Unger (1999), for example, emphasize that learners develop understanding through performance practice, including reflective engagement in challenging, applicable tasks, and in sequence properly geared for furthering breadth and depth of understandings. Schank et al. (1999) emphasizes the need to have opportunities to practice the skills and to seek knowledge, and that the learner needs lots of opportunities to practice.

Lastly, if we consider the concept of meaningfulness, four of the theorists seem to pay particular attention to this heuristic. For example, Mayer' s guidance (1999a) is that the instructional developer needs to organize the information for the learner with particular notice given to: structure of the text, outlines, headings, signal words, and graphic representations. Gardner (1999) and Perkins and Unger (1999) note the need to develop a few significant topics reasonably connected to powerful themes and disciplinary ideas and to use approaches which are central to the discipline or the domain, to make them interesting, as well as connecting them to diverse themes (as noted earlier in the discussion of multiple contexts).

Meaningfulness is a somewhat pervasive construct in the design recommendations. It is cited as being related to functional context both in Schank et al.'s discussion (1999) of providing meaningful, relevant, and interesting instruction and with the point made by Schwartz et al. (1999) that instruction needs to be anchored in meaningful, authentic tasks. The latter also advocate instruction that provides benchmarks for reflection and self-assessment on the part of the learner. Here, these theorists observe that meaningfulness should take on a personal note. At the same time, they emphasize the need for teams to develop shared mental models to achieve their learning goal.

The purpose and value of this section has been to illustrate how instructional design theorists have developed what we would call macro-variables of instructional strategies, which represent practical applications of the micro-variables of learning, which we have described earlier. We see a need for synthesizing the variables into a coherent context, understandable and useable by developers.

5. THE INTERRELATEDNESS OF DOMAINS OF LEARNING

Below, we present a taxonomy as a heuristic for organizing four domains of learning. While Table 1.1 seems to regard the domains as independent, the intention is simply to provide a separating device for ease of examination. Over the years there seems to have been enough evidence accumulated from research (e.g., Broadbent, 1952a, 1952b; Mayer, 2002; Murphy & Martin, 2002), clinical observation (e.g., Grinder & Bandler, 1981), and anecdotal evidence to establish the fact that the domains of cognitive, psychomotor, affect, and interpersonal act pretty much together. From the senior author's point of view we may characterize each experience not as an isolated domain experience, but rather as a multi-dimensional range of experience. By this we intend that each experience carries with it multi-channel sensory inputs, affective involvement, cognitive transformation, kinesthetic feedback, and some form of organized motor output. We can readily agree, therefore, with Rosenbaum, Carlson, & Gilmore (2001) that most abstract problem solving probably involves, even to the tiniest degree, some sort of real or imagined motor execution. Beyond that, it is our position that the other domains are also involved.

For example, to use a personal anecdote, the senior author had been trying to figure out how to repair a halogen desk lamp. The process involved taking it apart a couple of times, then re-twisting pairs of wires which seemed to become separated, as well as twice replacing the plastic covers which are required to be twisted over the wires in order to seal properly. Following each instance of repair, the lamp functioned for a day or two and then stopped. After experiencing such frustrations I was about to give in, throw out that lamp, and replace it with a new one. However, apparently I had not really totally given up. That night, after falling asleep I found myself working the problem again. And that night I visualized myself re-twisting both sets of pairs and following that, soldering the pairs together before re-covering them with the plastic covers. The next day I performed this solution; and found my lamp working successfully (It has been a week at the time of this writing.). The obvious point of the example is that my cognitive problem solving in the middle of the night involved a combination of modalities: visual, kinesthetic, auditory (imagining the sound of the solder as it melted onto the heated wire), and motor. The cognitive component involved the manipulation and transformation of the elements of the problem into an organized solution. In addition, the activity involved a focused affect, which we call motivation, to aid organizing and performing the task in order to solve the problem.

In describing their own unique method of guided imagery, Grinder and Bandler (1981) ask their clients to anchor their early experience memories with the "multiple components: visual, auditory, kinesthetic, olfactory, and gustatory. Anchoring refers to the tendency for any one element of an experience to bring back the entire experience" (p. 61). They have used this method for trance induction successfully over many years, and have given numerous workshops to clinicians who have also subsequently reported successful use of their techniques. It is most significant for the reader to understand that there are individual differences in how people access these experiences. While most individuals which seemed to be visual, many people access their early memories through the auditory channel, and perhaps even with the sense of taste (gustatory). Since a clinical purpose of their technique is to alter the meaning of early painful experiences, their anchoring procedure involves re-imaging a positive experience; and all of these emotional experiences recalled involved interpersonal relationships.

Murphy and Martin (2002) provide an excellent review of research concerning the use of imagery in sports psychology. In addition to establishing the validity of imagery as they help for improving athletes' performance, the research they reviewed also illustrates the contribution of all the modalities in the establishment of the image. For example, they cite the psychometric development of an imagery assessment instrument, which was submitted to a factor analysis and revealed a three factors solution. "The imagery factors identified by this measure (the Multidimensional Mental Imagery Scale, MMIS) are Sensory Skills (using olfactory, muscular, emotional, gustatory, and auditory dimensions of imagery), Controllability (the ability to hold images over time, prevent distractions, stay focused on task, and change easily from one image to another), and General Factors (items examining the content, purpose, and quality of imagery)" (p. 429). Moreover, in some of the research that they described comparing visual plus kinesthetic dimensions as contributors to imagery, researchers uncovered individual differences in persons' ability to form images, and that these were related to the ability to learn and perform psychomotor tasks. The research of Mayer and his associates (Mayer, 1999b; Mayer, 2002; Mayer & Moreno, 2003) in multimedia learning also provide support for this point of view. For example, the study with Moreno (2003) showing that students using a joystick or moving a bunny back and forth in a multimedia environment were superior to students not having that opportunity. While this is cited as evidence for students' being better able to understand what they are learning when they are required to be active, we would state also that for our purposes the study shows the interrelatedness of Cognitive and Psychomotor learning Domains (as well as the need in learning research with young children to keep examples concrete).

From another perspective, the evolutionary psychologists tell us that all our actions are wired from birth to be in service of a single basic purpose: perpetuation of the human. "The central premise... is that there is a universal human nature, but that this universality exists primarily at the level of the evolved psychological mechanisms, not of expressed cultural behaviors.... cultural variability is not a challenge to claims of universality, but rather data that can give one insight into the structure of the psychological mechanisms that helped generate" (Barkow, Cosmides, & Tooby, 1992, p. 5). These evolutionary psychologists take the long view of human existence, for example "... our ancestors spent the last 2 million years as Pleistocene hunter-gatherers, and, of course, several hundred million years before that as one kind of forager or another." On the other hand, agriculture appeared some few thousand years ago, "... but less than 1% of the 2,000,000 years..." of our predecessor hunter-gatherers. Along these lines, according to Lisle and Goldhammer (2003), there are three motives to guide us: pleasure seeking, pain avoidance, and conservation of energy. The many complex functions of society are said to be in service of these affective functions. Again, from this perspective, the interrelatedness of domains is a natural phenomenon. Similarly, automaticity of action serves the purpose of minimizing conscious attention to protective, basic actions while freeing us to concentrate on new features of our environment needing to be mastered. The research reviewed by Bargh and Chartrand (1999) forces the conclusion that much of our behavior is hard-wired to protect us and make us more efficient where, "...the non-conscious or automatic processes... are unintended, effortless, very fast, and many of them can operate at any given time" (p. 476). Such processes enable our limited, cognitive abilities to deal consciously with the requirements of our environment. However, we can also intentionally acquire automaticity through consistent experiences (e.g., to drive a car, to learn and play a sport, or to develop other skills).

6. A POTENTIAL TAXONOMY

In order to place these heuristics/principles into such a meaningful context for application to instruction, we propose the following taxonomy modified somewhat from Romiszowski (1999). The shaded areas indicate the modifications to the original taxonomy.

Table 1.1. Taxonomy

Process Requirements Knowledge Domains	Acquisition Learning elements of a new knowledge domain (e.g., acquiring nomenclature).	Automaticity Integrating and applying elements and procedures through extensive repetition (i.e., automating skills)	Transfer: Near term Developing ability to generalize- apply principles, and strategies (e.g., heuristics) within a domain	Transfer: Far term Learning to discover new principles in a domain (e.g., creative thinking, problem finding, meta-cognition) and applying them across domains
COGNITIVE *decision making *problem solving *logical thinking *critical thinking	Rote learning (e.g., learning alphabet); Part task learning; Learning new procedures of a domain	Applying a known procedure to a known category of problem (e.g., decoding words, adding numbers, and automating through repetitive practice)	Solving new problems in the domain, conceptual thinking, strategic learning, transfer learning (e.g., self-generating a definition, proving a theorem)	Extending knowledge of a domain (creative thinking) to other domains (e.g. applying schemas of reading acquired in science to math, social studies, etc.)
PSYCHOMOTOR *physical actions *perceptual acuity	Learning basic procedures (e.g., letter indentation on keyboard); Practicing the elements of the basics (e.g., typing letters, etc.)	Repetitive or automated skills (e.g., practicing typing procedures for automaticity; practicing competitive running)	Strategy or planning skills (e.g., playing football, defensive driving)	Inventing a new strategy or skill (e.g., use of the curve ball in baseball)
AFFECTIVE *dealing with oneself (motivations, habits, and self control)	Learning the boundaries of "self"'; Acquiring the skill of self-reflection	Conditioned habits and attitudes; approach and avoidance behaviors	Using personal control skills: attention, affective metacognitive skills, volitional skills, self-regulatory skills	Creating "flow" situations in learning, optimal engagement in activities; self-determination theory
INTERPERSONAL *dealing with others (social habits and skills)	Learning cooperative play; Learning to work in teams; Socialization skills	Conditioned social responses (e.g., socialized behaviors)	Interpersonal control skills (leadership, persuasion, prosocial skills, e.g., management skills)	Applying management skills from one domain to another (e.g., civilian to military life or vice versa)

Given our proposed universal set of dimensions, we then offer for the reader, heuristics and or algorithms from the learning research literature, which could then be applied through our taxonomy as prescriptions for instruction. The relevant theorists' research and paradigms will be cited as appropriate context for those categories of the taxonomy relevant to the mapping into particular instructional tasks.

It is perhaps useful at this point to compare our taxonomic approach with the revised Bloom taxonomy by Andersen and Krathwohl (2001). They break down the cognitive domain into six different categories of process. The first three they cite as remembering relevant knowledge from long-term memory, understanding or constructing meaning from messages, and applying or carrying out of a procedure in a given situation. We would propose that these processes involve acquiring the basic elements of a subject matter and automating the application of these in specific situations. In our taxonomy, Acquisition and Automaticity cover the basic acquisition including recall, simple understanding or meaning construction, and application. The other processes they cite are analyzing or breaking material in two parts for relational structuring, evaluating based on standards, and creation, involving integration of elements into a new functional structure. We would say these three processes involve activities for building schemas in order to transfer across examples within a domain or subject matter, and ultimately with proper, intentional instruction, to transfer such schemas or principles of planning or organization across domains. We feel our approach is parsimonious; and as we shall see shortly, it readily encompasses the interrelatedness of the various domains discussed above.

The taxonomy provides an overview of the Knowledge Domains and the Process Requirements during Acquisition, Automaticity, Near Term Transfer and Far Term Transfer that will be discussed in each chapter. Chapter 2 will discuss the development of cognitive skills in each of the Processes as they relate to instruction in Reading. Cognitive skills such as decision making, planning, problem solving, logical thinking and critical thinking are all necessary for becoming a strategic reader. Decision-making and planning skills enable the reader to identify several alternatives and to select the best alternative. Problem solving skills allow the reader to use techniques to distinguish between necessary and unnecessary information in order to find a solution. Logical thinking is the ability to make sound judgments and use reason. Critical thinking involves considering possible approaches and weighing the pros and cons of each. These cognitive skills are essential for the development of a strategic reader and will be addressed in relation to their perspective in the taxonomy.

The first set of skills in any cognitive domain requires mastery of the Acquisition Process. We propose that operant learning and conditioning principles operate at this level. In Reading, as an example, this requires developing initial skills of letter recognition through rote learning and extensive repetition. Specifically, the reader should first acquire the database elements. In reading these are: decoding, letter-sound relationship, phonemic awareness, and vocabulary. Students at the most basic level of reading should use rote learning to rehearse and memorize letters and words at the early stages of Reading skill acquisition. These early skills provide the foundation for automaticity and then learning more complex skills such as comprehension and elaboration.

The second set of cognitive skills in the taxonomy involves Automaticity processes. In Reading, these processes require skills such as applying a known procedure to a known category of problem. We call these reproductive skills. One such skill is word decoding. Again rote memorization and heavy reinforced repetition apply. Word decoding is the identification of sounds associated with the word's letters and blending them together to determine what the word is. In order to utilize reproductive skills, students should have prior knowledge such as the ability to identify a letter and its sound(s), to which the new information can be related. They should first be aware of the potential relationship between prior information and a known category of problem before they can relate new information to old. Both of these, Acquisition and Reproductive Skills, provide the novice, such as the emergent reader, or the novice basketball player, or the new Spanish student, with the elements of the subject matter necessary to transition to the development of strategies or schemas.

Near Term Transfer, such as using strategies and skills to solve new problems, is the third set of processes in the cognitive domain. For example, in order to use reproductive skills in reading, one must first formulate a problem and make initial attempts to solve it. This domain of problem solving involves learning and use of schemas involving conceptual thinking, strategic learning, transfer learning and self-generating a definition that all involve logical thinking. Logical thinking is the science of thinking that makes it possible to evaluate the correctness of the use of specific problem solving strategies and skills. When utilizing skills such as logical thinking, the thinking strategies and skills used in strategic reading are judged in terms of their accuracy and worth as they relate to solving the problem at hand.

The fourth cognitive process in the taxonomy, Far Term Transfer, allows the extension of existing knowledge of a domain using problem finding, and creative thinking. The skills developed here allow one to see novel relationships or unusual connections amongst seemingly unrelated things. Such skills allow the transfer of knowledge, in the form of schemas or rules, from one domain to the next. For example, one can speculate how acquiring this ability in Reading transfers to seeing novel relationships amongst elements in math. Also, learning the monitoring skills of meta-cognition, while helpful in Reading, can benefit learning in other domains. These critical thinking skills involve the manipulation of new and previous information and knowledge; and from a Far Term Transfer perspective should show up in the facilitation of learning in another domain (e.g., math, social studies, or learning Morse code). They are effective in Reading instruction when students are given many different examples and have numerous opportunities to practice these skills in a variety of situations. Support for this approach to instruction has been implied by Jacobson and Spiro (1995) in their cognitive flexibility theory. The emphasis is on the use of multiple perspectives to facilitate learning of complex materials. Spiro et al. (1995) provide an excellent example of this approach in the teaching of multiple possible interpretations of the themes in the movie *Citizen*

Kane. They emphasize out at various points in the film one can reenter nonlinearly with different themes for various scenes, thereby providing the opportunity for flexibility in interpretation, which they dub "...functional and context-sensitive (particularized) definitions..." (Spiro, et al., 1995, p. 98). In this way, themes and particular scenes can vary in their shades of meaning, especially if the learner is given the opportunity to have expert commentary associated with the particular scene. In such ill-structured domains we can certainly see the application of functional context in the extreme. Yet, paradoxically this concept in itself represents a meta-cognitive principle to be applied across various contexts. We would assert therefore that there are some rules or schemas (e.g., cognitive flexibility) needed to generalize across instantiations of the rule and are per force context-free and the epitome of tools for Far Term Transfer.

Following these processes, the emergent reader begins to acquire the skill of recognizing contextual cues. This stage begins the second, or strategic development phase. This phase begins with cues recognition and proceeds to strategies such as inferencing, analogizing, summarizing, and generalizing within a domain and across domains.

Iding, Klemm, Crosby, & Speitel (2002) propose a taxonomy of illustration types that provides a kind of graphic analog to text. They propose three stages: knowledge acquisition, knowledge application, and knowledge creation. Knowledge acquisition encompasses the first two steps of our taxonomy: Acquisition and Automaticity. This first step assumes the majority of the cognitive processes that readers should engage in to understand the material. Though Iding et al. suggest that their three stages encompasses this task, we feel that knowledge application and creation are similar to our stages of Near-Term and Far-Term Transfer. Knowledge application involves "applying processes learned in text" (Iding et al., 2002, p. 444) and knowledge creation involves "developing new models/theories/representations" (Iding et al., 2002, p. 445).

As underpinnings for the development of these skills and strategies during instruction, what kinds of learning principles can we identify? Broadly speaking, there are two sets of relevant principles: those dealing with operant learning and conditioning and secondly, those principles governing conceptual learning and problem solving. The research and theories of Skinner (1953), Thorndike (1931), Piaget (1957), Ausubel (1960, 1962, 1969), Rothkopf (1972; Rothkopf & Billington, 1974), Brunswik (1944), and cognitive theorists, such as Rumelhart and Norman (1988), and others, will be cited as relevant throughout the chapter where appropriate.

At this point it would be instructive to include a discussion of schema formation since it is our position that schema development is responsible for both Near-term and Far-term Transfer.

7. SCHEMA CONSTRUCTION

Schema theory asserts that schemas (or schemata) are our way of organizing our environment (Bartlett, 1932; Rumelhart & Norman, 1988; Sweller, 1989; Sweller et al., 1998). From these rules we know that certain objects go together and therefore are to be reacted to in a common and consistent manner even though specific elements of those objects may differ. Schemas therefore provide the basis for knowledge organization and storage. They also provide the function of reducing working memory load. Sweller et al. (1998) suggested the following:

> "When reading, we can derive meaning from an infinite variety of marks on a page because we have schemas that allow us to appropriately categorize letters, words, and combinations of words. Schemas provide the elements of knowledge. According to schema theory, it is through the building of increasing numbers of ever more complex schemas by combining elements consisting of lower-level schemas into higher level schemas that skilled performance develops. Often, this acquisition of schemas is an active, constructive process. Reading provides a clear example. In early school years, children construct schemas for letters that allow them to classify an infinite variety of shapes (as occurs in handwriting) into a very limited number of categories. These schemas provide the elements for higher order schemas when they are combined into words that in turn can be combined into phrases, and so forth. Ultimately this process allows readers to rapidly scan a page filled with a hugely complex array of squiggles and derive meaning from it" (p. 255).

We agree with the authors that learning the basic elements of any domain first and then automating these elements are important steps in order to form rules, heuristics, schemas, or any other characterization of principles which are required for transfer whether near-term or far-term. However, we propose in our 4 stage process model that acquisition of the basic data elements in the domain are best accomplished through rote memory and operant conditioning principles. We agree that extensive practice is required to automate and instill these elements into long-term memory, the Automaticity Phase. If one wishes to call the acquisition of letter elements to learn Reading, schemas, so be it. We simply take the position that no higher order event is required in order to do this and that the acquisition activity requires very "low interactivity" to use Sweller et al. (1998) terminology. Therefore, not only is there very little demand on working memory, but they are also almost truly sensory in nature and require very little cognitive load for processing.

Following the acquisition and automating of the basic elements, the letters in the case of Reading, the learner is able to acquire rules or schemas for the formation of words, phrases, and sentences. It is at this stage in development that near-term transfer takes place. That is, the learner can now develop a knowledge-base of rules for meaning, both in terms of vocabulary and grammar, in order to facilitate the emerging reading process. As we apply these Reading principles across subject-matters or domains, we are engaging in far-term transfer. For example, we are reading to solve mathematics problems, or we are reading a technical manual to repair a tank. Sticht (1975) captured these points in an anthology of functional literacy.

Before proceeding to the next chapter, it is useful to map the taxonomy onto a generic framework, which suggests a curricular approach to teaching for understanding. Figure 2 illustrates how a spiral curriculum might look. The organization is from simple to complex coupled with increasing breadth of domain coverage. Others have advocated a similar approach (e.g., Gagne & Merrill, 1990; Reigeluth, 1999; van Merriënboer et al., 2003; White & Frederiksen, 1990a, 1990b). Gagne and Merrill (1990), for example, use terms like "integrated multiple objectives" and "enterprises" to describe their view of the need for using a functionally appropriate context and holistic approach for structuring the learning environment. Some of the key features to our approach are to present functionally relevant contexts for all course materials from the outset. Secondly, this requires learning knowledge and applying it at even the simplest level, Acquisition. Multiple contexts and examples are also part of this approach from the beginning of domain learning. By moving up the spiral in this way, we facilitate the learner's ability to go beyond specific contexts (sometimes called situated learning) when required to transfer her or his understanding across domains. The approach itself, which we are advocating, viewed at a meta-level is an example of the Far Term Transfer process. This is so because we are advocating use of the multiple-context-spiral curriculum approach regardless of a specific discipline or subject matter.

Beyond this, one of the most significant examples of far term transfer is meta-cognition (see for example, Tobias & Everson, 2000, for a discussion of objective measures). The idea that one can evaluate, monitor, and self-regulate his or her behavior during learning by definition must be de-contextualized to be valuable to the learner across subject-matters (Zimmerman, 1990). To be maximally valuable to the learner, he or she should recognize that the monitoring and regulation process is extremely useful regardless of a particular curriculum or particular learning task. The topic of self-regulation has received considerable interest of late (Corno & Winne, 2002).

Gredler (2002) discussed the negative impacts that various classroom practices have on the development of self-regulation. The inhibiting factors are a focus on testing content knowledge and specific task performance plus the social contract in the classroom (continual comparisons with fellow students). Eliminated from this approach are activities relating to reading real books, solving problems as opposed to rote recognition, hands-on activities in science, and writing in authentic contexts.

One important factor that seems to be missing in these discussions is the recognition that in order for transfer to occur, multiple contexts (e.g., inside school and outside school) should be integral to the instruction for the learner to generalize the heuristic that monitoring and self-regulation is beneficial regardless of the learning context. Sweller et al. (1998) from their research also advocate variety of practice. The key for good instructional design is to build new principle capacity by adding just the right mix of multiple-example, surface structure to challenge with germane cognitive load for the learner without overloading her or him. Sweller and associates (1998) cite the benefits of variability of practice as follows, "Variability over problem situations is expected to encourage learners to develop schemas, because it increases the probability that similar features can be identified and that relevant features can be distinguished from a relevant ones" (Sweller et al, 1998, p. 286). Also, Seidel and Hunter (1970) obtained this effect when teaching computer programming in a programmed instruction format, either with or without a variety of example problems. Providing variety resulted in clear advantages for the learner. What we as teachers need to create then is the appropriate (functionally relevant) multiple-context environment in order for the learning of principles to occur. That means we include germane cognitive loads with low extraneous load placed on the learner. In this way, we teach for understanding or for transfer. Figure 2 shows this approach graphically as it would apply to any curriculum. The learner is aided by including all three features of knowledge (K), examples (E), and applications (A) through all the processes, expanding the K, E, A as understanding grows.

In describing the process of learning Mayer's approach (2003) characterizes the learner as an active transformer and organizer of information encountered in the learner's environment. In this regard, as noted, it is very similar to Dewey's approach (1910, 1949) around the turn of the 20th century, and one that is reflective of many cognitive psychologists. In the broadest sense he defines a three-stage theory, which in the cybernetics sense can be broken down into input, process, and output. The input component consists of sensory images. These are then transformed into a usable symbolic representation by the learner, who then organizes the information to make it understandable allowing a meaningful performance. Mayer uses as an example for his position that information theory is inadequate to explain meaningful learning studies involving students' receiving animation, concurrently with narration versus students receiving animation with onscreen text and other studies where students received the animation, concurrently with the narration as opposed to preceding or following narration. Mayer asserts that they all should, from an information processing perspective, learn equally well because they receive the same information. We would assert that this is a very restricted view of information and that it is quite possible to assert that every form of presentation represents another type or another dimension of information and is therefore not identical.

Our position is that all experience can be characterized as a range of modalities (visual, auditory, kinesthetic, olfactory, affective) plus the verbal. We add the verbal dimension as a separate one superimposed upon the other modalities, and assert that they all provide unique dimensions of information. Moreover, contrary to Mayer's theory of the learning processes that the visual input but not the auditory is in the form of an image, we would assert that the sensory input is in the form of an image, irrespective of whether it is presented visually or as auditory input, when initially given to the naïve learner. We would maintain that there are sound images as well as visual images, and that the learner organizes these images into his or her available symbol system. If that symbol system includes words, apropos of the earlier point, they represent another form of information. We therefore feel that the learner can organize visually words as well as pictures and in an auditory manner can organize sounds into words. Both of these operations require a transformation from sensory input to another form of information. We agree with the position that the next process involves organization; and that the last stage requires integration.

While Mayer (2003) apparently attributes this focus on learning by understanding, the quality of acquired knowledge, uniquely to the constructivists, we would not. As an example of the contrary approach to acquiring knowledge by memorizing,

Mayer (2003) cites the blind use of a formula in Wertheimer's work (1945) on problem solving as an example of rote learning. We would say that it's not totally rote learning. It is probably also a result of the power of mental set (see also Dember, 1960 for a discussion of set related to perception and perceptual learning). As Bargh and Chartrand (1999) discuss reducing certain of our mental processes to automaticity serves an important survival function. As they note, "...how impossible it would be to function effectively if conscious, controlled, and aware mental processing had to deal with every aspect of life, from perceptual comprehension of the environment (both physical and social) to choosing and guiding every action in response to the environment" (p. 464). For our purposes, in the most general case, even though we, as instructors, may be teaching for understanding we may not be covering the total landscape or sample space, except for the objectives, which we are trying to achieve, providing therefore an insufficient variety of examples and contexts. In such a case the learners may have some understanding but it may be very limited. The learning may or may not also be affected to some degree by rote memorization. The key of course from our perspective is to concentrate always on helping the learner by instructing within what we might label a Functional Context Spiral. This spiral involves from the beginning the use of advanced organizers to give an overview of the ultimate task, with multiple examples in functionally relevant contexts (some might call this, authentic). We note a similar approach in van Merriënboer and associates' "four component instructional design model" (see, for example, van Merriënboer, Clark, & de Crock, 2002; van Merriënboer, Kirschner, & Kester, 2003). They propose organizing tasks as "...simple-to-complex versions of the whole task" (van Merriënboer, Kirschner, & Kester, 2003, p. 11), and we would say, applying operant principles of high support followed by fading as the constituent tasks become more complex, and even within the same class of tasks following greater experience. Spector (2000) notes in his Introduction that in the "...technology-intensive learning situations..." (p. xviii) highlighted in his volume on instruction and technology, the primary focus by the authors is on understanding as the ultimate goal of learning. It is useful also to relate our framework and conceptualization of transfer to the three dimensions of mastery model given by Michenbaum & Biemiller (1998, pp. 70-80). We would agree with the authors that all learning is facilitated by moving from simple to complex and that meaningful learning takes place when the tasks are functionally relevant in context. In their framework, however, "*far transfer*, usually involving complex decisions" implies learning increasingly complex tasks within the same domain. In their transfer dimension called "the planning complexity dimension" they state, "can be assessed in terms of the complexity of domain-relevant tasks that the student can construct and perform."

In our recommendation for designing a spiral curriculum, we feel that the focus should always be on understanding, and therefore, on transfer; however, when learning the elements of a new subject matter, there is a place initially for rote memory and operant conditioning procedures. Drills can aid the initial Acquisition phase of learning, as well as moving towards Automaticity of the basic elements. Stated another way, we would propose that you need to acquire both a database, with the help of rote procedures, for retention purposes and principles or schemas for transfer purposes; and clearly you need to build the schemas if you're going to have either near term or far term transfer.

In the next chapter therefore, we will exemplify the cognitive domain in more detail with the set of tasks that an emerging reader must master in terms of the processes, Acquisition, Automaticity, Near Term Transfer, and Far Term Transfer, at which she or he must succeed in order to understand. The learning principles and or heuristics will be noted as appropriate to the various instructional task requirements. It is difficult indeed to conceive of a task in everyday life or in formal schooling where Reading for understanding is not required. Our choice of Reading as the cognitive exemplar, therefore, is based on the fact that Reading provides the best and most universal case for illustrating far term transfer.

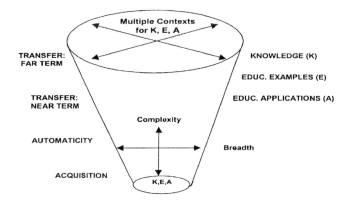

Figure 1.1. The Functional Context Spiral Curriculum: Teaching for Understanding

REFERENCES

Anderson, L. W. & Krathwohl, D. R. (Eds.). (2001). A taxonomy for learning, teaching, and assessing: A revision of Bloom's taxonomy of educational objectives. New York: Longman.

Ausubel, D. P. (1960). The use of advance organizers in the learning and retention of meaningful verbal material. *Journal of Educational Psychology, 51,* 267-272.

Ausubel, D. P. (1962). A subsumption theory of meaningful verbal learning and retention. *Journal of General Psychology, 66,* 213-224.

Ausubel, D. P. (1969). A cognitive theory of school learning. *Psychology in the Schools, 6*(4), 331-335.

Barkow, J. H., Cosmides, L., & Tooby, J. (Eds.). (1992). *The adapted mind: Evolutionary psychology and the generation of culture.* New York: Oxford University Press.

Bargh, J. A. & Chartrand, T. L. (1999). The unbearable automaticity of being. *American Psychologist, 54*(7), 462-479.

Bartlett, F. C. (1932). *Remembering.* New York: Cambridge University Press.

Broadbent, D. E. (1952a). Speaking and listening simultaneously. *Journal of Experimental Psychology, 43*, 267-273.

Broadbent, D. E. (1952b). Listening to one of two synchronous messages. *Journal of Experimental Psychology, 44*, 51-55.

Brunswik, E. (1944). Distal focusing of perception: Size-constancy in a representative sample of situations. *Psychological Monographs, 56*(1), 1-49.

Corno, L. & Winne, P. H. (Eds.). (2002). Using qualitative methods to enrich understandings of self-regulated learning. *Educational Psychologist, Special Issue, 37*(1), 1-65.

Dember, W. N. (1960). *The Psychology of Perception*. New York: Henry Holt and Company.

Dewey, J. (1910). *How we think*. Boston: D.C. Heath.

Dewey, J. & Bentley, A. F. (1949). *Knowing and the known*. Boston: Beacon Press.

Dochy, F., Segers, M., & Buehl, M. M. (1999). The relation between assessment practices and outcomes of studies: The case of research on prior knowledge. *Review of Educational Research, 69*(2), 145-186.

Druckman, D. & Bjork, R. A. (Eds.). (1991). *In the mind's eye: Enhancing human performance*. Committee on Techniques for the Enhancement of Human Performance, National Research Council. Washington, D.C.: National Academy Press.

Druckman, D. & Bjork, R. A. (Eds.). (1994). *Learning, remembering, believing: Enhancing human performance*. Committee on Techniques for the Enhancement of Human Performance, National Research Council. Washington, D.C.: National Academy Press.

Estes, W. K. (1975). The state of the field: General problems and issues of theory and metatheory. In W. K. Estes (Ed.), *Handbook of learning and cognitive processes* (pp. 1-24). Hillsdale, NJ: Lawrence Erlbaum Associates, Publishers.

Gagne, R. M. & Merrill, M. D. (1990). Integrative goals for instructional design. *Educational Technology Research and Development, 38*(1), 23-30.

Gardner, H. (1999). Multiple approaches to understanding. In C. M. Reigeluth (Ed.), *Instructional-design theories and models, Volume II: A new paradigm of instructional theory* (pp. 69-89). Mahwah, NJ: Lawrence Erlbaum Associates, Publishers.

Gredler, M. E. (2002, April). Pseudo theory and classroom practice: Reciprocal inhibitors to self-regulation. Paper presented at American Educational Research Association, New Orleans, Louisiana.

Grinder, J. & Bandler, R. (1981). *Trans-formations: Neuro-linguistic programming and the structure of hypnosis*. Moab, Utah: Real People Press:

Iding, M., Klemm, E. B., Crosby, M. E., & Speitel, T. (2002). Interactive texts, figures, and tables for learning science: Constructivism in text design. *International Journal of Instructional Media, 29*(4), 441-452.

Jacobson, M. J. & Spiro, R. J. (1995). Hypertext learning environments, cognitive flexibility, and the transfer of complex knowledge: An empirical investigation. *Journal of Educational Computing Research, 12*(4), 301-333.

Kimble, G. A. & Garmezy, N. (1963). *Principles of general psychology, (2nd edition)*. New York: The Ronald Press Company.

Lave, J. & Wenger, E. (1991). *Situated learning: Legitimate peripheral participation*. Cambridge, England: Cambridge University Press.

Lisle, D. J. & Goldhammer, A. (2003). *The pleasure trap*. Summertown, Tennessee: Healthy Living Publications.

Mayer, R. E. (1999a). Designing instruction for constructivist learning. In C. M. Reigeluth (Ed.), *Instructional-design theories and models, Volume II: A new paradigm of instructional theory* (pp. 141-159). Mahwah, NJ: Lawrence Erlbaum Associates, Publishers.

Mayer, R. E. (1999b). *The promise of educational psychology: Volume 1, Learning in the content areas*. Upper Saddle River, NJ: Prentice Hall.

Mayer, R. E. (2002). *The promise of educational psychology: Volume 2, Teaching for meaningful learning*. Upper Saddle River, NJ: Prentice Hall.

Mayer, R. E. (2003). Theories of learning and their application to technology. In H. F. O'Neill & R. S. Perez (Eds.), *Technology applications in education: A learning view* (pp.127-157). Mahwah, NJ: Lawrence Erlbaum Associates, Publishers.

Mayer, R. E. & Moreno, R. (2003). Nine ways to reduce cognitive load in multimedia learning. *Educational Psychologist, 38*(1), 43-52.

Meichenbaum, D. & Biemiller, A. (1998) *Nurturing independent learners*. Cambridge, MA: Brookline Books.

Murphy, S. M. & Martin, K. A. (2002). The use of imagery in sport. In T. S. Horn (Ed.), *Advances in sport psychology* (2nd ed.) (pp. 405-439). Champaign, IL: Human Kinetics.

Perkins, D. N. & Unger, C. (1999). Teaching and learning for understanding. In C. M. Reigeluth (Ed.), *Instructional-design theories and models, Volume II: A new paradigm of instructional theory* (pp. 91-114). Mahwah, NJ: Lawrence Erlbaum Associates, Publishers.

Piaget, J. (1957). *Logic and psychology*. New York: Basic Books.

Reigeluth, C. M. (Ed.). (1999). *Instructional-design theories and models, Volume II: A new paradigm of instructional theory*, Mahwah, NJ: Lawrence Erlbaum Associates, Publishers.

Robinson, D. N. (1976). Adaptation by learning and memory. In. D. N. Robinson, *Psychology: Traditions and perspectives*. New York: D. Van Nostrand Company.

Romiszowski, A. (1999). The development of physical skills: Instruction in the psychomotor domain. In C. M. Reigeluth (Ed.), *Instructional-design theories and models, Volume II: A new paradigm of instructional theory* (pp. 457-481). Mahwah, NJ: Lawrence Erlbaum Associates, Publishers.

Rosenbaum, D. A., Carlson, R. A., & Gilmore, R. O. (2001). Acquisition of intellectual and perceptual-motor skills. *Annual Review of Psychology, 52*, 453-470.

Rothkopf, E. Z. (1972). Variable adjunct question schedules, interpersonal interaction, and incidental learning from written material. *Journal of Educational Psychology, 63*(2), 87-92.

Rothkopf, E. Z. & Billington, M. J. (1974). Indirect review and priming through questions. *Journal of Educational Psychology, 66*(5), 669-679.

Rumelhart, D. E. & Norman, D. A. (1988). Representation in memory. In R. C. Atkinson, R. J. Herrnstein, G. Lindzey, & R. D. Luce (Eds.), *Stevens' handbook of experimental psychology, (2nd Ed.), Volume 2: Learning and cognition* (pp. 511-587). New York: Wiley.

Schank, R. C., Berman, T. R., & Machpherson, K. A. (1999). Learning by doing. In C. M. Reigeluth (Ed.), *Instructional-design theories and models, Volume II: A new paradigm of instructional theory* (pp. 161-181). Mahwah, NJ: Lawrence Erlbaum Associates, Publishers.

Schwartz, D., Lin, X., Brophy, S., & Bransford, J. D. (1999). Toward the development of flexibly adaptive instructional designs. In C. M. Reigeluth (Ed.), *Instructional-design theories and models, Volume II: A new paradigm of instructional theory* (pp. 183-213). Mahwah, NJ: Lawrence Erlbaum Associates, Publishers.

Seidel. R. J. & Hunter, H. G. (1970). The application of theoretical factors in teaching problem-solving by programmed instruction. *International Review of Applied Psychology, 19*(1), 41-81.

Shoemaker, H. A. (1967). The functional context method of instruction. HumRRO Professional Paper, 35-67.

Skinner, B. F. (1953). *Science and human behavior*. New York: Macmillan.

Spector, J. M. (2000). Building theory into practice in learning and instruction. In J. M. Spector & T. M. Anderson (Eds.), *Integrated and holistic perspectives on learning, instruction, and technology: Understanding complexity* (pp. 79-90). The Netherlands: Kluwer Academic Publishers.

Spiro, R. J., Feltovich, P. J., Jacobson M. J., & Coulson R. L. (1995). Cognitive flexibility, constructivism, and hypertext: Random-access instruction for advanced knowledge acquisition in ill-structured domains. In L. P. Steffe & J. E. Gale (Eds.), Constructivism in education (pp. 85-107). Hillsdale, NJ: Lawrence Erlbaum Asssociates.

Sticht, T. (1975) *Reading for working: A functional literacy anthology*. HumRRO Paperback Book.

Sweller, J. (1989). Cognitive technology: Some procedures for facilitating learning and problem solving in mathematics and science. *Journal of Educational Psychology, 81*(4), 457-466.

Sweller, J., van Merriënboer, J. J. G., & Paas, F. G. W. C. (1998). Cognitive architecture and instructional design. *Educational Psychology Review, 10*(3), 251-296.

Thorndike, E. L. (1931). *Human learning*. New York: Century.

Tobias, S. & Everson, H. T. (2000). Assessing metacognitive knowledge monitoring. In G. Schraw & J. C. Impara (Eds.), *Issues in the measurement of metacognition* (pp. 147-222). Lincoln NE: Buros Institute of Mental Measurements.

van Merriënboer, J. J. G., Clark, R. E., & de Crock, M. B. M. (2002). Blueprints for complex learning: The 4C/ID Model. *Educational Technology Research & Development, 50*(2), 39-64.

van Merriënboer, J. J. G., Kirschner, P. A., & Kester, L. (2003). Taking the load off a learner's mind: Instructional design for complex learning. *Educational Psychologist, 38*(1), 5-13.

Wellman, H. M. & Gelman, S. A. (1992). Cognitive development: Foundational theories of core domains. *Annual Review of Psychology, 43*, 337-375.

Wertheimer, M. (1945). *Productive thinking.* New York: Harper & Row.

White, B. Y. & Frederiksen, J. R. (1990a). Causal model progressions as a foundation for intelligent learning environments. In. W. J. Clancey & E. Soloway (Eds.), *Artificial intelligence and learning environments* (pp. 99-157). Cambridge, MA: MIT Press.

White, B. Y. & Frederiksen, J. R. (1990b). Intelligent tutors as intelligent testers. In. N. Frederiksen, M. Shafto, A. M. Lesgold, & R. Glaser, (Eds.), *Diagnostic monitoring of skill and knowledge acquisition* (pp. 1-25). Mahwah, NJ: Lawrence Erlbaum Associates, Inc.

Zimmerman, B.J. (1990). Self-regulated learning and academic achievement: An overview. *Educational Psychologist, 25*, 3-17.

CHAPTER 2

A COGNITIVE DOMAIN EXAMPLE: READING

Table 2.1. Taxonomy of the Cognitive Domain

Process Requirements ⟍ Knowledge Domains	Acquisition	Automaticity	Transfer: Near term	Transfer: Far term
	Learning elements of a new knowledge domain (e.g., acquiring nomenclature).	Integrating and applying elements and procedures through extensive repetition (i.e., automating skills)	Developing ability to generalize- apply principles, and strategies (e.g., heuristics) within a domain	Learning to discover new principles in a domain (e.g., creative thinking, problem finding, meta-cognition) and applying them across domains
COGNITIVE *decision making *problem solving *logical thinking *critical thinking	Rote learning (e.g., learning alphabet); Part task learning; Learning new procedures of a domain	Applying a known procedure to a known category of problem (e.g., decoding words, adding numbers, and automating through repetitive practice)	Solving new problems in the domain, conceptual thinking, strategic learning, transfer learning (e.g., self-generating a definition, proving a theorem)	Extending knowledge of a domain (creative thinking) to other domains (e.g. applying schemas of reading acquired in science to math, social studies, etc.

In this Chapter we will be highlighting the following learning heuristics as they apply to the developing reader:

- ♦ *Operant principles of minimizing errors, using small steps, and providing immediate reinforcement for acquisition of initial elements of domain knowledge;*
- ♦ *Advanced organizers to facilitate integrative skill acquisition and capitalize on prior knowledge;*
- ♦ *Continual use of active learning in functional context;*
- ♦ *Part-task training to break up complex tasks into manageable chunks;*
- ♦ *Providing multiple-context environments to facilitate positive transfer within and across domains.*

INTRODUCTION

In this chapter, we cover the four learning processes as they relate to the Cognitive domain. The Cognitive example we have chosen to illustrate our approach in this chapter is Reading. When we teach people to read, we are trying to enhance or facilitate their ability to manipulate a symbol system, we call it language. The purpose this serves is to help the learner to better organize his world. Therefore, we are aiding the development of thinking and reasoning, the abstract representation and manipulation of a symbol system. We would submit that Reading represents the primordial ooze of such a complex, cognitive process and is essential for all future abstract manipulations (see Whorf, 1956, on language and thought).

Perceptually, the gestalt psychologists, working in the visual domain, helped us to note that certain primary structures exist from birth and then are built upon later; e.g., the curve, the line, etc. (Köhler, 1947). When we teach our children early on we give them concrete manipulanda and attach abstract names to them. This facilitates organizing the primary, perceptual structures into higher order categories or groupings, for example, trees, dogs, cats, cars, etc. Developmentally, we note the success in such categorizations by use of the term "perceptual constancies." The research on brightness, shape, size, and color constancies indicate that their appearance occurs respectively at chronologically increasing ages (brightness first at a few months, next shape, size, and lastly, color, the last at about eight to nine years of age; See Woodworth & Schlosberg, 1955). Note also that while we are teaching our children to attach names to objects, we are also providing motivation, emotional involvement, and motor involvement as we smile, clap our hands and in other ways with our body language show approval for what the child is accomplishing. In turn the child smiles back, points to or manipulates the object, and may even mimic the approval-making applause. This example illustrates that the interrelatedness, therefore, of all our domains is reinforced from the child's earliest learnings.

The point of this discussion is to emphasize that in instruction we capitalize on the developmental sequence by moving from the concrete to the abstract, simple to complex, and provide multiple examples for the learner to aid the organizational process. Language learning facilitated by listening, reading, and writing is the primary means by which we gain the basis for our learning increasingly abstract organization and symbol manipulation for thinking and reasoning. Learning to read by its very nature, manipulating an abstract symbol system, represents the learning of an ill-structured domain, an open task if you will, and is the epitome of a complex, cognitive ability. This is especially so in the learning of the English language with its many rules, exceptions to rules, and irregular characteristics. Moreover, the fruits of this learning are felt in every other domain and subject matter. In their research on memory, comparing novices to experts, Ericsson, Patel, and Kintsch (2000) provide additional support for our selection of Reading as a cognitive domain example. They note, "It is necessary to keep large amounts of information accessible in WM [working memory] during text comprehension and expert performance in domains such as chess and medicine." Furthermore they assert "… that the same type of memory mechanisms mediate the comprehension of texts, chess, and medical diagnosis" (pp. 582-83).

The value of choosing Reading as our example of the Cognitive domain is that it is the clearest illustration of learning to transfer principles or schemas across all other areas of human learning. We call this, as noted above, Far Term Transfer. In education, or training, transfer might otherwise be called teaching or instructing for understanding. The schemas for grammatical construction, sentence or paragraph comprehension, application of cognitive strategies in reading, etc. are not learned typically as ends in themselves. Rather, their meaning is attained when we apply them to learning other cognitive examples, such as math, science, etc. as well as learning skills in other domains: psychomotor, affective, and interpersonal. Thus, learning to read for understanding means learning the verbal skills and the schemas necessary to learning other domain skills, such as, playing the piano, typing, playing sports, solving a physics problem or describing a historical event, and expressing ourselves emotionally and socially. Becoming expert in these skills would be severely limited, if not impossible, without the ability to read.

The limitations of Reading in serving far term transfer result from the fact that we encode our experiences in a number of ways. First, in the visual domain we encode verbally and pictorially (Pavio, 1986). We also encode with multiple channels (Broadbent, 1952a, 1952b; Mayer & Moreno, 2003), such as the mix of auditory and visual information. In training with simulations, especially in virtual reality, the military is experimenting with including the haptic sense (feel, touch) as well (Bakker, Werkhoven, & Passenier, 1999; Dupont, Schulteis, Millman, & Howe, 1999). Nevertheless, our world is heavily visual, and reading to do something or act on something to understand our world is one of the first and most important cognitive skills we learn.

The format of the chapter will be two sections following the Introduction. First, we suggest possible strategies or guidance that the developer might apply to the targeted training or educational materials under consideration for this domain. Secondly, we provide the research and theoretical support from the literature. The reader may wish only to use Section I without reading the backup material. The value of Section II is to provide a more comprehensive basis for the practical suggestions given first; but it is not necessary in order to apply the recommended strategies.

Acquisition

The process of learning all the elements of the domain (in this case, Reading), regardless of specific theorist descriptions, we are calling: Acquisition. As the chart above illustrates, this would include rote learning of such items as the alphabet among others in order to develop a basic skill set from which further instruction in reading can progress.

When children move into reading, they shift from visual cue processing of words to phonetic cue processing. The phonetic processing requires familiarity with letters and their names or sounds and knowledge of how letters symbolize phonetic units detected in the pronunciation. It also entails recognizing and remembering associations between letters in spellings and sounds in pronunciations and explains how children first become able to read single words reliably. At this stage, the emerging reader (from approximately birth to age 5) is learning the alphabet, becoming familiar with storybook reading, and building important letter-sound relationships (Chall, 1983/1996).

Automaticity

Reading is a complex skill that requires a great deal of attention and integrates many processes in a short period of time. The Automaticity Phase requires integrating the basic elements and automating the earlier processes. Reading is also a continuously developed skill and the instructional materials should match the changing abilities and skills of the reader. Initial skills such as word decoding, learning letter-sound relationships, and using contextual cues are ones that beginning readers use as they begin to become familiar with print and the processes of reading (Chall, 1993/1996). Word recognition becomes automatic at a fairly early level of reading development. The processing of words takes only a few seconds for the fluent reader but there are many who do not succeed in becoming fluent readers although they may quickly and easily understand speech (LaBerge & Samuels, 1974). When these basic skills are automatized, little attention is needed to perform these skills. This allows the readers' full attention to focus on the comprehension of the text. As readers develop and become more proficient, their learning shifts to more complex tasks, such as the development of cognitive schemas, which require higher-order constructive, cognitive processes including the use of complex reading strategies.

Transfer: Near Term

As the reading task gets more complex, it requires conceptual thinking and strategic learning. It involves developing the ability to interpret and generalize (i.e., to transfer principles). The reader interprets what he or she reads, associates it with past experiences, and projects beyond it in terms of ideas, relations, and categorizations. Chall (1983/1996) categorizes this stage of reading as *learning the new*. The supporting research for near term transfer is classified in broad Reading categories of strategic reading and conceptual learning from text. The reader can be aided in his or her quest for developing such transfer capabilities by competent authors. "In a well written text, the author facilitates the integration of new sentences with earlier presented information through the organization of the text and the use of explicit and implicit references. For example, when a skilled reader encounters the words 'that all policemen' in a sentence, then these words provide a semantically based retrieval cue to relevant information about the associated character in the text that the reader generated during the prior reading of the text" (Ericcson, Patel, & Kintsch, 2000, p. 583).

Transfer: Far Term

The key to far term transfer is developing strategies that apply beyond the domain one is currently learning, in this case techniques for learning how to read better that might apply to other curricula, say, math or social studies (Bransford & Stein, 1993). It may include, for example, such strategies as meta-cognitive strategy use, comprehension monitoring and decision-making. The supporting research for far term transfer includes reading engagement, reading in multi-text environments and amount and breadth of reading. These will be discussed further in Section II.

SECTION I:

INSTRUCTIONAL GUIDANCE

Acquisition Process

Table 2.2. Acquisition Process of the Cognitive Domain

Process Requirements	Acquisition	Automaticity	Transfer: Near term	Transfer: Far term
COGNITIVE *decision making *problem solving *logical thinking *critical thinking	Rote learning (e.g., learning alphabet); Part task learning; Learning new procedures of a domain	Applying a known procedure to a known category of problem (e.g., decoding words, adding numbers, and automating through repetitive practice)	Solving new problems in the domain, conceptual thinking, strategic learning, transfer learning (e.g., self-generating a definition, proving a theorem)	Extending knowledge of a domain (creative thinking) to other domains (e.g. applying schemas of reading acquired in science to math, social studies, etc.

In order to maximize performance during the Acquisition phase of early reading, the following strategies will apply:

- **Exposure to storybook reading;**
- **Practice in sound and letter recognition;**
- **Teach word-decoding skills and help develop vocabulary words;**
- **Teach word recognition and sight reading skills.**

Exposure to Storybook Reading
Preschool children who are read to consistently usually associate reading with pleasure and enjoyment and learn to read more easily once they reach the kindergarten and first grade age (Whitehurst et al., 1994). Activities such as storybook reading, storytelling, object and picture identification, practice with the alphabet and rhyming games confer skills that are essential to the reading process. Through these learning activities, emerging readers begin to understand important associations between the spoken and written language. Importantly, research indicates that the quality of the reading experience is essential to reading development (Heath, 1983). How parents and teachers mediate the reading process with regard to positive social interactions surrounding the book reading is as important as the reading itself. Some milestones for the emerging reader occur when she or he begins to recognize commercial establishment signs such as "McDonald's" or when she or he can recognize his or her own name in print. It also involves learning that: (1) Reading proceeds from left to right and from the top of the page to the bottom; (2) Spoken language is represented in a consistent fashion in the written language; (3) Each letter of the alphabet is associated with one or more sounds in spoken language. Studies in emergent literacy have focused on the following points (Sulzby & Teale, 1991):

1. The presence of people who read and write in the child's environment is vital to emergent literacy. This includes social interactions with parents and caretakers in activities that integrate reading and writing.
2. Create a routine to foster storybook reading. Being read to daily (or as often as possible) is crucial in the development of reading in children. Routine in dialogue creates a predictable atmosphere, which helps children learn how to participate in the reading event.
3. When print is present, children begin to take an interest in reading and writing, so one should introduce storybooks as early as infancy. There are "soft fabric" books and sturdy cardboard books that they can begin to play with and manipulate on their own.
4. Reading and writing reinforce one another and develop simultaneously rather than sequentially so one should provide reading and writing materials (e.g. books, coloring books, crayons, and plain writing paper) in the play area so that they will be viewed as exciting activities.

5. Have children reenact their favorite stories and read familiar stories in unconventional ways in order to create independence with reading.
6. Allow children to create, write and retell their own stories in order to reinforce the connection between the spoken and written word.
7. Watch *Sesame Street* or television with captioning to improve readiness (Pressley, 2002).
8. Create a positive social interaction around reading. Tell children how the story relates to their own personal experiences.

Practice Sound and Letter Recognition

Instruction in reading begins when the student is able to recognize each letter of the alphabet and its corresponding sound(s). The student should also be able to distinguish letters of the alphabet in uppercase and lowercase forms. Students should be versed in hearing phonemes that are the distinct sounds within a spoken word. Phonemic awareness refers to the ability to recognize units of sounds or phonemes in words, and to manipulate individual sounds in words. When children have the understanding that words are made up of phonemes, their reading improves significantly (Adams, 1990; Ball & Blachman, 1991; Pressley, 1998; Stahl & Murray, 1994). The initial emphasis is placed on auditory recognition because 1) the auditory processing of language helps differentiate sounds in words, and 2) often, words that sound the same do not share visually similar characteristics, such as words "friend" and "mend." The following exercises can assist children in being skilled in the beginning stages of reading:

1. Explicitly teach skills for phonemic awareness. Help children practice the skill of isolating the initial letter in the sound of a word.
2. Ask children to identify words all beginning with the same sound. Initial letter isolation differs from the ability to produce words that have the same beginning sound, as it requires the child to separate the initial sound of a word from a whole word as opposed to producing words that begin with the same sound, which is a more difficult skill.
3. Say several words and/or show pictures of several objects and ask children to choose the one that begins and/or ends with a different sound from the others.
4. Play games that incorporate words that rhyme and words that have the same beginning sounds.
5. Read alphabet books embedded with individual letters in colorful pictures and meaningful stories. Have children practice writing letters, first by tracing, then copying, and eventually retrieving them from memory.

Teach Word-Decoding Skills

Students should be taught how particular letters and letter combinations are pronounced (Stanovich, 1991). Word decoding involves identifying the sounds associated with the word's letters and blending them together to determine the word. The letters used to spell a word often give some indication of the way in which the word is pronounced. However, the English language is not always reliable because it does not have one concrete correspondence between sounds and symbols. To assist students in learning to read words:

1. Focus on spelling patterns. Help the reader become familiar with riming clusters and repeating patterns in letters (e.g., ate).
2. Clap out the syllables of new words to help students hear and pronounce all of the sounds in the word.
3. Teach the rules of reading words that apply most of the time (e.g., the *e* at the end of a word is usually silent).
4. Show patterns in similarly spelled and pronounced words (e.g., the *end* in *bend, mend, send*).
5. Have students create nonsense words using common letter combinations (e.g., *brip, shwing*).
6. Give students a lot of practice sounding out unfamiliar words.
7. Teach students how to spell the words they are learning to read.

Using Examples and Non-examples to Reinforce Decoding of Words
This type of part-task training presents contrasting examples that are accurate representations with those that are "non-examples." Non-examples help to refine definitions of concepts being understood by a learner. The contrast between examples and non-examples helps to develop learners' representation of knowledge (Montague, 1987). In teaching a student to read, this approach can be easily applied. First, provide examples of how the task should be accomplished; Start off simple and proceed to the more difficult task at hand. Next provide the contrasting non-example to reinforce the concept or word being learned.

With regard to word decoding, if you are teaching a student to read the word *placemat*, first present the child with each syllable of the compound word starting with *place* and then *mat*. Complete the instruction with sounding the whole word out. The letter "c" can be pronounced differently depending upon its placement in a word. The teacher can present to the student a non-example of the word's pronunciation. The letter "c" is sometimes pronounced like "k" making the word *plakemat*. Explain why this is not the correct way to pronounce "c" in this context; in turn, the non-example further defines how to read *placemat*.

Importantly, the use of examples and non-examples applies not only to word decoding, but also is useful in other phases of learning (e.g., conceptual development, near term transfer).

Automaticity Process

Table 2.3. Automaticity Process of the Cognitive Domain

Process Requirements	Acquisition	Automaticity	Transfer: Near term	Transfer: Far term
COGNITIVE *decision making *problem solving *logical thinking *critical thinking	Rote learning (e.g., learning alphabet); Part task learning; Learning new procedures of a domain	Applying a known procedure to a known category of problem (e.g., decoding words, adding numbers, and automating through repetitive practice)	Solving new problems in the domain, conceptual thinking, strategic learning, transfer learning (e.g., self-generating a definition, proving a theorem)	Extending knowledge of a domain (creative thinking) to other domains (e.g. applying schemas of reading acquired in science to math, social studies, etc.

In order to maximize performance during the Automaticity stage, the following strategies will apply:

- **Teach word recognition and vocabulary;**
- **Use oral and expressive reading to develop fluency;**
- **Practice with appropriate levels of familiar texts;**
- **Maximize time spent reading.**

Teach Word Recognition and Vocabulary
Word recognition must become automatic in two ways. First students should be able to sight-read words quickly and automatically, without having to decode them letter-by-letter. Secondly, they should be able to retrieve the meanings of words immediately. Importantly, research shows that any one process of reading, like Automaticity, need not develop incrementally (Stanovich, 1991); rather, students can simultaneously gain meaning from text while developing automatic word decoding skills. Also, students need to expand their repertoire of word meanings through the development of an extensive vocabulary. Automaticity in word recognition develops through constant practice:

1. Utilize activities that incorporate environmental print such as logos, cereal boxes, household products, etc that can support emerging control over the conventions of print.
2. Provide many opportunities for the students to write to help them see connections among speech, sounds in words, and written words.
3. Use flashcards of individual words to promote more automatic word recognition.

Emphasize vocabulary development through:

1. Teaching the meanings of words through explicit vocabulary lessons;
2. Helping students activate their prior knowledge and experiences when encountering new words;
3. Providing word-building activities that pay attention to spelling, prefixes and suffixes;
4. Using both definitions and contextual examples when introducing new words;
5. Practicing the use of new words in several contexts and through two or three sensory modes;
6. Using semantic mapping for vocabulary expansion that extends knowledge of how words are related to one another (see also Near Term Transfer Section for more discussion and guidance);
7. Using analogies to portray the meaning of a word through comparisons that show its relationship to other words;
8. Encouraging students to read a variety of texts and materials as often as possible.

Use of Context to Facilitate Word Recognition
Word order is important in understanding the relationship between language and reading. The syntactic patterns in language are the same patterns followed in reading and writing. Words are recognized more easily when seen within the context of a sentence than when seen in isolation. Both the syntax and the overall meaning of the sentence provide context clues that help. Context is especially important for beginning readers who are not familiar with the new words or who have not fully developed automaticity. Some instructional techniques for effectively using context are listed below. An important caveat for the reading teacher is to provide multiple contexts of word representation. In this way, the beginning reader does not restrict the meaning of a word to a specific graphic representation (for further explanation see Stanovich, 2000).

1. Reading stories aloud provide opportunities to hear sounds in words within the context of the connected text.

2. When the student comes to an unknown word, instruct them to complete the sentence and then come back to the unknown word to figure it out.
3. Present the reader with a sentence in which one word has been omitted but the initial consonant is present.
4. Present a sentence with a blank that could be filled with just one word and no other.
5. Use exercises in which the vowels are absent from a word in the sentence and the student relies upon meanings, language cues and consonant cues in order to decipher the word.
6. Provide incomplete sentences in which the missing word can be identified among a group of words.

Use Oral and Expressive Reading to Develop Fluency

Students can gain oral fluency and expressiveness in reading through daily practice with familiar text. Fluency involves: (1) the rate and accuracy with which students recognize words (LaBerge & Samuels, 1974); and (2) the intonation, tone, and expressiveness of reading. Advanced readers are fluent, in the sense that they can read isolated words rapidly and accurately. They can read a whole passage aloud to communicate its meaning by adjusting their inflection, rate, and speed to match the intended meaning of the author. There are a number of variants of reading aloud to gain fluency including:

- Repeated readings—reading the same material more than once;
- Paired readings—pairs read orally to one another;
- Choral readings—a group of students read together simultaneously;
- Expressive readings—students dramatize oral readings through assuming roles in books or choosing favorite passages to read aloud. Books with rhyming patterns or ones that use two voices are very good for this type of reading (e.g., *Joyful Noise: Poems for Two Voices* by Paul Fleischman (1988) or *Under One Rock: Bugs, Slugs, and other Ughs* by Anthony D. Fredericks (2001) would be good selections to use).

Practice with Appropriate Levels of Interesting Texts and Maximize Time Spent Reading

Book access is an especially crucial aspect of early reading development (Pressley, 2002). Readers should have access to multiple levels and genres of text (see also Davis & Tonks, 2004; Guthrie & Cox, 1998). Guthrie and Cox (1998) recommend:

- Provide an ample supply of books about a theme of instruction;
- Provide books that are culturally responsive to students;
- Provide time for self-selected reading;
- Balance self-selected reading with guided reading.

Transfer Process: Near Term

Table 2.4. Near Term Transfer Process of the Cognitive Domain

Process Requirements	Acquisition	Automaticity	Transfer: Near term	Transfer: Far term
COGNITIVE *decision making *problem solving *logical thinking *critical thinking	Rote learning (e.g., learning alphabet); Part task learning; Learning new procedures of a domain	Applying a known procedure to a known category of problem (e.g., decoding words, adding numbers, and automating through repetitive practice)	Solving new problems in the domain, conceptual thinking, strategic learning, transfer learning (e.g., self-generating a definition, proving a theorem)	Extending knowledge of a domain (creative thinking) to other domains (e.g. applying schemas of reading acquired in science to math, social studies, etc.

In order to maximize performance during the Near Term Transfer stage, the following strategies will apply:

- **Teach reading comprehension strategies, such as activating background knowledge, questioning, searching, summarizing, and graphic organizing, text structure, and story grammar, among others;**
- **Use tasks that help readers transform their knowledge, including metaphorical reasoning;**
- **Integrate reading and writing whenever possible.**

Teach Reading Comprehension Strategies
Since reading is a constructive process in which readers identify main ideas, draw inferences, and usually go beyond the words in order to construct authors' intended meanings, reading strategy instruction is essential. *Reading Strategy Instruction* refers to the explicit teaching of strategic behaviors in reading. The National Reading Panel (2000) reviewed the current reading research in comprehension strategy instruction and concluded that several reading strategies are beneficial to students' meaning construction. These include: activating background knowledge, questioning, searching, summarizing, self-explanation, and graphic organizing, etc. that enable students to acquire relevant knowledge from text. Instruction using

teacher modeling, scaffolding, and coaching, with direct explanation for why strategies are valuable, and how and when to use them, is important for strategy use to develop. Other researchers (e.g., Meichenbaum & Biemiller, 1998) similarly point to the importance of a variety of instructional strategies to nurture learning. According to Meichenbaum and Biemiller (1998), it is important for teachers to use explicit direct instruction with clear instructional goals, modeling, independent practice, and appropriate feedback (see pp. 124-130 for more detail). Taboada and Guthrie (2004) have created benchmarks for strategy learning in the elementary grades and explicated the necessary components of competence, awareness, and self-initiation when teaching comprehension strategies. Guthrie, Wigfield, and Perencevich (2004) offer the following instructional recommendations:

- **Activating background knowledge**—Effective meaning instruction is enhanced by the amount of knowledge the reader already has about the topic (Alexander & Jetton, 1996; van Dijk & Kintsch, 1983).
  1. When first teaching activation, use books with the following qualities in order to reduce cognitive load:
     - Familiar topics relating to personal experiences,
     - Pictures that relate to students' experiences,
     - Title matched to content,
     - Vivid pictures,
     - Minimal text,
     - Situationally interesting,
     - Avoid topics about which students have many misconceptions.
  2. Later, the topics should be slightly unfamiliar; so that students can identify a number of new ideas they learned.
  3. The teacher can lead a discussion based on a book walk, previewing the text and illustrations and helping students to recall their knowledge about the topic.
  4. The teacher can use photographs, videos, demonstrations, props, hands-on activities, or even a field trip *before* reading to help students activate their knowledge.
  5. After reading, students can identify something new and important that they learned but did not express in prior knowledge statements. That is, they can revise and update their prior knowledge to include new knowledge learned after reading.
- **Question answering** – Students answer questions posed by the teacher and receive immediate feedback.
- **Self-questioning** – Students ask themselves questions about various aspects of an informational text or story.
  1. Specific instruction on how to ask questions needs to be provided by the teacher.
  2. When first teaching self-questioning, books with the following qualities will help students ask "good" questions:

- Visually enticing/vivid pictures,
- Concept-rich texts with related details,
- High quality text features such as, headings, sub-headings, captions, and
- Title, heading, and sub-headings matched to content.

3. In the initial stages of questioning, the teacher can first give one-half a question and have the students finish it. Or teacher can also provide a question word and have students finish the question. Students can also do these in pairs finishing each other's questions.

4. The teacher should highlight the difference between factual questions and conceptual questions. Teacher can emphasize that higher-order questions request *explanations* rather than facts. Taboada and Guthrie (2004) have developed a very useful questioning rubric for teachers and instructors to utilize.

5. Teachers can model questioning both before and during reading.

6. After reading (amount of text to be decided by teacher), teacher and students identify which questions were answered and which were not. Questions that could not be answered by the text can be reformulated or search for answers can be extended across multiple texts.

7. Be aware of individual differences, including students' personal characteristics, and social factors (Van Der Meij, 1994) when having students complete this task.

- **Searching** – Students are taught how to search for information in the text (i.e. table of contents, headings, index, etc.) (see also Dreher, 1993; Guthrie, Weber, & Kimmerly, 1993).

1. When first teaching search, choose books with the following qualities:
   - High quality text features such as, headings, sub-headings, captions;
   - Title, heading, and sub-headings matched to content.

2. Give students the choice of which book to search for information (Reynolds & Symons, 2001; Symons, McLatchy-Gaudet, & Stone, 2001).

3. When first teaching search, introduce students to text features, such as table of contents (TOC), index, glossary, bolded words, captions, illustrations, boxed text, etc., and have the students practice finding answers to questions using various text features.

4. Teach the students how to identify indexed terms, skim the text carefully, and monitor how well extracted information fulfills the search goal (Symons et al., 2001).

5. When first teaching the use of index, select a book with simple index and choose straightforward search terms where the student does not have to figure out synonyms. Later, students can build a "synonym journal" and have insert synonyms about re-occurring topics to help with finding terms in the index.

6. Discuss with students why captions and pictures go together. To help students become aware of the use of bold in headings, ask them to provide alternative titles or headings. Similarly, ask students to develop better captions for text illustrations.

7. Have students compare two books with different search features and have them evaluate how books differ in their text features and which books are more conducive to searching.

8. Give learners a worked example as a high scaffold for searching. For example, students can be given a research question, a list with books, and the search processes used to elicit the book selection. Students can identify the quality of the book selection and search processes utilized (van Merrienboer, Kirschner, & Kester, 2003).

9. Give learners a ½ worked example and have students complete the search process. For example, students can be given a research question, a list of books, and students can complete the search task by reducing the number of books to a predefined number (van Merrienboer, Kirschner, & Kester, 2003).

10. Present the task in an appealing format to arouse the student's interest (Reynolds & Symons, 2001).

- **Explanation and elaborative interrogation** – Students are taught to explain information to themselves and others and ask *why* questions about text material.

  1. Have pairs of students read a text selection silently. Next have one student read a sentence aloud. Have the partner ask a why question, such as, "Why would that be true?" or "Why is that important? to which the reader responds by connecting text ideas.

  2. Both partners can gain information from the process. The reader should think deeply to connect text information and the *why* question asker should choose an appropriate question to ask that makes sense in the context of the text information.

  3. Have students explain text material aloud to ensure comprehension (Chi et al., 1994).

  4. Have readers use think-alouds wherein they talk out loud about hurdles they face during reading. Also teachers can think-aloud to model their thinking processes about how to fix difficulties that might arise during the reading process (Afflerbach, & Pressley, 1995).

- **Summarizing** – Students are taught to integrate ideas and generalize from the text information (see also Brown & Day, 1983).

  1. Books for teaching summarizing should have the following qualities:
     - Concept information that is contained in one page or one section of text,
     - Section organized with main idea and supporting details,
     - Concept-related rather than fact-based (e.g., Eyewitness books are already summarized for the reader),
     - Familiar content.

2. The teacher can tell students about a movie he or she recently saw, using a detailed, long, description with irrelevant details. Next, the teacher can summarize what the movie was about in 2 to 3 sentences. Discuss the differences between the 2 statements in order for students to understand the purpose of a summary.

3. To summarize, have students identify and circle the main idea, underline all of the supporting details, and cross out all of the unimportant details (Brown & Day, 1983).

4. Have students highlight key words and then use those words to write a summary sentence.

5. Partners can trade summaries and verbally explain to summary-writer what the book was about.

- **Using Graphic and Semantic Organizers** – Students make graphic representations of the material.

  1. Have students identify clusters of related words within lists and then arrange word clusters and build a concept map.

  2. Teachers can provide a list of the main words (e.g. word-cards or word-slips with the main-idea word(s)) and supporting-detail words. Students can read a section of text and then build a class concept map with the words provided by the teacher. Discussion of word choice and word organization should be a central part of the direct instruction process (e.g. Why do we put this word in the center? Which words should branch out from the main idea? etc.). When students decide on the organization of words and provide their rationales for word organization they should be able to back up their concept-maps organization with text information.

  3. Concept maps should have a hierarchical form. Each level should express a similar level of generality and inclusiveness; however, as the student moves from top to bottom, the information should get progressively more specific and less inclusive of the specific context (Novak & Musonda, 1991).

  4. There should be consecutive map revisions by the students with the assistance of the tech to increase clarification of the concepts being learned and the connections between them (Starr & Krajcik, 1990).

- **Teaching "Story grammar"** (i.e. story structure) – Students learn how to use the structure of the story texts (morals, plot, obstacles, etc.) as a means of helping them recall story content in narratives (Baumann, & Bergeron, 1993; Meyer, 1984). Narrative texts have different purposes than expository texts. Expository text is intended to present information. Narrative texts, on the other hand, explore literary themes emphasizing character development and plot occurrences. Students need to be aware of these differences between genres in order to use strategies appropriate for each text type (see also Guthrie, Wigfield, & Perencevich, 2004).

1. Have students think about the crafting of the plot: *What is the author's purpose for writing this? What is the author trying to say?* Have students generate questions to help them develop awareness of the plot's progression and understanding of what is happening in the story and why.

2. Students can search for evidence of characters' main motivations and obstacles facing the main characters. Students can make predictions on how the obstacles could be handled by the characters based on what they found about the character's motivations.

3. To build cognitive flexibility, expose students to literary texts, which can support multiple interpretations, and have students search for multiple, possible themes and develop arguments to substantiate their positions. (see Spiro, et al., 1989, 1990, 1995).

Transfer Process: Far Term

Table 2.4. Far Term Transfer Process of the Cognitive Domain

Process Requirements	Acquisition	Automaticity	Transfer: Near term	Transfer: Far term
COGNITIVE *decision making *problem solving *logical thinking *critical thinking	Rote learning (e.g., learning alphabet); Part task learning; Learning new procedures of a domain	Applying a known procedure to a known category of problem (e.g., decoding words, adding numbers, and automating through repetitive practice)	Solving new problems in the domain, conceptual thinking, strategic learning, transfer learning (e.g., self-generating a definition, proving a theorem)	Extending knowledge of a domain (creative thinking) to other domains (e.g. applying schemas of reading acquired in science to math, social studies, etc.

At this level of transfer processes, multiple-contexts are applied in an even broader application of the principle.

- **Reading is presented as a context in itself as an example of structure.**
- **Positive far term transfer is expected across domains; e.g., with history, from attending to concepts of form and meta-cognitive awareness,**
- **Self-initiation of strategy use, and**

- **Strategies that integrate reading and writing.**

Metacognitive Awareness
Metacognitive awareness refers to the ability of the reader to recognize that reading is a construct in itself as well as a conveyor of information about ideas and events in the physical world. Many metacognitive strategies, such as elaborating and comprehension monitoring, are important in reading. Good readers spend a great deal more time on parts of a passage that are likely to be critical to their overall understanding (Afflerbach & Pressley, 1995; Garner, 1987; Palincsar & Brown, 1984). Good readers often set goals for their reading and ask themselves questions that they hope to answer as they read (Baker & Brown, 1984; Webb & Palincsar, 1996). Metacognitive processes in reading can be encouraged in readers through:

1. Utilizing activities that require the reader to attend to the structure, form, and or semantic character of words or sentences to develop skills in attention to critical detail or to important cue words or phrases.
2. Deleting trivial and redundant information.
3. Identifying general ideas that incorporate several more specific ideas (Bean & Steenwyk, 1984).
4. Instructing students to make predictions as they read.
5. Providing opportunities for group discussions of material (Gambrell & Almasi, 1996).
6. Asking students to give a verbal retelling of why what they read is important to increase the sophistication of the beginner/novice reader; i.e. elaborative interrogation (Willoughby et al., 1994; Willoughby et al., 1999, Woloshyn et al., 1994).

Generalizing these techniques to other cognitive domains is illustrated by Meichenbaum and Biemiller (1998). They suggest six useful strategies for self-instructional guidance, including: "defining the problem, accessing and summarizing relevant information, focusing attention and planning, self-monitoring (e.g., evaluating performance, catching and correcting errors), using coping self-statements, and self-reinforcing [statements]" (p. 131).

Comprehension Monitoring
Students learn how to be aware of their understanding of their reading material. Instructing by using metaphors can be helpful here. Metaphorical reasoning uses a schema-based approach for comprehension of the subject at hand. Using schemas to construct meaning during reading involves the reader's use of prior knowledge, context, and other linguistic cues (Kincade, 1991). Through this interaction, each reader constructs an individualized interpretation of the material read by integrating both explicitly and implicitly stated information. An example of the use of the skills in metaphorical reasoning in Reading would be figurative language such as sentence metaphors. The individual uses abstract problem-solving strategies to successfully

comprehend a methaphorical text. In other words, a problem or concept is presented to an individual that they cannot understand. For comprehension, the problem is put into metaphorical terms using prior knowledge or schemas already developed by the individual. This way, the individual learns new material by understanding it in other comprehensible terms.

1. Teach students detection cues for when a breakdown in understanding occurs. For example, during reading students can ask themselves, "does this make sense? or "what did the paragraph say?" After reading, students can explain the meaning of the text to a peer or identify the main ideas of the passage. If this cannot be accomplished, students need to use fix-up strategies.

2. Comprehension monitoring occurs at various levels, including the word, sentence, paragraph, page, and book levels. Therefore, students must have a repertoire of fix-up strategies at each level where a breakdown occurs. Word and sentence meaning fix up strategies include, rereading the sentence, using context clues, consulting an expert (e.g., glossary, dictionary, other person). Higher level fix up strategies include, summarizing the text, drawing illustrations or graphic organizers, or explaining the meaning of the text to another person.

3. Teach students text structures (e.g., compare/contrast, problem/solution, and persuasion for information texts and poetry or legends for narrative). Prompt these text structures to help students recognize patterns that authors often use.

4. Remind students of the ideas they already know about the reading topic.

5. Give students' specific training in drawing inferences from reading material (see suggestions above for developing cognitive flexibility in Near Term Transfer).

6. Relate events in a story or information in an expository text to students' own lives.

7. Ask students to form mental images of the people or events depicted in a reading passage.

8. Ask students to retell, elaborate, or summarize what they have read after each sentence, paragraph, or section to foster concept learning.

9. Remind students to use reading strategies, such as elaborative interrogation, graphic organizing, drawing pictures, creating mental images, or questioning, to overcome hurdles in the comprehension process.

Reading with Technology: Reducing Cognitive Load
When teaching for fluency or comprehension skills, use as many familiar contexts as you can. Make the text easily accessible, i.e. simple vocabulary, recognizable spelling, and patterns. Otherwise, a cognitive overload could prevent an individual from taking in, processing, or integrating new information. Below, we suggest some

guidance when using multimedia learning supported by learning research principles (see Section II for a discussion of cognitive overload) to avoid this from happening:

1. *When presenting new information to an individual on a computer, instead of overusing one channel, such as the visual channel, use two channels to spread out the cognitive processing to prevent overload.* (e.g., Sweller's split-attention effect, 1999). For example (Mayer & Moreno, 2003), an individual wants to learn about lightning. On the screen appears an animation depicting the steps in lightning formation. Instead of presenting on-screen text describing the steps of lightning formation, a narrative can be sounded. This way the visual channel is not overloaded by watching the animation as well as reading the text.

2. *When organizing the information being presented, use illustrations* (Foshay, Silber, & Stelnicki, 2003). When presented with a picture/illustration, people actually code them twice. They 1) assign meaning to them and 2) interpret the visual image. This is referred to as dual coding and makes it easier for the individual to store and retrieve information in long term memory as well as prevent cognitive overload.

3. *To avoid both channels being overloaded, the information presented to the individual could be broken up into parts divided by breaks in time* (Mayer & Moreno, 2003). This way, the individual can process all the information presented to them before moving on to new information. Use principles of part-task training and distributed practice (discussed in more detail in Chapter 3).

4. *Another way of avoiding overload in both channels, is pre-training the individual on the information that will be presented to them* (Mayer & Moreno, 2003). If they have a background on the components, when the information is presented in full, the student will not try to understand each component and the causal links between them.

5. *Unnecessary information must be weeded out that may cause overload* (Mayer & Moreno, 2003; Sweller et al., 1998). For instance, with the lightning example, an instructional developer might want to include extra features in the presentation of information, such as background music, distracting graphics, etc. This additional information may just overload either channel; therefore, to avoid this, don't include any unnecessary additional information. Training examples are: 1) training pilots to recognize landing info on carriers, black and white outline figures better (or at least as good as) than full color 3-D pictures). 2) training Army helicopter pilots on cockpit procedures with cardboard mockups superior to use of copter itself (Prophet & Boyd, 1970). In addition to being better for the learner, such procedures are less costly.

6. *If this unnecessary information cannot be weeded out, then something should be done do draw attention to the information that is necessary* (Mayer & Moreno, 2003). In the lightning example, this can include putting words in bold, adding arrows to the animation, stressing words in the

narration, or organizing images by adding a map showing which of the parts of the lesson was being presented, using the principle of saliency.

7. *Make sure that you are not displaying the information in a confusing manner that would cause cognitive overload* (Mayer & Moreno, 2003). For example, pictures are on one screen and the words to go with them are displayed on another screen. This would require the individual to go back and forth to integrate all the information. Instead, present pictures and corresponding words/explanations together in an integrated presentation.

8. *Do not be redundant in presenting information* (Mayer & Moreno, 2003). You do not need a narration, animation, and test for presenting one piece of information. Too many things to listen to and look at may cause an overload in processing. In this situation, one should also take into account individual differences. Some persons' needs may warrant redundancy (novices) and others (experts) may not depending on their experience and level of education (Kalyuga et al., 2003).

9. The learner sometimes will have to hold onto the material previously presented to them to understand the next set of information presented. "Cognitive capacity must be used to hold a representation in working memory, thus depleting the learner's capacity for engaging in the cognitive processes of selecting, organizing and integrating" (Mayer & Moreno, 2003, p. 50). *In order to minimize the amount of material required to be held in working memory, the recommendation is to synchronize the material.* Present both pieces of material at the same time without presenting too much, (Foshay et al., 2003; also Miller's 1956, 5 to 7 items, maximum capacity for short-term memory), which may cause an overload. For example, present the narration and the animation of the steps of the lightning at the same time. Do not present the animation, than afterwards present a narrative explanation. The learner may have to jump back to the animation in order to integrate all of the information, which may result in confusion and time lost. If this suggestion is not possible, then training in holding mental representations in memory can be done.

Foster Far Term Transfer through Reading Engagement

Our engagement perspective on reading focuses on the mutual functioning of motivation, cognitive skills, strategy use, and knowledge during reading (see also Guthrie & Wigfield, 2000). Because reading is an effortful activity that often involves choice, motivation is crucial to reading engagement (see Chapter 4 in this volume for further discussion of motivation as task-oriented focus of energy). Even the reader with the strongest cognitive skills may not spend much time reading if she or he is not motivated to read. This discussion offers instructional recommendations that answer the question, how do you increase long-term reading engagement in and outside the classroom? We and other researchers suggest using the following motivational practices to foster engagement in reading (Guthrie & Cox, 2001; Guthrie, Wigfield, & Perencevich, 2004).

- *Learning and Knowledge Goals* – construct instructional goals that emphasize conceptual understanding in a specific topic within a knowledge domain (Ames, 1992; Ames & Archer, 1988).
  - o For example, within a unit on life sciences for elementary school students, a conceptual theme may be "adaptation". There are many subtopics within this theme, such as physical body features of animals, their behavioral functions, and species-biome relationships.
- *Hands on experience* – provide a sensory interaction (e.g., seeing, hearing, feeling, or smelling) with tangible objects or events as they appear in their natural environment to increase curiosity in a topic, which in turn, evokes intrinsically motivated behaviors (Paris, Yambor, & Packard, 1998).
  - o For example, in science, real-world interactions consist of inquiry science activities such as observing predatory beetles or conducting experiments with guppies. In history, real-world interactions may consist of reenacting a historical event or visiting the American History Museum.
- *Interesting texts* – provide an ample supply of texts that are relevant to the learning and knowledge goals being studied as well as matched to the cognitive competence of the learners (Davis & Tonks, 2004)
- *Autonomy support* – give the students opportunities for choices and control over their learning (see also Cordova & Lepper, 1996; Deci & Ryan, 1987; Stefanou, Perencevich, DiCintio, & Turner, 2004; also see discussion on self-regulation in Chapter 4 of this volume).
  - o For example, to provide support for student choice, allow students to select a subtopic as their learning goal and allow students to identify texts that they believe will be informative and understandable for them.
- *Collaboration in instruction* – provide structures for social interchange around learning the content (Meichenbaum & Biemiller, 1998; Turner, 1995; also discussed under Strategies Section in Chapter 5).
  - o For example, work in teams to learn. In learning about adaptation in mammals, different students may elect the subtopics of feeding, defense, shelter, and reproduction. As students integrate their diverse information, they form higher-order principles about the topic. Students can choose who to work with on specific learning tasks and how to distribute their expertise.
  - o For example, students may consult with others in the classroom in a variety of ways, including, tutoring, think-pair-share, idea circles (Perencevich, 2004), or reciprocal teaching (see also Meichenbaum & Biemiller, 1998).

Concept Instruction with Text

This topic refers to three central aspects of instruction that foster in-depth conceptual learning of expository text (informational text). Concept instruction with text is defined as providing extensive opportunities for students to interact with multi-layered knowledge, to transform meaning by manipulating information, and to experience optimal challenge during reading. Conceptual learning from text occurs when students have formed a mental representation consisting of four schematic elements. Those elements include: (a) basic propositions about the domain (e.g., facts), (b) relations among the propositions, (c) concepts or generalizations that broadly relate propositions (facts) to each other, and (d) a network of concepts. Students with conceptual knowledge can use this schema network flexibly to solve problems or serve as an analogy for new learning. This flexible schema and all its parts constitute an explanatory understanding of the domain (network of interrelated concepts and rules that serve as a critical component in a discipline of knowledge). To acquire a domain of richly elaborated knowledge, students should encounter and interact with all these levels of knowledge. To improve concept learning, Cox and Guthrie (2001) recommend:

- Teachers rely on texts that contain all levels of knowledge (e.g., propositional, relational, and conceptual levels).
- Students read, discuss, and write about such texts in a setting in which this material is relevant and useful.
- Use hands-on activities to provide concrete referents for the basic propositions and to create opportunities for spontaneous questioning.
- Have students create new representations of text, such as concept mapping, constructing projects, building models or drawing graphical representations so that they rely on deep structural knowledge of a domain.
- Use optimally challenging reading activities to heighten conceptual learning from text
- Help students meet increasingly difficult goals and see concrete evidence of their growth.
- Expose students to multiple texts with multiple perspectives on a topic or theme.

Time Spent in Multiple Contexts
The teacher should provide learners with multiple contexts (i.e. different topics, different subject matters) and reading opportunities in which the learner can practice the development of comprehension strategies. The more variety of example contexts and content that the learner practices, the greater the likelihood of developing domain independent strategies. In Far Term Transfer, this translates into greater "time on task" where the task is to develop cross-domain schemas. This theme will be noted repeatedly throughout the book because we feel it is of paramount importance for all higher-order, schematic learning, or transfer. Stanovich (2000) compared this idea of time on task to the "rich get richer effect", which translates into the more you read the better you get. The amount that students read for enjoyment and for school strongly contributes to students' reading achievement and knowledge of the world (Cipielewski & Stanovich, 1992; Cox & Guthrie, 2001; Guthrie & Wigfield, 2000).

More than simply time on task however, it is essential that the quality of the material and the instruction permit and encourage the development of multiple interpretations when the learner is faced with complex contexts. Spiro et al. (1989, 1990, 1995) advocate the use of a hypertext-learning environment as especially useful when the learner is trying to read and understand complex concepts, which can take on different meanings dependent upon the context (i.e., in ill-structured domains). In an extension of this discussion, Feltovich, Spiro, and Coulson (1993) point to the need for using techniques of multiple representation (including analogies) as opposed to a single isolated and oversimplified perspective in order to teach complex learning, especially in ill structured domains. We would submit that in teaching Reading, it is quite clear that word meaning is dependent on the semantic context of a story, implied in a sentence. For example, "He caught the fly," at the very least could mean a baseball or an insect. Instruction involving our proposed functional context spiral can certainly help avoid the oversimplification and isolated concept problems. Spiro and his associates cite as one of their prime domain examples the field of "medical education, [which] has traditionally had separated 'basic science' and clinical parts..." with the clinical parts occurring much later in the program (Feltovich, Spiro, & Coulson, 1993, p. 204) We would submit that following Sticht's early work on functional literacy (1975), it became quite clear to those teaching Reading that it suffered from the same problems. Since Reading involves the basic symbol system by which we learn early on to encode and build transfer schemas, it is our position, as stated earlier in Chapter 1, that it is fundamental as an example of learning in the cognitive domain.

Therefore:

- Provide a wide array of texts in multiple levels & genres for students to read, and
- Give supplementary guidance about the way meanings can vary in particular situations.
- Provide extensive time for students, to read and then in class, to discuss alternative interpretations.

Classroom Environment
An integral part of Reading education is a conducive learning environment, indeed, it is for all learning, as we discuss in Chapter 4. In the Reading context, Pressley et al. (2001) suggest:

- The teacher should emphasize a positive, reinforcing, cooperative setting.
- Instructors should set high but realistic expectations, and make accomplishing these expectations accessible to them by providing and encouraging more challenging tasks.
- Books of all contexts and subject matters should be readily available to the students along with the time (long, uninterrupted periods) to read them. This

time as well as organization and work habits should be self-monitored by the students.

- Finally the teacher should make their rules and expectations clear to the student and meaningfully engage assistants in assisting in these tasks.

SECTION II:

SUPPORTING RESEARCH

Gray (1950) describes reading as consisting of four processes: word recognition, comprehension, reaction, and assimilation. Robinson (1966) expanded the model to include rate of reading. Beginning readers need a wide range of skills and abilities for making sense of text at the word and sentence levels (Adams, 1990). A reader should first learn how to recognize individual sounds and letters, use word-decoding skills, recognize words automatically, use of context clues to facilitate word recognition, and develop meanings of vocabulary words for story comprehension (Adams, 1990; Ehri, 1991; Stanovich, 1991; Sulzby, & Teale, 1991).

More advanced readers can use high-order reading strategies to develop an understanding of the writer's intended meaning and metacognitively regulate the reading process (Meyer, 1984; National Reading Research Panel, 2000). Some of these skills include: activating background knowledge, questioning, searching, summarizing, organizing graphically, structuring story grammars, and monitoring comprehension. Along with these cognitive skills, readers use self-regulatory and motivational strategies to persist in the effortful task of reading. Following is a review of the skills, abilities, and cognitive and motivational strategies necessary for reading to develop.

Research Supporting Acquisition and Automaticity

One common observation in reading research is that the beginning reader must rely on visual information much more than the advanced reader, who is able to use both visual and non-visual sources of information, both syntactic and semantic. Beginning readers typically deduce meaning from the surface structure or the visual array of letters on the page. Often the beginning reader becomes so absorbed with the mechanical aspects of reading, specifically word identification and pronunciation, that comprehension becomes problematic. The advanced reader on the other hand, attends selectively to the more important words in the text and uses other strategies to comprehend the text effectively. In the Instructional Guidance section of this chapter, we described exercises to facilitate this transition between beginning and advanced reading (e.g., practice in efficient methods for decoding written words and using context cues).

Ehri (1991, 1994) synthesized strategy development in word reading, and revealed that development occurs in three phases: logographic, alphabetic, and orthographic. The first phase, logographic, refers to the visual features of a word that are nonphonemic, contextual, or graphic. Children in this stage use visual images of a word, rather than letter-sound correspondences to read a word (e.g., a store logo). Logographic readers move to the alphabetic stage when they stop attending to visual cues and begin to read the print.

The alphabetic stage begins when readers can read words by processing and recognizing letter-sound relationships. Alphabetic readers can phonologically recode written words into pronunciations, meaning that they know the names and sounds of letters and have the ability to break words into pronounceable segments or chunks; This skill allows readers at this stage to decode unfamiliar words accurately. Alphabetic readers are also able to store the spellings of sight words and letter-sound connections in memory. Treiman (1985) found that onsets (initial consonants) and rimes (remaining vowel stems) are natural ways to divide words and are stable spelling patterns. Adams (1990) contends that a major difference between good and poor readers is their proficiency to use such spelling patterns and their ability to translate spelling and sound relationships.

Children in the orthographic stage have word knowledge that includes prefixes, suffixes, and digraphs. These readers are able to use grapheme-phoneme patterns that recur across words that they have learned to read. Orthographic readers are able to recognize spelling patterns (e.g., -ate, -ment, -ed) and are able to store these patterns in memory. The ability to read words can also happen by decoding words by analogy through the use of spelling patterns and using contextual clues (Ehri, 1991). Decoding is the process of making letter-sound connections into pronunciations that may include blending and sounding out letters to make meaning. Decoding by analogy and the use of spelling patterns are other ways to read unfamiliar words. Analogy is the strategy that teaches readers to compare a word they don't know to a word they do know. For example, if students know the word *cat,* they can read the word *mat* by comparing the rhyming part of the word and changing the initial consonant from *c to m.* They learn that this "at" pattern is stable and remains the same in the words *hat, fat, rat, that.* Contextual clues are important in the decoding of unfamiliar words because the text preceding a word enables readers to form expectations about what the word is (Goodman, 1965). Researchers have found that young readers' expectations are working because they substitute words that are semantically and syntactically consistent with the text up to the point of the unfamiliar word (Biemiller, 1970).

One effective way of strengthening low or high-order skills and transform a non-strategic reader into a strategic reader is to apply techniques such as reinforcement and contingency. These operant learning and conditioning principles should be consistently applied while the reader is learning to read, as well as during the utilization of low-order and high-order reading skills and strategies. An example of applying the principles is when an individual uses appropriate strategies or skills, an extrinsic reinforcer such as positive feedback (e.g., words of praise) immediately follow. Intrinsic motivations, such as enjoying what one reads or simply getting pleasure out of gaining knowledge from the materials read, are often considered superior measures of reinforcement. Whatever the reinforcer, it should increase the frequency of the individual's utilization of the correct skills and strategies. In order for the reinforcer to be effective, it must be appropriate and contingent upon the voluntary desired behavior of the reader. (see Honig, 1966, for general discussion of reinforcers).

The way in which students read, whether reading expressively to an audience, reading aloud to oneself, silent reading, or silent reading while listening, may also affect comprehension. Some researchers speculate reading orally to oneself aids comprehension because it focuses closer attention on the words and involves a second modality. When there are distracting noises in the environment or when the concept load of the text increases the difficulty level to a near frustration point, readers often resort to reading aloud. Under these conditions, the reader is not concerned with perfect intonation or pronunciation, but rather with their own understanding of the text.

Holmes (1985) conducted a study to determine which of mode of reading best facilitated the answering of post comprehension questions. In the study, students read an expository passage in each reading mode (i.e., silent reading, silent reading while listening, oral reading to one self, expressive reading to an audience) and answered comprehension questions that included gist, literal recall of details, inferences and scriptal comparisons. Silent and oral reading to oneself were both found to be superior to oral reading to an audience. Additionally, silent reading was also found to facilitate comprehension to a greater extent than did silent reading while listening to the text being read. When reading to oneself silently or orally, the reader is able to concentrate on understanding the text and can re-read portions that were not clearly understood or utilize various comprehension techniques because he/she does not have to divide attention. This study supported the findings of Poulton and Brown (1967), which showed that when the reader is concerned about his vocal output as the case may be when reading to someone, attention is diverted away from comprehension. However, when reading to ones-self, these factors were not relevant because of the absence of an audience.

A plethora of research indicates the importance of explicit instruction in processes to help students acquire phonological awareness, word recognition, spelling patterns, and vocabulary development (Adams, 1990; Ball & Blachman, 1991; Stahl & Murray, 1994; Whitehurst et al., 1994).

Transitioning from Automaticity to Transfer: Reading Comprehension

Reading comprehension is "the process of simultaneously extracting and constructing meaning through interaction and involvement with written language" (RAND Reading Study Group, 2002, p. 11) and there are three elements required in comprehension: the reader, the text, and the activity. The reader comprises all the capacities and abilities as well as the knowledge and experience it entails in order to comprehend information. The text is what the reader is attempting to comprehend and includes any printed or electronic text. Reading has a purpose and this is the activity. The activity comprises all the processes and consequences used in reading that is motivated by the purpose. (RAND Reading Study Group, 2002).

Summarized by Dole, Duffy, & Roehler (1991), comprehension techniques include grasping the critical elements of a single text, questioning, summarizing, making inferences, and drawing conclusions about the theme for a narrative or the moral of a fable (Graesser, Golding, & Long, 1991). In their work, Britton and Graesser (1996) define text understanding as "the dynamic process of constructing coherent representations and inferences at multiple levels of text and context, within the bottleneck of a limited-capacity working memory" (p. 350). Indeed, the successful comprehender should connect incoming textual information with prior knowledge in such a way that she constructs a coherent and stable representation of the passage rather than a random list of ideas. Also, she should recognize the main idea of a text, generate relevant inferences, and reconcile multiple interpretations of the text reading. One of our goals as educators is to help readers move from recalling simple sentences to the construction of internal representations of meaning.

Ausubel (1960, 1962, 1969) used the Piagetian theory to argue that learning new materials greatly depend upon the existing cognitive structure or what the person already knows. New information will be more easily learned if it is explained and also related to prior ideas in the student's cognitive structure. Accordingly, instruction should begin with a general concept, the advanced organizer, and move to more specific information. This principle includes teaching the most general ideas of a subject first, and then integrating new information with the information previously taught. Reading instruction should include real-world (authentic or functionally relevant) tasks, use many examples and concentrate on similarities and differences. The most important factor in instruction is what the student already knows. The process of meaningful learning involves recognizing the relationship between new information and what is already known. We have discussed this in Chapter 1 as the spiral curriculum. Harvey and Goudvis (2000) describe this from an instructional perspective as aligning the teaching content and teaching process.

In order to differentiate conceptual text learning from mere recall of text, Kintsch and van Dijk (1978) developed a theory of expository text comprehension (see also van Dijk & Kintsch, 1983). In this model, Kintsch and his colleagues (1983) defined three levels of text representation: a linguistic model, a textbase model and a situational model.

The linguistic representation comprises the meaning of specific words in memory often at a verbatim level. At this level of meaning, the reader typically recalls explicit information and preserves the surface structure of the text. At this level of text representation, content from the text is subject to rapid decay.

The text-base representation includes information expressed in the text that is organized such that it remains relatively faithful to the passage. Though the text structure may be modified to emphasize the more important information from the text, these representations consist of the direct textual propositions along with necessary inferences that satisfy coherence among the propositions. This representation is more stable than the linguistic level of representation because it contains a macrostructure that ties the main ideas together and a microstructure that reflects the interrelated semantic details of the passage.

The situational level of representation captures readers' integration and restructuring of text information such that it has connected meaningfully with prior knowledge. The situation model shows a higher-level integration process wherein vital information is inferred and made part of the representation. Thus, the reader gains a deeper understanding of the material, resulting in the transfer of knowledge to novel situations and problem-solving tasks (Kintsch & van Dijk, 1978).

How do we know when students have made these integrated knowledge connections suggested in the situation model? Michelene Chi's work (1994) has been particularly informative in describing the organization and quality of conceptual knowledge gained from text. The degree to which knowledge is connected and integrated depends on the number of connections between nodes of knowledge. Nodes are connected with regard to structures, functions, and relationships. Using the atrium, a feature of the heart, as an example, Chi and her colleagues (1994) describe differing nodes of knowledge that must connect and co-exist in order to achieve conceptual understanding. She explains that the local features of the atrium include a structural property, that it is a muscular chamber, a behavioral component, that it squeezes blood, and a functional aspect, that it is a holding bin. The connections between these three components represent one network of relations. As the web of relations expand, however, the reader understands connections among the various features and form hierarchical relations. The greater the number of connections, both at the micro-level (between structures) and at the macro-level (among structures) defines the level of conceptual learning.

Viewed from a schema perspective (e.g., Sweller et al, 1998), these micro- and macro-structural developments might also be seen as the basis for complex schema learning. Certainly we would see these structures as aiding transfer both within the topic of focus; and as the complexities develop, and with multiple-example contexts, they would provide the foundation for transfer of these rules (schemas) to apply across domains as well. Guthrie and his colleagues (2004) have developed similar rubrics to understand elementary-aged students' levels of conceptual learning from text.

Strategic Reading
There are two important aspects of reading comprehension. One aspect involves reading becoming more automatic with strategy use. Strategies such as making inferences, using analogies, predicting, and questioning all become automatic as readers become more proficient and have familiarity with text. The other aspect is the ability to use complex reading strategies deliberately and consciously.

Harvey & Goudvis (2000) discuss strategies used by proficient readers that support these two aspects. They suggest that a reader must make connections between prior knowledge and the test, ask questions, visualize, draw inferences, determine important ideas, synthesize the information and repair and misunderstandings. These skills "interact and intersect to help readers make meaning and often occur simultaneously during reading" (p. 12). Strategies students need to become more efficient readers include acquiring initial associative skills as emergent readers and high-order strategies as more experienced readers.

Many reading theorists believe reading is very much a constructive process (Hiebert & Raphael, 1996), involving the development of these higher-order strategies. A strategy is a plan of action that can be applied to different situations or tasks and it helps increase understanding, improve memory, solve a particular problem, reach a desired goal, or increase efficiency in performance. Strategies are crucial when planning a vacation, playing a game of chess, a championship basketball game, golf, or tennis. In Reading, strategies are cognitive processes that are controllable and conscious activities. They help learners increase their abilities to become efficient in decoding, comprehension, memory, problem solving, and transferring conceptual understanding from one text to another. Being a strategic reader requires effort, time, careful planning, and persistence. Strategies are necessary when students are learning how to read, solve problems, or when reading material that is unfamiliar or too difficult (Paris, Lipson, & Wixon, 1983).

Strategies differ from skills in the sense that skills are more automatic strategies. Gagne (1977) and Fischer (1980) define skills as automatic sequences of complex actions. Skills are continuous changes in performance that are compared to normative standards such as speed and complexity. Strategies are skills that can be broken down and analyzed, modeled, shared, and examined more closely. Strategic behavior adds motivational intent to skills and is personalized from learner to learner. There is not a uniform pattern to which each learner applies strategies. Readers individualize strategy use based on his or her personal needs and methods (Paris, Lipson, & Wixon, 1983).

Strategic readers have control over their strategy execution and are meta-cognitive about monitoring their comprehension and strategy use. These readers take into consideration the task at hand, which may include evaluating different strategies and deciding which ones are most appropriate and necessary. They are aware of what strategies to apply in a given situation in order to increase comprehension of the text. They also use more strategies as they read and they use them more efficiently than poor readers. For example, they may use context clues in order to decipher the syntax and meaning of a text. Strategic readers employ techniques such as looking at the words around the word that they do not know in order to construct meaning. These readers also know when a strategy they are using is not working, and are able to evaluate and change their strategies to one that will facilitate understanding of a particular text. This evaluation may include an assessment of the learner's effort, intelligence, and amount of prior knowledge that they might need to accomplish the task.

Thus, a major distinction between experts and novices in any domain is self-controlled strategic behavior. An expert reader and/or problem solver is someone who can read and comprehend different and various types of texts by transferring their strategic knowledge to different genres (e.g., expository, narrative, goal-based expository). These readers are also able to monitor their strategy use and transfer this knowledge to different domains (e.g., writing). Higher-order skills and effective reading strategies are quite valuable, yet they are rarely learned well. Since they are difficult to acquire, readers, both emergent and skilled, need intrinsic motivations, sustaining reinforcers, and purposes for learning to aid in the successful acquisition and use of cognitive strategies (Guthrie & Wigfield, 2000). In order to encourage reading and the utilization of skills and strategies reading activities should as often as possible be enjoyable and this enthusiasm should either be inherent to the task itself or an internal desire of the learner. The key to effective strategy use, however, is the way in which these strategies get moved from teacher to students through effective and explicit instruction within meaningful contexts and authentic, or functionally relevant, literacy tasks.

Near Term Transfer Processes

Early behaviorist theories believed that transfer occurred only to the extent that the original and transfer tasks had identical or similar elements (Thorndike, 1931). Behaviorist views have since focused on how transfer is affected by stimulus and response characteristics in both the original and transfer situations. In specific transfer, the original learning task and transfer task overlap in content. In general transfer or transfer of principles, the original task and the transfer task are different in content.

The cognitive perspective views transfer as involving a process of retrieval in which people are apt to transfer previously learned information and skills to a new situation only when they retrieve the information and skills at the appropriate time. In order to make the connection between their current situation and prior knowledge, they must have both things in working memory at the same time. The presence or absence of retrieval cues in the transfer situation determines what relevant knowledge is retrieved in working memory. According to cognitive theorists, the probability of retrieving any particular piece of information is considered low considering the limited capacity of working memory and many relevant pieces of information may very well not be transferred in situations in which they would be helpful. More recently, cognitivists proposed that most learning is context specific and is unlikely to result in transfer to new contexts, especially when they are very different from the ones in which learning originally occurred (see Druckman & Bjork, 1994, for a review of transfer; Lave & Wenger, 1991, for a discussion of situated learning; and Sweller et al., 1998, for a cognitive view of how transfer occurs).

A slightly different view of transfer worthy of discussion, captures the notion of "situated" learning and cognition and comes from Gestalt theory roots (e.g. Köhler, 1947). Linder's (1993) theory of transfer (conceptual dispersion), called phenomenagraphic, focuses on enhancing the learner's appreciation of context and the ability to make conceptual distinctions based on a concept's appropriateness to a given context. This appreciation or lack thereof results in the facilitation or inhibition of the learning of new tasks from previous experiences. Learning is viewed as a function of ""experienced variation ...explored in relation... to make sense of things in confusing and complex situations" (Linder & Marshall, 2003, p. 271). Linder and Marshall (2003) introduce the concept of "mindful conceptual dispersion". This is characterized by: (1) experiencing a phenomenon in different ways in different contexts, and (2) developing an explicit conceptual appreciation of the variation in context. Taken together these attributes provide the basis for learning. The learner solves problems by being able to shift his or her conscious or mindful appreciation of context, so that s/he can establish new figure from ground relationships. Thereby, we are able to reason from the familiar to the unfamiliar; or in our terms, to accomplish near or far term transfer.

One of Piaget's (1957) basic assumptions is that children are active and motivational learners. They construct knowledge from their prior experiences and seek out information that will help them understand and make sense of what they encounter. He identified schemas as groups of similar thoughts or actions that organize the things that are learned. While searching for information, one uses the processes of assimilation and accommodation to modify and recognize the relationship of existing schemas. According to Piaget (1957), assimilation is the process of using prior knowledge in existing schemas to understand new information. Successful assimilation results in a state of equilibrium. Disequilibrium occurs if the new information does not fit within existing schemas. One will modify existing schemata or form an entirely new schema in order to accommodate the new information. Equilibration is the process of moving between the states of equilibrium and disequilibrium. This process promotes development of higher levels of comprehension and complex thought. Readers use these processes to make meaning from text. In a derivative way, Perfetti (1995) sees Reading as a perceptual process, an interpretive process, a conceptual and thinking process. Strategic learners continually expand the scope of their cognitive grasp through *problem solving* by transferring knowledge to new situations. Their degree of transfer of knowledge depends primarily on the level of previous conceptual knowledge. Strategic learners continually test old schemas against new information and tailor the information for a better understanding.

Strategic readers are better than non-strategic readers, not only at reading, but also at monitoring, controlling, and adapting their strategic processes while reading (Dole, Duffy, & Roehler, 1991). Effective meaning construction in reading is enhanced by the amount of knowledge the reader already has about the topic in question (van Dijk & Kintsch, 1983). Knowing what strategies to employ will only result from practice in reading and using problem solving techniques. Non-strategic readers, on the other hand, are unaware of what strategy works for them. If poor readers have difficulty understanding text, they may not know what will help them gain an understanding. If a strategy is not working, poor readers are less likely to be aware of this problem and are unable to adjust their strategy use to increase understanding of various texts (Baker & Brown, 1984; Garner, 1987). Poor readers face these difficulties due to their lack of ample experience in reading and employing problem solving strategies.

It is well documented that some reading strategies help foster deep understanding with text (Baker & Brown, 1984; Brown & Day, 1983; Collins-Block & Pressley, 2002; Harris & Graham, 1992; Paris, Wasik, & Turner, 1991; Symons, McLatchy-Gaudet, & Stone, 2001). A few powerful reading strategies that are widely recognized include: (1) using prior knowledge, (2) questioning (self and teacher) (3) searching for information (4) summarizing, (5) using graphic and semantic organizers, and (6) elaborative interrogation. We explicate these cognitive reading strategies in the following research discussion. The reader will note that the procedures for implementing these strategies were described in Section I of this chapter.

Using Prior Knowledge

First, using prior knowledge is essential to comprehending new information (Anderson & Pearson, 1984; Spires & Donley, 1998), and it is imperative to the advancement of conceptual knowledge (Alexander & Jetton, 1996). Activating students' prior knowledge about a topic provides students with a way to connect their new knowledge to their previous understanding, which is how comprehension and learning occurs. Past experiences can help create *schemas* (Anderson, 1994) that are recalled when cued from text. For example, we have schemas about how to order dinner in a restaurant, how to travel by airplane, and how to get ready for school or work each week morning. These common events in our lives are loaded with different kinds of declarative and procedural knowledge. When reading new text, activating students' prior knowledge allows students the opportunity to reflect upon what they already know about the topic, which enhances their understanding of new information. Inferences can be made in reading the new text, which allows for meaning to be made by the student. Activated schemata guide attention to text and allow inferencing to occur with the new information.

Questioning

Questioning is one comprehension strategy that aids in the understanding of new information in single texts (Rosenshine, Meister, & Chapman, 1996). Students are typically eager to pose questions that address what they needed and wanted to understand about literature and life (Commeyras & Sumner, 1998; Taboada & Guthrie, 2004). Questioning is a strategy that triggers students' prior knowledge and allow them to attach new knowledge and meaning to their previous knowledge. Asking students to question and predict outcomes helps to engage them in the text. Self-questioning is also suggested to increase comprehension. While students are questioning themselves, they are thinking, seeking meaning, and connecting new ideas to already learned concepts (King, 1995), which generates more learning.

Miyake and Norman (1979) believe that asking questions is helpful in comprehension; however, the interaction between the level of knowledge of the student and the material should also be considered. Their 1979 study suggested that with easier material beginning readers asked more questions than advanced readers; with the harder material, advanced readers asked more questions than the beginning readers. Also, Scardamalia and Bereiter (1992) performed a study examining the ability of elementary school children to ask and recognize constructive and beneficial questions. They found that there were two different types of questions: knowledge-based and text-based questions. Knowledge-based questions (including "basic questions" asking for information and "wonderment questions" asking for explanations), questions formulated in advance of instruction, were found to be more sophisticated than text-based questions, which were produced after exposure to the text being learned. The researchers concluded that knowledge-based questions would better lead to conceptual learning than the text-based questions.

Taboada and Guthrie (2004) developed a rubric for questioning asserting that there are four levels of students questions consisting of Level 1, Factual questions, Level 2, Questions requesting simple descriptions, Level 3, Questions requesting complex explanations, and Level 4, Questions requesting patterns of relationships. In a study of third grade students, Taboada and Guthrie (2004) showed that students who asked lower-level or factual questions (Level 1) showed lower levels of comprehension on the passage comprehension task whereas students who asked complex explanation questions had the highest levels of comprehension. The value of questions in comprehension learning has also been found when they are strategically posed in written materials given to students (Rothkopf, 1972; Rothkopf & Billington, 1974).

Searching For Information
When engaged, learners are motivated to understand and explain the world they see around them. As they explore their environment, they are inevitably involved in a process of *searching for information.* Pursuing their personal goals, they seek information from multiple sources including libraries, multiple media, and informational books. They browse multiple texts, examine a variety of documents, and extract critical details during their search (Guthrie, Weber, & Kimmerly, 1993). Searching for information refers to students seeking and finding a subset of information in the total text by forming specific goals, selecting particular sections of text, extracting information accurately, combining new and old information, and continuing until goals are fulfilled (Guthrie, Weber, & Kimmerly, 1993). Searching for information is a reading strategy that will help students in both a single text environment and a multi-text environment.

Reynolds and Symons (2001) performed three studies on 3rd, 4th, and 5th graders, which provided experimental evidence of the effects of choice and response format on children's search of informational text. They found that choice and context were motivating factors for information seeking. When students were given a choice of which book to search, they were faster at locating information and they used more efficient search strategies than if they were assigned a book to search. The context or format of the task improved the children's approach to the task. In addition, it was found that prior knowledge and topic interest might contribute to the child's performance as well.

Multiple scaffolds can be used to support learning search processes (van Merrienboer, Kirschner, & Keester, 2003). van Merrienboer, Kirschner, and Keester, submit that scaffolds, such as "worked out examples, goal-free problems, or completion tasks are associated with a lower extraneous cognitive load than conventional problem solving" (p. 8). Therefore, depending on the goal of instruction, students can use worked examples, completion tasks, or reverse tasks to support the teaching of search. For example, learners can be given a full worked example as a scaffold and the task of evaluating the search process in the example. Further, students can be given a ½ worked example to be completed. Lastly, students can receive a list of books and the search process used to produce the list of books and students can make predictions about what the research question for the search was.

Summarizing
Summarizing refers to students forming an accurate abstract representation (summary) of text after reading (Brown & Day, 1983). During summarizing, students may copy verbatim from a text or may use text-explicit information only. Often, they follow the sequence of information in a text, rather than form their own coherent conceptual organization. Therefore, instruction in summarizing is geared toward helping students to reconstruct the text by identifying main ideas and supporting details.

Using Graphic and Semantic Organizers
The construction of concept maps facilitates meaningful learning by requiring students to integrate information from the text into existing knowledge structures. Concepts maps are visual representations of a student's knowledge which organize concepts in a hierarchical fashion to represent the relationships among concepts (Novak, 1995). Using graphic and semantic organizers relies on "the need for deeper understanding of concepts as a prerequisite for meaningful learning" (Starr & Krajcik, 1990, p. 999). Novak (1995) developed the idea of hierarchical representation of concepts based on Ausubel's (1968) assimilation theory of cognitive learning, which briefly states that all cognition is hierarchically organized and that any new conceptual meaning must build upon existing concepts. Concept maps can be used to represent a variety of domains (Novak, 1995) for all age levels (Novak & Musonda, 1991).

Concept mapping supports students' generation of multi-layered knowledge. When students generate concept maps they retain knowledge (Novak & Musonda, 1991) and increase awareness of relationships among concepts (Novak, 1995). In a meta-analysis of 10 studies using concept maps as instruction tools, Horton et al. (1993) found that while the effect size for teacher versus student-prepared maps were similar, the greatest effect size was observed for student-construed maps in which students identified key terms. Since students must specify the hierarchical relationships and create valid links among concepts, it is a significant predictor of text comprehension and conceptual learning from text.

Starr and Krajcik (1990) recommended that teachers use graphic and semantic organizers to enhance activity designed to aid the learner's conceptual development. The mapping process itself is an opportunity for teachers to consider and discuss the importance of individual concepts, the placement of the concepts on the map (including the relationships between concepts), and the propositions, which are used to connect concepts.

Elaborative Interrogation

Simply asking the question "why" often leads students to discern facts from concepts and increase elaboration and integration of knowledge. The elaborative interrogation method is a higher-order questioning strategy that requires students to explain why phenomenona described in text occur. It has been found that students make significant improvements in integrating prior knowledge with text information when they explain the answer to the question, "Why is that true?" In a study of 6th and 7th graders recall of knowledge, Woloshyn, Paivio, and Pressley (1994) found that students performed significantly better in an elaborative interrogation condition compared to a condition in which children were simply asked to read for understanding. The elaborative interrogation condition supported short and long-term knowledge growth even when facts were inconsistent with students' prior knowledge.

Far Term Transfer Process

When instruction is coherent, far term transfer is likely to occur. Guthrie et al. (2000) define coherent instruction as "teaching that connects. It connects the student's reading skills to writing. It connects reading and writing to content. It links the content of learning to student interests. Coherent teaching makes it easy for students to learn because it combines the strange-new with the familiar-old. When the classroom is coherent, teachers help students make connections among reading, writing, and content" (Guthrie et al., 2000, p. 209). Coherent instruction is essential to aide the transfer process.

Research has also revealed that students read more energetically and persistently, use more metacognitive strategies, and remember more content when they are interested in what they are reading (Alexander, Schallert, & Hare, 1991). Reading is said to require metacognitive, reflective knowledge. That is, a reader must possess: (1) the awareness of whether or not comprehension is occurring, and (2) the ability to consciously apply one or more strategies to correct comprehension difficulties.

Comprehension monitoring is one strategy that fosters far term transfer. Effective comprehension monitoring requires students to set goals, focus their attention, engage in self-reinforcement, and cope with hurtles in the reading process. Students can use "think alouds" to help with comprehension monitoring. Another instructional method that encourages students to be reflective about their reading processes is explanation both to oneself and others (Chi, de Leeuw, Chiu, & Lavancher, 1994). Explaining concepts supports conceptual learning from text because it requires students to become more reflective about their knowledge (Brown, 1997). Explaining can be facilitated through writing, private speech, or with peers. For example, King, Staffieri, and Adelgais (1998) studied the effects of explanation on knowledge acquisition. In their study students were assigned to one of three groups: explanation only, inquiry plus explanation, and sequenced inquiry plus explanation. When students received training in asking each other thought-provoking questions and explaining the concept to each other, they increased conceptual understanding in measures of knowledge integration and retention. A large body of evidence indicates that self-explanations increase conceptual learning from text and transfer propensity (Chi, de Leeuw, Chiu, & Lavancher, 1994).

Metaphorical Reasoning
Students can benefit from metaphorical reasoning in several ways: understanding concepts, interpreting representations, connecting concepts, improving recall, computing solutions, and detecting and correcting errors (Chiu, 2001). In addition, metaphorical reasoning functions as a valuable teaching tool with those learners having difficulties in comprehension. However, there are some possible limitations to metaphorical reasoning. These include: invalid inferences, unreliable justifications, and inefficient procedures (Chiu, 2001). The learner must be careful of these possible difficulties when using this technique. The instructor as well needs to be selective in its use so that the metaphor can capitalize on the prior knowledge of the learner, thereby minimizing possibilities for communicating confusing material to the learner.

This type of confusion could have been the problem in a study where children were found to use metaphors more often than adults to compute, detect and correct errors, and justify their answers; however adults used more metaphors with fewer details during understanding tasks (Chiu, 2001). Children as young as second graders are able to engage in metaphorical reasoning (Kincade, 1991). Not only can they recall metaphorical propositions in text, but they truly understand the metaphorical meaning. Kincade's study (1991) suggested that providing externally generated, structured probes can greatly enhance children's reading recall. This is suggested to enable children to demonstrate metaphorical comprehension prior to the age at which it spontaneously appears. This concept allows for far-term transfer to occur at earlier ages which can enhance education and learning in many areas.

Metaphorical reasoning does not just apply to the example of Reading. Kincade (1991) stated it best: "School learning at all levels of science, social studies, and mathematics involves reading to acquire knowledge and the use of analogical-metaphorical examples to facilitate the acquisition of new concepts" (p. 94). An individual uses prior knowledge or developed schemas from many domains as part of the far term transfer process to allow for the acquisition and comprehension of new ideas and concepts. For example, Carreira (2001) suggested "that the activity of applied situations, as it fosters metaphorical thinking, offers students' reasoning a double anchoring for mathematical concepts" (p. 261). In addition, Chiu (2001) suggested that the metaphors used by both the children and adults are central to understanding arithmetic. Novices uncertain about their mathematical knowledge while solving an applied mathematics problem can create a chain of metaphors" (Chiu, 2001, p. 95). The trick in teaching the learners to use metaphors and facilitate far term transfer is to capitalize on the relevant experience base of the individual learner. As teachers, we probably do a better job with less care instructing adult learners in this manner because of the broader experience base of the adult learner.

Multiple Text Environments
In a multi-text environment, readers must integrate information across texts, combine new knowledge with prior knowledge, connect information across texts, link illustrations with accompanying prose, and abstract common themes from multiple frameworks. When students are capable of integrating content from multiple texts their comprehension of the topic is evident. Stahl & Hynd (1998) found that for high school students, instruction is necessary for students to profit from multiple texts, especially those presenting conflicting opinions. Students do not automatically know how to integrate multiple texts even in the presence of an integrative goal and a multi-text environment. These multi-text comprehension strategies have to be taught directly and explicitly. In a study examining students multiple perspectives on historical events. These strategies may entail drawing, charting, note taking, and composing either in narrative, expository, or persuasive rhetorical structures (Harris & Graham, 1992).

Strategies for solving problems include identifying the problem, defining terms, exploring various strategies, acting on strategies, and looking at the effects (Bransford & Stein, 1993). These five stages of problem solving can be used with a variety of curricula (i.e., far term transfer) but are especially helpful when reading in multiple text environments. All of the above are classic examples of positive transfer being facilitated by the use of multiple-context learning, and provide an excellent transition to our next topic concerning problem solving and transfer.

Reading Engagement and Motivation
Reading engagement is important to facilitate reading later in one's academic life, career, and personal enjoyment. Engaged readers are students who are intrinsically motivated to read for knowledge and enjoyment (Guthrie & Cox, 2001) and are highly achieving and strategic readers. Engaged readers "exchange ideas and interpretations of text with peers. Their devotion to reading spans across time, transfers to a variety of genre, and culminates in valued learning outcomes" (Guthrie & Wigfield, 2000, p. 403).

Intrinsic reading motivation refers to students' enjoyment of reading activities as well as their disposition to participate in reading events (Deci, Vallerand, Pelletier & Ryan, 1991; Wigfield & Guthrie, 1997). Intrinsically motivated reading practices and dispositions include students' curiosities for learning, preference for challenge, and involvement in reading. Empirical research has indicated that high levels of intrinsic motivation are associated with a sense of competence (Miller, Behrens, Green, & Newman, 1993), coping with failure (Leitenen et al., 1995) and high achievement in reading (Benware & Deci, 1984). Consistent with previous motivation research, we believe that a teacher plays a large role in creating and maintaining students' intrinsic motivation.

Another aspect of reading motivation is readers' efficacy, or their belief that they can accomplish a given reading task (Bandura, 1998). When students think they can accomplish an assignment in English class, they are likely to choose to do it, to continue working despite difficulties in the reading process, and ultimately persist until the task is accomplished (Schunk & Zimmerman, 1997). Reading efficacy has been linked to achievement (Pajares, 1996), goals for understanding (Schunk & Zimmerman, 1997), and intrinsic motivation. For instance, Schunk (1991) reported that school students with strong efficacy beliefs were able to successfully master reading comprehension tasks even after prior achievement and cognitive skills were accounted for. Finally, Stipek (1996) prescribed some classroom practices that lead to positive self-efficacy beliefs, such as providing challenging tasks and attributing student success and failure to effort.

Past research has been done that supports these suggested instructional strategies. For instance, Stipek (1996) and Guthrie et al. (2004) state that "stimulating activities" will support motivation; and we believe that *real-world interactions* represents a class of highly stimulating activities (see also, Paris, Yambor, & Packard, 1998). Also, regarding using *interesting texts*, Wade et al. (1999) found that texts with important, new, and valued information were associated with student interest and Morrow and Young (1997) found that an abundance of texts within the classroom and availability to community resources are known to directly facilitate motivation.

With regard to *autonomy support*, Stefanou, Perencevich, DiCintio, and Turner (2004) found that when students are supported in making important decisions in school, they are highly motivated. Specifically, they refer to three levels of autonomy support, organizational autonomy wherein students can make decisions over classroom management procedures, procedural autonomy wherein students have decisions about how to present their ideas, and the most important, cognitive autonomy support, wherein students are afforded a wide array of choices that are significant and important. Moreover, Guthrie, Wigfield and Perencevich (2004) and Cordova and Lepper (1996) have found that significant choices over reading materials leads to sustained reading and measured achievement increase.

Self-perceived competence and *self-efficacy* is related to intrinsically motivated reading, students are given a sense of self-perceived competence when they are supported to use strategies and be successful readers (Bandura, 1998).

Brown (1997) and Turner (1995) emphasized that social discourse in learning communities, *collaboration support*, is intrinsically motivating and Wentzel (1993, 2000) demonstrated that students' possession of prosocial goals leads to constructive social behaviors in the classroom (read more on this in Chapter 5).

Several programs have also utilized conceptual instruction in science with beneficial results on reading engagement and conceptual learning from text. Guthrie and his colleagues (1998) implemented a classroom intervention to emphasize conceptual instruction in reading and science, called Concept-Oriented Reading Instruction (CORI). CORI teachers were trained to provide multi-layered instruction, knowledge transformation activities, and optimal challenge during an integrated reading/science unit. CORI teachers used conceptual themes to organize central disciplinary principles in a multi-layered fashion. The conceptual theme was accessible to all students and allowed for an ebb and flow between the facts and principles of the domain. Using the theme of "birds around the world" teachers helped their students to embrace nine ecological principles (such as defense and predation). CORI teachers enabled students to search through multiple trade books to integrate information about the theme. After reading, students often summarized, made graphic organizers (student construction of a spatial representation of text-based knowledge, such as concept map or Venn diagram), drew and labeled illustrations of the text information, and created models and artifacts based on their new understandings gleaned from the multiple texts. In terms of optimal challenge, CORI teachers used a wide array of interesting texts to accommodate a range of ability levels in order to ensure students worked at the edge of their competencies.

In a typical CORI classroom, students conduct science activities within a conceptual theme of study. In the midst of a conceptual theme on aquatic life, a science activity might be to visit a freshwater habitat for students to collect pond water and specimens. Students would then ask personal questions about the animals and plants they observed. Next, they would search through multiple texts to find the answers to their questions and they would choose from an abundance of books ranging in difficulty level. For example, students may have begun with an easy text when the topic was new and knowledge relatively fragmented. As students gained knowledge, they would become increasingly able to read and gain information from more challenging texts. Students would use multiple knowledge transformation activities to learn knowledge from the text. This would include concept mapping, illustrating and labeling text ideas, or conducting experiments based on text information. Finally, students would present a display of their knowledge to classmates. This, too, would be accomplished using a variety of knowledge transformation activities, ranging from poster presentations to the creation of artifacts. In several quantitative studies of CORI, Guthrie and his associates have documented the benefits of concept instruction on conceptual learning from text, reading strategy-use, and reading motivation (see Guthrie, Wigfield & Perencevich, 2004, for review).

Among other classroom intervention programs that have also emphasized concept instruction with text, Marlene Scardamalia and her colleagues (1994) implemented a classroom intervention called Computer Supported Intentional Learning Environments (CSILE). CSILE classrooms contained networked computers connected to a communal database. During a typical day in a CSILE classroom, students researched topics using the computers for 30 minutes per day. Students browsed through expert and classmates' notes and information, attached notes and graphics found in databases, and recorded information found through other avenues. Used simultaneously by students were multiple text sources to gather information (see entry multiple text in this chapter). Personal inquiries were posted in the database to which other students responded, thus, an ongoing communication among students provided the impetus for knowledge growth.

In a series of studies, the effects of CSILE on students' ability to construct knowledge from multiple texts and other sources were reported. For instance, CSILE students exhibited their ability to represent knowledge in multiple forms, including graphics, and to better comprehend expository text. In one study, students' cognitive actions were analyzed in order to examine whether student usage of the computer system resulted in differential conceptual learning from text (Oshima, Scardamalia and Bereiter, 1996). Indeed, students who treated information flow from computer to self as a unidirectional exchange learned relatively few principles and higher order relations. In contrast, students who sought to construct meaning in a bi-directional interchange of textual information with other students and sources, gained higher levels of knowledge. These students questioned and rebutted information and acted as co-creators of the knowledge. In addition, high conceptual learners took notes that were coordinated with the principles of the domain; whereas low conceptual learners wrote many fragmented notes.

Ann Brown (1997) designed a curriculum to Foster a Community of Learners (FCL) in 2nd through 5th grade science classrooms. Her general philosophy was that students develop their knowledge through dialogue in a social learning community. Students were expected to research some subset of a topic, and produce an artifact based on the content. In one study, three groups of students were compared with regard to conceptual learning outcomes. One group received instruction characterized by a jigsaw approach (teams of students studying various sub-themes of a topic and sharing their subset of expertise with classmates in order for all students to integrate sub-theme information with the overall conceptual theme) to learn sub-themes of a conceptual unit. During various phases of learning, students were involved in three participant structures: composing on the computer, conducting research using multiple texts, and interacting with the teacher. In these structures, jigsaw groups worked simultaneously on sub-topics of a conceptual theme. Students gathered and presented findings to each other and engaged in asking questions of peers and clarifying concepts. A summary of the Fostering Communities of Learners studies showed that students gained deep level understandings about the scientific topics of study as expressed in problem solving by analogy tasks.

Taken together, the CORI, CSILE, and Fostering Communities of Learner studies show the powerful effects of a conceptual emphasis in instruction. In each of these programs students were given multiple opportunities to create relations between the facts and principles of the conceptual domain, to experience optimal challenge, and to manipulate information in order to transform meaning. It has been shown that concept instruction helps students to understand that there exist multiple, often rival viewpoints within a domain of knowledge. Students should learn to create their personal understandings based on text and to reconcile discrepancies among diverse texts and their own knowledge. Thus, searching for information in multiple trade books or original documents, being presented with diverse viewpoints, and manipulating incoming information into a variety of forms are instrumental in being able to accomplish these understandings.

Amount and Breadth of Reading

Reading amount and breadth is defined as wide and frequent reading for a variety of purposes (Cox & Guthrie, 2001). Reading amount has been defined and characterized by many researchers and thus has been referred to as voluntary reading (Morrow, 1996), print exposure (Cunningham & Stanovich, 1997; Stanovich & Cunningham, 1993), leisure reading, and time spent reading. It is well documented that students who read frequently and widely have higher reading achievement and possess more knowledge than those students who read less often. Essentially, this activity can be described as increasing time on task, a factor important for all types of learning.

Amount of reading is important because it enhances both reading comprehension and conceptual learning from text. First, among elementary school children reading comprehension is substantially predicted by amount of independent reading (Cipielewski & Stanovich, 1992). This strong contribution of reading amount to reading comprehension has been documented with a wide variety of indicators including, activity diaries (Wigfield & Guthrie, 1997), self-report questionnaires, such as the Reading Activity Inventory (RAI) (Guthrie, Wigfield, Metsala, & Cox, 1999), and measures of print exposure, such as a title recognition tests (TRT) and author recognition tests (ART) (Cunningham & Stanovich, 1993, 1997).

Amount and breadth of reading is significantly correlated with reading comprehension (Guthrie, Wigfield, Metsala, & Cox, 1999). It may seem obvious that children who read widely and frequently are high achievers. However, amount of reading is not only correlated to achievement in a simple association, but is a source of growth in reading comprehension (Cunningham & Stanovich, 1997). In a zero order correlation, of course, the causal influence may point in either direction or it may be reciprocal. However, longitudinal studies and studies that control for previous reading achievement help to explain growth in reading achievement.

Additionally, Cunningham and Stanovich (1997) argue that amount of time reading measured by print exposure techniques, is a causal factor in reading achievement (see Cunningham & Stanovich, 1997 for a review). In a series of longitudinal investigations, using multiple control variables, Stanovich and his colleagues (1997) have shown that wide and frequent reading (measured by print exposure) accounts for growth in reading comprehension and knowledge gains. The print exposure method is one in which children are presented with titles and authors of books and they are asked to indicate which titles and authors they recognize. Combined with actual titles and authors are non-author and non-book title names. In a 2-year longitudinal study of students in grades 3, 4, and 5, fifth graders' amount of reading (as measured by print exposure) predicted reading comprehension after prior achievement and prior amount of reading, as well as intelligence and parental income had been controlled (Cipielewski & Stanovich, 1992).

It is plausible that students who read frequently and widely should gain knowledge about the topics and domains in which they read and this expectation has been confirmed (Cunningham & Stanovich, 1997; Cipielewski & Stanovich, 1992).

Several studies have also shown that the increase in reading comprehension during an academic year, from fall to spring, is predicted by children's amount of reading (Cipielewski & Stanovich, 1992; Guthrie, Wigfield, Metsala, & Cox, 1999). For instance, in a study of 117 third and 154 fifth graders, Guthrie, Wigfield, Metsala and Cox (1999) found that reading for school and reading for enjoyment predicted passage comprehension and conceptual learning from text on a performance assessment task.

The influence of the amount and breadth of reading is not limited to one locality or even one country. For instance, Elley (1994) showed that for nine-year-old students frequency of reading silently significantly contributed to achievement in 32 nations after statistically controlling for a variety of health, wealth, and school resource indicators within and across countries.

In classroom and school settings, student time engaged in reading is a stable predictor of reading comprehension (Morrow, 1996). In Morrow's study an experimental group was exposed to literacy centers including a volume and diverse array of reading materials, teacher-modeled literacy activities, and time for sharing information about books. They proved superior to a control group receiving traditional reading instruction from basal readers with occasional storybook reading. The experimental group scored significantly better on measures of reading comprehension, vocabulary, and creating original stories. Additionally, experimental students were asked to record the amount of books they took home from the literacy center. From the total amount of books taken home, 15% were taken home in the beginning of the school year whereas 50% of books were taken home after the literacy center was introduced.

Taken together the evidence indicates that amount and breadth of reading contributes to reading comprehension and conceptual learning from text and is supported by a network of cognitive and contextual supports within the classroom.

Reducing Cognitive Load
We save this topic for last because the danger of cognitive overload reaches across all of the processes: Acquisition, Automaticity, Near and Far Term Transfer. Key features of cognitive overload are found in the research dealing with dual channel receiving, processing, storing, and retrieval. Broadbent was the first researcher to notice the effects of interference or facilitation involving the dual channel processing (1952a, 1952b). (Strategies were recommended by this theoretical position in Section I.) The following is the cognitive theory of multimedia learning proposed by Mayer & Moreno (2003):

- ▪ Information processing consists of two channels: auditory/verbal and visual/pictorial (Pavio, 1986; Baddeley, 1998; Mayer & Moreno, 2003).
- ● Each channel has a limited capacity; therefore, only a limited amount of cognitive processing can take place in one channel at any one time (Chandler & Sweller, 1991; Sweller, 1999; Mayer & Moreno, 2003).
- ● Cognitive processing occurs in each channel: selecting (paying attention to the material), organizing (into a coherent structure), and integrating with existing knowledge (Mayer, 1999, 2002) (as shown in the diagram below).

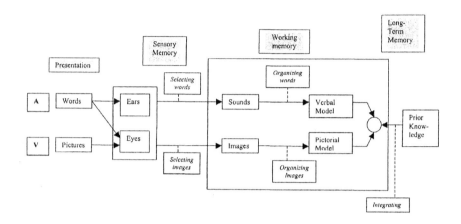

A=auditory channel
V=visual channel

Figure 3.1. Mayer & Moreno's Cognitive Theory of multimedia learning (2003)

Implications of Cognitive Load Theory for Instructional Design

Sweller et al. (1998) report on studies of problem solvers distinguishing between problem solving where the schema is automated vs. problem solving where surface structure differences in the problems required conscious attempts at use of rules rather than the use of automated rules . "Problem solvers using automated rules had substantial working memory reserves to search for problem solution" (Sweller et al., 1998, p. 257). We would add for the reader that the automaticity of the schema tied to a limited surface structure (i.e., few concrete example types) restricts the "meaning" of that schema to the concrete level and inhibits 1) abstraction, and 2) generalization, and therefore, 3) limits near term positive transfer, and prevents far term transfer. Further, it is precisely the use of multiple "surface structure" differences in problem examples, which use encourages the learning of abstract, transferable principles, which in agreement with Sweller, et al. (1998), promotes the development of new schemas. Thus, the key for good instructional design is to build new principle capacity by adding just the right mix of multiple-example, surface structures to challenge with germane cognitive load for the learner without overloading her or him. We discussed this approach earlier as exemplified with the teaching of Reading.

As noted in Chapter 1, according to Sweller et al. (1998), schemas provide the basis for knowledge organization and storage. They also provide the function of reducing working memory load. This approach is extremely important for teaching

Reading as well as being the foundation for learning all other cognitive subject matters as well as Psychomotor, Affective, and even Interpersonal skills.

REFERENCES

Adams, M. J. (1990). *Beginning to read: Thinking and learning about print.* Cambridge, MA: MIT Press.

Afflerbach, P. & Pressley, M. (1995). *Verbal protocols of reading: The nature of constructively responsive reading.* Hillsdale, NJ: Lawrence Erlbaum Associates, Inc.

Alexander, P. A. & Jetton, T. L. (1996). The role of importance and interest in the processing of text. *Educational Psychology Review, 8*(1), 89-122.

Alexander, P. A., Schallert, D. L., & Hare, V. C. (1991). Coming to terms: How researchers in learning and literacy talk about knowledge. *Review of Educational Research, 61*, 315-343.

Ames, C. (1992). Classrooms: Goals, structures, and student motivation. *Journal of Educational Psychology, 84(3)*, 261-271.

Ames, C. & Archer, J. (1988). Achievement goals in the classroom: Students' learning strategies and motivation processes. *Journal of Educational Psychology, 80*(3), 260-267.

Anderson, R. C. (1994). Role of the reader's schema in comprehension, learning, and memory. In R. B. Ruddell, M. R. Ruddell, & H. Singer (Eds.), *Theoretical models and processes of reading, 4th Edition* (pp. 469-482). Newark, DE: International Reading Association.

Anderson, R. C. & Pearson, P. D. (1984). A schema-theoretic view of basic processes in reading. In P. D. Pearson (Ed.), *Handbook of reading research* (pp. 255-291). New York: Longman.

Ausubel, D. P. (1960). The use of advance organizers in the learning and retention of meaningful verbal material. *Journal of Educational Psychology, 51*, 267-272.

Ausubel, D. P. (1962). A subsumption theory of meaningful verbal learning and retention. *Journal of General Psychology, 66*, 213-224.

Ausubel, D. P. (1968). *Educational psychology: A cognitive view.* New York: Holt, Rinehart, & Winston.

Ausubel, D. P. (1969). A cognitive theory of school learning. *Psychology in the Schools, 6*(4), 331-335.

Baddeley, A. (1998). *Human memory.* Boston: Allyn & Bacon.

Ball, E. W., & Blachman, B. A. (1991). Does phoneme segmentation training in kindergarten make a difference in early word recognition and developmental spelling? *Reading Research Quarterly, 26*, 49-66.

Baker, L., & Brown, A. L. (1984). Metacognitive skills and reading. In P. D. Pearson (Ed.), *Handbook of research in reading* (pp. 353-395). New York: Longman.

Bakker, N. H., Werkhoven, P. J., & Passenier, P. O. (1999). The effects of proprioceptive and visual feedback on geographical orientation in virtual environments. *Presence, 8*(1), 36-53.

Bandura, A. (1998). *Self-efficacy: The exercise of control.* New York: Freeman.

Baumann, J. F. & Bergeron, B. S. (1993). Story map instruction using children's literature: Effects on first graders' comprehension of central narrative elements. *Journal of Reading Behavior, 25*(4), 407-437.

Bean, T. W. & Steenwyk, F. L. (1984). The effect of three forms of summarization instruction on sixth graders' summary writing and comprehension. *Journal of Reading Behavior, 16*(4), 297-306.

Benware, C. & Deci, E. L. (1984). Quality of learning with an active versus passive motivational set. *American Educational Research Journal, 21*, 755-765.

Biemiller, A. J., Jr. (1970). Changes in the use of graphic and contextual information as children learn to read. *Dissertation Abstracts International, 30*(7-B), 3368-3369.

Bransford, J. D. & Stein, B. S. (1993). *The IDEAL problem solver (2nd edition).* New York: Freeman.

Britton, B. K. & Graesser, A. C. (Eds.). (1996). *Models of understanding text.* Hillsdale, NJ: Lawrence Erlbaum Associates, Inc.

Broadbent, D. E. (1952a). Speaking and listening simultaneously. *Journal of Experimental Psychology, 43*, 267-273.

Broadbent, D. E. (1952b). Listening to one of two synchronous messages. *Journal of Experimental Psychology, 44*, 51-55.

Brown, A. (1997). Transforming schools into communities of thinking and learning about serious matters. *American Psychologist, 52(3)*, 399-413.

Brown, A. L. & Day, J. D. (1983). Macrorules for summarizing texts: The development of expertise. *Journal of Verbal Learning and Verbal Behavior, 22,* 1-14.

Carreira, S. (2001). Where there's a model, there's a metaphor: Metaphorical thinking in students' understanding of a mathematical model. *Mathematical Thinking & Learning, 3*(4), 261-287.

Chall, J. S. (1983/1996). *Stages of reading development.* New York: McGraw Hill.

Chandler, P. & Sweller, J. (1991). Cognitive load theory and the format of instruction. *Cognition and Instruction, 8,* 293-332.

Chi, M. T. H., de Leeuw, N., Chiu, M., & Lavancher, C. (1994). Eliciting self-explanations improves understanding. *Cognitive Science, 18*(3), 439-477.

Chiu, M. M. (2001). Using metaphors to understand and solve arithmetic problems: Novices and experts working with negative numbers. *Mathematical Thinking and Learning, 3*(2&3), 93-124.

Cipielewski, J. & Stanovich, K. (1992). Predicting growth in reading ability from children's exposure to print. *Journal of Experimental Child Psychology, 54,* 74-89.

Commeyras, M. & Sumner, M. (1998). Literature questions children want to discuss: What teachers and students learned in a second-grade classroom. *Elementary School Journal, 99*(2), 129-152.

Collins-Block, C. & Pressley, M. (2002). *Comprehension instruction: Research-based best practices.* New York: Guilford.

Cox, K. E. & Guthrie, J. T. (2001). Motivational and cognitive contributions to students' amount of reading. *Contemporary Educational Psychology, 26*(1), 116-131.

Cordova, D. I., & Lepper, M. R. (1996). Intrinsic motivation and the process of learning: Beneficial effects of contextualization, personalization, and choice. *Journal of Educational Psychology, 88*(4), 715-730.

Cunningham, A. E. & Stanovich, K. E. (1997). Early reading acquisition and its relation to reading experience and ability 10 years later. *Developmental Psychology, 33*(6), 934-945.

Davis, M. & Tonks, S. (2004). Diverse text and techonology for reading. In J. T. Guthrie, A. Wigfield, & K. C. Perencevich (Eds.), *Motivating reading comprehension: Concept-oriented reading instruction.* Mahwah, NJ: Erlbaum.

Deci, E. L. & Ryan, R. M. (1987). The support of autonomy and the control of behavior. *Journal of Personality and Social Psychology, 53*(6), 1024-1037.

Deci, E. L, Vallerand, R. J., Pelletier, L. G., & Ryan, R. M. (1991). Motivation and education: The self-determination perspective. *Educational Psychologist, 26,* 325-346.

Dole, J. A., Duffy, G. G., & Roehler, L. R. (1991). Moving from the old to the new: Research on reading comprehension instruction. *Review of Educational Research, 61*(2), 239-264.

Dreher, M. J. (1993). Reading to locate information: Societal and educational perspectives. *Contemporary Educational Psychology, 18,* 129-138.

Druckman, D. & Bjork, R. A. (Eds.). (1994). *Learning, remembering, believing: Enhancing human performance.* Committee on Techniques for the Enhancement of Human Performance, National Research Council. Washington, D.C.: National Academy Press.

Dupont, P. E., Schulteis, T. M., Millman, P. A., & Howe, R. D. (1999). Automatic identification of environment haptic properties. *Presence, 8*(4), 394-411.

Ehri, L. C. (1991). Development of the ability to read words. In R. Barr & M. L. Kamil, (Eds.), *Handbook of reading research, Volume 2* (pp. 383-417). Hillsdale, NJ: Lawrence Erlbaum Associates, Inc.

Ehri, L. C. (1994). Cognitive development of the ability to read words: Update. In R. B. Ruddell, & M. R. Ruddell (Eds.), *Theoretical models and processes of reading, (4th ed.)* (pp. 323-358). Newark, DE: International Reading Association.

Elley, W. B. (1994). *How in the world do students read?* Hamburg, Germany: International Reading Association.

Ericsson, K. A., Patel, V., & Kintsch, W. (2000). How experts' adaptations to representative task demands account for the expertise effect in memory recall: Comment on Vicente and Wang. *Psychological Review, 107*(3), 578-592.

Feltovich, P. J., Spiro, R. J., & Coulson, R. L. (1993). Learning, teaching, and testing for complex conceptual understanding. In N. Frederiksen, R. J. Mislevy, & I. I. Bejar (Eds.), *Test theory for a new generation of tests* (pp. 181-217). Hillsdale, NJ: Lawrence Erlbaum Associates, Publishers.

Fischer, K. W. (1980). A theory of cognitive development: The control and construction of hierarchies of skills. *Psychological Review, 87*(6), 477-531.

Fleischman, P. (1988). *Joyful noise: Poems for two voices.* New York: HarperCollins Publishers.

Foshay, W. R., Silber, K. H., & Stelnicki, M. B. (2003). *Writing training materials that work: How to train anyone to do anything.* San Francisco: Jossey-Bass/Pfeiffer.

Fredericks, A. D. (2001). *Under one rock: Bugs, slugs, and other ughs.* Nevada City, CA: Dawn Publishing.

Gagne, R. M. (1977). *The conditions of learning.* New York: Holt, Rinehart, & Winston.

Gambrell, L. & Almasi, J. (1996). *Lively discussions! Fostering engaged reading.* Newark: DE: International Reading Association.

Garner, R. (1987). Strategies for reading and studying expository text. *Educational Psychologist, Special Issue: Current issues in reading comprehension, 22*(3-4), 299-312.

Goodman, K. S. (1965). A linguistic study of cues and miscues in reading. *Elementary English, 42,* 639-642.

Graesser, A., Golding, J. M., & Long, D. L. (1991). Narrative representation and comprehension. In R. Barr & M. L. Kamil (Eds.), *Handbook of reading research, Volume 2* (pp. 171-205). Hillsdale, NJ: Lawrence Erlbaum Associates, Inc.

Gray, W. S. (1950). Growth in understanding of reading and its development among youth. *Supplementary Educational Monographs, 72,* 8-13.

Guthrie, J. T., Weber, S., & Kimmerly, N. (1993). Searching documents: Cognitive processes and deficits in understanding graphs, tables, and illustrations. *Contemporary Educational Psychology, 18*(2), 186-221.

Guthrie, J. T. & Cox, K. E. (2001). Classroom conditions for motivation and engagement in reading. *Educational Psychology Review, 13,* 283-302.

Guthrie, J. T. & Cox, K. E. (1998). Portrait of an engaging classroom: Principles of concept-oriented reading instruction for diverse students. In K. Harris and S. Graham (Eds.), *Teaching every child every day* (pp. 77-130). Newton Upper Falls, MA: Brookline Books Inc.

Guthrie, J. T. & Wigfield, A. (2000). Engagement and motivation in reading. In M. L. Kamil, P. B. Mosenthal, P. D. Pearson, & R. Barr (Eds.) *Handbook of reading research, Volume III* (pp. 403-422). Mahwah, NJ: Erlbaum.

Guthrie, J. T., Wigfield, A., Metsala, J., & Cox, K. E. (1999). Predicting text comprehension and reading activity with motivational and cognitive variables. *Scientific Studies of Reading, 3,* 231-256.

Guthrie, J. T., Wigfield, A., & Perencevich, K. C. (2004). *Motivating reading comprehension: Concept-oriented reading instruction.* Mahwah, NJ: Erlbaum.

Harris, K. R. & Graham, S. (1992). Self-regulated strategy development: A part of the writing process. In M. Pressley & K. R. Harris (Eds.), *Promoting academic competence and literacy in school* (pp. 277-309). San Diego, CA: Academic Press, Inc.

Harvey, S. & Goudvis, A. (2000). *Strategies that work: Teaching comprehension to enhance understanding.* York, ME: Stenhouse Publishers.

Heath, S. B. (1983). *Ways with words: Language, life and work in communities and classrooms.* Cambridge, MA: Cambridge University Press.

Hiebert, E. H. & Raphael, T. E. (1996). Psychological perspectives on literacy and extensions to educational practice. In D. C. Berliner & R. C. Calfee (Eds.), *Handbook of educational psychology* (pp. 550-602). New York: Wiley, John & Sons, Inc.

Holmes, B. C. (1985). The effect of four different modes of reading on comprehension. *Reading Research Quarterly, 20*(5), 575-585.

Honig, W. K. (Ed.). (1966). *Operant behavior: Areas of research and application.* New York: Meredith Publishing Company.

Horton, P. B., McConney, A. A., & Gallo, M. (1993). An investigation of the effectiveness of concept mapping as an instructional tool. *Science Education, 77*(1), 95-111.

Kalyuga, S., Ayres, P., Chandler, P., & Sweller, J. (2003). The expertise reversal effect. *Educational Psychologist, 38*(1), 23-31.

Kincade, K. M. (1991). Patterns in children's ability to recall explicit, implicit, and metaphorical information. *Journal of Research in Reading, 14*(2), 81-98.

King, A. (1995). Designing the instructional process to enhance critical thinking across the curriculum. *Teaching of Technology, 22,* 13-17.

King, A., Staffieri, A., & Adelgais, A. (1998). Mutual peer tutoring: Effects of structuring tutorial interaction to scaffold peer learning. *Journal of Educational Psychology, 90*(1), 134-152.

Kintsch, W. & van Dijk, T. (1978). Toward a model of text comprehension and production. *Psychological Review, 85*(5), 363-394.

Köhler, W. (1947). *Gestalt psychology.* New York: Liveright Publishing Corporation.

LaBerge, D. & Saumuels, S. J. (1974). Toward a theory of automatic information processing in reading. *Cognitive Psychology, 6,* 293-323.

Lave, J. & Wenger, E. (1991). *Situated learning: Legitimate peripheral participation.* Cambridge, MA: Cambridge University Press.

Leitenen, E., Vaurus, M., Salonen, P., Olkinuora, E., & Kinnunen, R. (1995). Long-term development of learning activity: Motivational, cognitive, and social interaction. *Educational Psychologist, 30,* 21-35.

Linder, C. L. (1993) A challenge to conceptual change. *Science Education, 77*(3), 293-300.

Linder, C. L. & Marshall, D. (2003). Reflection and phenomenongraphy: Towards theoretical and educational development possibilities. *Learning and Instruction, 13,* 271-284

Mayer, R. E. (1999). *The promise of educational psychology: Volume 1, Learning in the content areas.* Upper Saddle River, NJ: Prentice Hall.

Mayer, R. E. (2002). *The promise of educational psychology: Volume 2, Teaching for meaningful learning.* Upper Saddle River, NJ: Prentice Hall.

Mayer, R. E. & Moreno, R. (2003). Nine ways to reduce cognitive load in multimedia learning. *Educational Psychologist, 38*(1), 43-52.

Meichenbaum, D. & Biemiller, A. (1998). *Nurturing independent learners: Helping students take charge of their learning.* Cambridge, MA: Brookline Books.

Meyer, B. J. F. (1984). Text dimensions and cognitive processing. In H. Mandl, N. L. Stein, & T. Trabasso (Eds.), *Learning and comprehension of text* (pp. 3-51). Hillsdale, NJ: Erlbaum.

Miller, G. A. (1956). The magical number seven, plus or minus two: Some limits on our capacity for processing information. *Psychological Review, 53,* 81-97.

Miller, R. B., Behrens, J. T., Green, B. A., & Newman, D. (1993). Goals and perceived ability: Impact on student valuing, self-regulation and persistence. *Contemporary Educational Psychology, 18,* 2-14.

Miyake, N. & Norman, D. A. (1979). To ask a question, one must know enough to know what is not known. *Journal of Verbal Learning and Verbal Behavior, 18,* 357-364.

Montague, W. (1987). *What works: Research findings about navy instruction and learning.* Washington, D.C.: Direction of Chief of Naval Education & Training.

Morrow, L. M. (1996). *Motivating reading and writing in diverse classrooms: Social and physical contexts in a literature-based program.* Urbana, IL: NCTE.

Morrow, L. M. & Young, J. (1997). Parent, teacher, and child participation in a collaborative family literacy program: The effects of attitude, motivation, and literacy achievement. *Journal of Educational Psychology, 89,* 736-742.

National Reading Panel. (2000). *Teaching children to read.* (NIH Publication No. 00-4769). Bethesda, MD: National Institute of Child Health and Human Development.

Novak, J. D. (1995). Concept mapping: A strategy for organizing knowledge. In S. Glynn and R. Duit (Eds.), *Learning science in the schools: Research reforming practice* (pp. 229-245). Mahwak: N.J: Lawrence Erlbaum Associates.

Novak, J. & Musonda, D. (1991). A twelve-year longitudinal study of science concept learning. *American Educational Research Journal, 28,* 1153-1171.

Oshima, J., Scardamalia, M., & Bereiter, C. (1996). Collaborative learning processes associated with high and low conceptual progress. *Instructional Science, 24*(2), 125-155.

Pajares, F. (1996). Self-efficacy beliefs in academic settings. *Review of Educational Research, 66,* 543-578.

Palincsar, A. S. & Brown, A. L. (1984). Reciprocal teaching of comprehension-fostering and comprehension-monitoring activities. *Cognition & Instruction, 1*(2), 117-175.

Paris, S. G., Lipson, M. Y., & Wixon, K. K. (1983). Becoming a strategic reader. *Contemporary Educational Psychology, 8,* 293-316.

Paris, S. G., Wasik, B., & Turner, J. C. (1991). The development of strategic readers. In M. L. Kamil, P. Mosenthal, & P. D. Pearson (Eds.), *Handbook of reading research, Volume 2* (pp. 609-640). Mahwah, NJ: Erlbaum.

Paris, S. G., Yambor, K. M., & Packard, B. W. (1998). Hands-on biology: A museum-school-university partnership for enhancing students' interest and learning in science. *Elementary School Journal, 98(3)*, 267-288.

Pavio, A. (1986). *Mental representations: A dual coding approach.* Oxford, England: Oxford University Press.

Perfetti, C. A. (1995). *Text-based learning and reasoning: Studies in history.* Hillsdale, NJ: Lawrence Erlbaum Associates.

Perencevich, K. C. (2004). What CORI looks like in the classroom. In J. T. Guthrie, A. Wigfield, & K. C. Perencevich (Eds.), *Motivating reading comprehension: Concept-oriented reading instruction.* Mahwah, NJ: Erlbaum.

Piaget, J. (1957). *Logic and psychology.* New York: Basic Books.

Poulton, E. C. & Brown, C. H. (1967). Memory after reading aloud and reading silently. *British Journal of Psychology, 58*(3-4), 219-222.

Pressley, M. (1998). *Reading instruction that works: The case for balanced teaching.* New York: Guilford Press.

Pressley, M. (April, 2002). Effective beginning reading instruction: The rest of the story from research. Paper presented at the National Reading Conference, New Orleans, LA.

Pressley, M., Wharton-McDonald, R., & Allington, R. (2001). A study of effective first grade literacy instruction. *Scientific Studies of Reading, 15*(1), 35-58.

Prophet, W. W. & Boyd, H. A. (1970). Device-task fidelity and transfer of training: Aircraft cockpit procedures training. HumRRO Technical Report, 70-100.

RAND Reading Study Group. (2002). Reading for understanding: Toward an R&D program in reading comprehension. Arlington, VA: RAND.

Reynolds, P. L. & Symons, S. (2001). Motivational variables and children's text search. *Journal of Educational Psychology, 93*(1), 14-22.

Robinson, H. A. (1966). Reliability of measures related to reading success of average, disadvantaged, and advantaged kindergarten children. *Reading Teacher, 20*(3), 203-209.

Rosenshine, B., Meister, C., & Chapman, S. (1996). Teaching students to generate questions: A review of the intervention studies. *Review of Educational Research, 66*(2), 181-221.

Rothkopf, E. Z. (1972). Variable adjunct question schedules, interpersonal interaction, and incidental learning from written material. *Journal of Educational Psychology, 63*(2), 87-92.

Rothkopf, E. & Billington, M. J. (1974). Indirect review and priming through questions. *Journal of Educational Psychology, 66*(5), 669-679.

Scardamalia, M. & Bereiter, C. (1992). Text-based and knowledge-based questioning by children. *Cognition and Instruction, 9*(3), 177-199.

Scardamalia, M., Bereiter, C., and Lamon, M. (1994). The CSILE Project: Trying to bridge the classroom into world 3. In K. McGilly (Ed), *Classroom lessons: Integrating cognitive theory and classroom practice* (pp. 201-228). Cambridge: MIT Press.

Schunk, D. H. (1991). Self-efficacy and academic motivation. *Educational Psychologist, 26*, 207-232.

Schunk, D. H. & Zimmerman, B. J. (1997). Developing self-efficacious readers and writers: The role of social and self-regulatory processes. In J. T. Guthrie & A. Wigfield (Eds.), *Reading engagement: Motivating readers through integrated instruction* (pp. 34-50). Newark, DE: International Reading Association.

Spires, H. A. & Donley, J. (1998). Prior knowledge activation: Inducing engagement with informational texts. *Journal of Educational Psychology, 90*(2), 249-261.

Spiro, R. J., Feltovich, P. J., Coulson, R. L., & Anderson, D. K. (1989). Multiple analogies for complex concepts: Antidotes for analogy-induced misconception in advanced knowledge acquisition. In S. Vosniadou & O. Andrew (Eds.), *Similarity and analogical reasoning* (pp. 498-531). New York: Cambridge University Press.

Spiro, R. J., Feltovich, P. J., Jacobson M. J., & Coulson R. L. (1995). Cognitive flexibility, constructivism, and hypertext: Random-access instruction for advanced knowledge acquisition in ill-structured domains. In L. P. Steffe & J. E. Gale (Eds.), *Constructivism in education* (pp. 85-107). Hillsdale, NJ: Lawrence Erlbaum Asssociates.

72 CHAPTER 2

Spiro, R. J. & Jehng, J-C. (1990). Cognitive flexibility and hypertext: Theory and technology for the nonlinear and multidimensional traversal of complex subject matter. In D. Nix, & R. J. Spiro, (Eds.), *Cognition, education, and multimedia: Exploring ideas in high technology* (pp. 163-205). Hillsdale, NJ, England: Lawrence Erlbaum Associates, Inc.

Stahl, S. A. & Hynd, C. R. (1998). What do we mean by knowledge and learning? In C. R. Hynd, S. A. Stahl, & M. Carr (Eds.), *Learning from text across conceptual domains* (pp. 15-44). Mahwah, NJ: Lawrence Erlbaum Associates, Inc.

Stahl, S. A. & Murray, B. A. (1994). Defining phonological awareness and its relationship to early reading. *Journal of Educational Psychology, 86*(2), 221-234.

Stanovich, K. E. (1991). Word recognition: Changing perspectives. In R. Barr, M. L. Kamil, & P. B. Mosenthal (Eds.), *Handbook of reading research, Volume 2* (pp. 418-452). Mahwah, NJ: Lawrence Erlbaum Associates, Inc.

Stanovich, K. E. (2000). *Progress in understanding reading: Scientific foundations and new frontiers.* New York: Guilford Press.

Stanovich, K. E. & Cunningham, A. E. (1993). Where does knowledge come from? Specific associations between print exposure and information acquisition. *Journal of Educational Psychology, 85,* 211-229.

Starr, M. L. & Krajcik, J. S. (1990). Concept maps as a heuristic for science curriculum development: Toward improvement in process and product. *Journal of Research in Science Teaching, 27*(10), 987-1000.

Stefanou, C., Perencevich, K. C., DiCintio, M., & Turner, J. C. (2004). Supporting autonomy in the classroom: Ways teachers encourage student decision making and ownership. *Educational Psychologist.*

Sticht, T. (1975) *Reading for working: A functional literacy anthology.* HumRRO Paperback Book.

Stipek, D. (1996). Motivation and instruction. In D. C. Berliner & R. C. Calfee (Eds.), *Handbook of educational psychology* (pp. 85-113). New York: Macmillan.

Sulzby, E. & Teale, W. (1991). Emergent literacy. In R. Barr, M. L. Kamil, & P. B. Mosenthal (Eds.), *Handbook of reading research, Volume 2,* (pp. 725-758). Mahwah, NJ: Lawrence Erlbaum Associates, Inc.

Symons, S., McLatchy-Gaudet, H., & Stone, T. D. (2001). Strategy instruction for elementary students searching informational text. *Scientific Studies of Reading, 15*(1), 1-33.

Sweller, J. (1999). *Instructional design in technical areas.* Camberwell, Australia: ACER Press.

Sweller, J., van Merrienboer, J. J. G., & Paas, F. G. W. C. (1998). Cognitive architecture and instructional design. *Educational Psychology Review, 10(3),* 251-296.

Taboada, A. & Guthrie, J. T. (2004). Growth of cognitive strategies for reading comprehension. In J. T. Guthrie, A. Wigfield, K. Perencevich (Eds.), *Motivating reading comprehension: Concept-oriented reading instruction.* Mahwah, NJ: Erlbaum.

Thorndike, E. L. (1931). *Human learning.* New York: Century.

Treiman, R. (1985). Onsets and rimes as units of spoken syllables: Evidence from children. *Journal of Experimental Child Psychology, 39,* 161-181.

Turner, J. C. (1995). The influence of classroom contexts on young children's motivation for literacy. *Reading Research Quarterly, 30,* 410-441.

van Dijk, T. A. & Kintsch, W. (1983). *Strategies of discourse comprehension.* New York: Academic Press.

van Der Meij, H. (1994). Student questioning: A componential analysis. *Learning and Individual Differences, 6*(2), 137-161.

van Merrienboer, J. J., Kirschner, P. A., & Kester, L. (2003). Taking the load off a learner's mind: Instructional design for complex learning. *Educational Psychologist,* 38(1), 5-13.

Wade, S., Buxton, W. M., & Kelly, M. (1999). Using think-alouds to examine reader-text interest. *Reading Research Quarterly, 34*(2), 194-216.

Webb, N. M. & Palincsar, A. S. (1996). Group processes in the classroom. In D. C. Berliner & R. C. Calfee, (Eds.), *Handbook of educational psychology* (pp. 841-873). New York: Wiley, John & Sons, Inc.

Whitehurst, G., Epstein, J. N., Angell, A. L., Payne, A. C., Crone, D. A., & Fischel, J. E. (1994). Outcomes of an emergent literacy intervention in Head Start. *Journal of Educational Psychology, 86*, 542-555.

Wentzel, K. R. (1993). Social and academic goals at school: Motivation and achievement in early adolescence. *Journal of Early Adolescence, 13*, 4-20.

Wentzel, K. R. (2000). What is it that I'm trying to achieve? Classroom goals from a content perspective. *Contemporary Educational Psychology, 25*(1), 105-115.

Whorf, B. L. (1956). *Language, thought, and reality: selected writings.* Cambridge: MA: Technology Press of Massachusetts Institute of Technology.

Wigfield, A. & Guthrie, J. T. (1997). Relations of children's motivation for reading to the amount and breadth of their reading. *Journal of Educational Psychology, 89(3)*, 420-432.

Willoughby, T., Wood, E., & Khan, M. (1994). Isolating variables that impact on or detract from the effectiveness of elaboration strategies. *Journal of Educational Psychology, 86*(2), 279-289.

Willoughby, T., Porter, L., Belsito, L., & Yearsley, T. (1999). Use of elaboration strategies by students in grades two, four, and six. *The Elementary School Journal, 99(3)*, 221-231

Woloshyn, V. E., Paivio, A., & Pressley, M. (1994). Use of elaborative interrogation to help students acquire information consistent with prior knowledge and information inconsistent with prior knowledge. *Journal of Educational Psychology, 86*(1), 79-89.

Woodworth, R. S. & Schlosberg, H. (1955). *Experimental psychology*, Revised edition. New York: Henry Hold and Company.

CHAPTER 3

PSYCHOMOTOR DOMAIN

Table 3.1. Taxonomy of the Psychomotor Domain

Process Requirements / Knowledge Domains	Acquisition	Automaticity	Transfer: Near term	Transfer: Far term
	Learning elements of a new knowledge domain (e.g., acquiring nomenclature).	Integrating and applying elements and procedures through extensive repetition (i.e., automating skills)	Developing ability to generalize- apply principles and strategies (e.g., heuristics) within a domain	Learning to discover new principles in a domain (e.g., creative thinking, problem finding, meta-cognition) and applying them across domains
PSYCHOMOTOR *physical actions *perceptual acuity	Learning basic procedures (e.g., letter indentation on keyboard); Practicing the elements of the basics (e.g., typing letters, etc.)	Repetitive or automated skills (e.g., practicing typing procedures for automaticity; practicing competitive running)	Strategy or planning skills (e.g., playing football, defensive driving)	Inventing a new strategy or skill (e.g., use of the curve ball in baseball)

Heuristics highlighted in this chapter on Psychomotor Development:

 ➢ *Task analysis within a consistent Motor Skill Taxonomy*
 ➢ *Part-task Learning with complex skills*
 ➢ *Use of Imagery to prepare for overt practice*
 ➢ *Observational learning from modeled performances*
 ➢ *Systematic Repetitive Practice*
 ➢ *Knowledge of Performance (Results)*
 ➢ *Transitioning from Cognitive Involvement to Automatic Movement*
 ➢ *Designing Instruction for Transfer.*

INTRODUCTION

Psychomotor learning has been characterized as relating to organismic and situational factors necessary for the acquisition and performance of behaviors that are generally reflected by movement (Singer, 1975, 1980). Psychomotor skills include actions such as contacting, manipulating, or moving an object and controlling the body or parts of the body. These types of motor skills require a great deal of information processing (see Ackerman & Cianciolo, 2000; Adams, 1987 discussed in Section II). Adams (1987) preferred to use "skill" to encompass "motor," "perceptual-motor," or any other term to cover the broadest behavioral definition of learning involving the use of movement. Rosenbaum et al. (2001) go further, and propose that there is virtually no difference between "intellectual" and "perceptual-motor" skill development. So, the very nature of the term "psychomotor" implies that the "domain" is more a convenient heuristic rather than an independent entity. Regardless of the ambiguity in definition, there seems to be some consensus on the skills we examine for clues concerning how to instruct the learner.

Athletic, secretarial, agricultural, dance, musical, and industrial production activities are examples of a few activities that include the more motor types of skills. Some actions involve many of the large muscles of the body, such as tennis, and others require the coordination and precision of fine muscles, like typing. As we move from Acquisition through Automaticity, there is less and less cognitive involvement as the skill becomes automated. However, to accomplish transfer, especially far term transfer, these actions involve increasing amounts of cognitive functioning in the skill development process to master new situations. Again, tennis is a prime example, since a new opponent, different surfaces, and higher skill level demands in tournament play all require conscious readjustment of one's game. In this sense, it is characterized as an open task (see Section II of this chapter). Once the new situation has been solved, the skill can recycle back to an automated state. This illustrates the fact that these categories interrelate, and that the processes are recursive for some types of skills (see Section II for a framework to characterize the nature of such developments). Therefore, one should not take the chart literally as indicating totally separate and isolated processes. As Bargh and Chartrand (1999) note, "automatic mental processes free one's limited conscious attentional capacity from tasks in which they are no longer needed" (p. 464). However, to take our tennis example again, facing new, more skilled opponents represents a new task requiring the reversion to using conscious, cognitive processes. Therefore, our active attention is demanded once again.

Another content example, which shows this interrelatedness, comes from a small muscle, high precision task, learning to copy high-speed Morse code (Wisher, Sabol, & Kern, 1995). This skill also clearly illustrates the requirement for integration of part-task skills. The acquisition of basic elements, a stream of "dahs" and "dits," is a perceptual component, which is then connected with the basic keyboard entries. The task is to copy strings of random, or encrypted, characters. Since the keyboard requirements are rather simple, the initial stage of perceptual-motor development is largely a cognitively driven activity. Later, larger elements are added, greater number of groupings of letters, and faster speeds, all of which require a continual integration and automating of prior skills, and fine-tuning of the motor requirement.

The ultimate criterion requirement is to copy at speeds exceeding 100 characters per minute. This criterion demands an interesting kind of integration of part-task skills at about 70 characters per minute. It is almost impossible to keep up with the stream of characters by matching the sensory input with motor output. Therefore, the successful copier, to move beyond this plateau, must develop a new strategy, which is to hold off his or her output by retaining one or two characters in short-term memory while cognitively identifying the characters arriving. This strategy involves both integrating the earlier part-task skills of copying faster with a new skill of learning to store some characters in memory before making the required motor output. This also could be called a secondary, higher order, Acquisition phase, which is then automated, and can be transferred to a work environment. The more commonly known skill of typing parallels the process of identifying the elements and letters, locating them on the keyboard, and then stringing them together into larger and larger, meaningful chunks (words, phrases, sentences, paragraphs, etc.). The same sort of buffering of characters and integrating the part-task skills to go beyond a plateau exists here as well.

For elaboration of the concepts of motor learning and performance, the reader is referred to Wrisberg's *Study Guild for Motor Learning and Performance* (2000). The guide provides exercises for students to further his or her understanding of motor learning. For example, Schmidt and Wrisberg (2000) review the three stages of information processing in their book, *Motor Learning and Performance* (2nd ed.). These three stages can be mapped into the Wisher et al.'s model (1995) to be discussed later in this chapter. The three stages are detecting and perceiving external cues (the sensing stage of the Wisher et al. model), selecting the appropriate response (the cognitive decision making and response selection stages), and organizing the response into an action (the response execution stage). Wrisberg's study guide provides an exercise for the student to better understand information processing during the performance of an open task. The exercise requests the student to pick an open task that he or she is familiar with and list examples of the information-processing activities that might take place in each of the stages when someone performs the skill. When offering a solution, the student is advised to include the following:

- "Describe the skill, emphasizing the goal of the movement and the basic actions that are required of the performer.
- Describe the person performing the skill, including personal characteristics that might affect the quality of the individual's information processing.
- Highlight an example of information-processing activity that might take place in each of these stages.
- Identify one factor that might influence the speed of processing each of the stages" (pp. 30).

These exercises enable the student to demonstrate his or her understanding of key concepts and principles of motor learning and performance.

Once again, we divide the remainder of the chapter into the two sections. Section I presents suggested guidance and Section II provides the supporting research from the literature.

SECTION I:

POSSIBLE INSTRUCTIONAL GUIDANCE

The availability and usage of necessary psychological and physiological factors are important determinants in the acquisition of psychomotor skills. Some necessary psychological factors include motivation, attention, feedback, and retention. Vision, hearing, kinesthesia, and fatigue are examples of a few of the physical factors that affect the acquisition and performance of a skill. Any instructional guidance must take into account these factors acting together and with differing emphases as the transition is made through the various stages and types of psychomotor learning. Romiszowski (1999) and Adams (1987) have provided a number of useful strategy suggestions and we have included, adapted, and expanded upon these to arrive at our listing.

During the Acquisition phase it is important to recognize that the learner's first task will always consist of identifying the elements; and, therefore, s/he must build up a knowledge base of these elements. The elements themselves must be presented for best learning in the context of the procedures to be performed using the knowledge elements. This requirement follows from the spiral curriculum approach described in Chapter 1 as a method for teaching or training for understanding or transfer. (Also, see Romiszowski's discussion (1999) on teaching for transfer.) We discussed this need in Morse code training to build up a knowledge base regarding the succession of "dahs" and "dits" as representing specific letters. In addition to the cognitive association between any sequence or groupings and the corresponding alphabetic characters, there must be the motor link relating to transcribing the appropriate alphabetic groupings (and later, increasingly more complex characters).

Acquisition Process

Table 3.2. Acquisition Process of the Psychomotor Domain

Process Requirements	Acquisition	Automaticity	Transfer: Near term	Transfer: Far term
PSYCHOMOTOR *physical actions *perceptual acuity	Learning basic procedures (e.g., letter indentation on keyboard); Practicing the elements of the basics (e.g., typing letters, etc.)	Repetitive or automated skills (e.g., practicing typing procedures for automaticity; practicing competitive running)	Strategy or planning skills (e.g., playing football, defensive driving)	Inventing a new strategy or skill (e.g., use of the curve ball in baseball)

Briefly, in this phase, the suggested strategy sequence is:

o **Conduct task analysis to identify specific knowledge and behavioral elements;**
o **Separate task into appropriate part-tasks;**
o **Teacher/instructor provides visual demonstration of the overall task performance, and the part-tasks, verbalizing appropriately as he or she performs;**
o **Learner identifies these basic elements, verbalizing overtly, in the part-task format;**
o **Learner commits these to memory; and**
o **Practices the association of the knowledge and motor elements to criterion;**
o **Learner facilitates the association by using mental rehearsal, as well as overt practice.**

Details of implementing these suggestions are as follows:

Task and Part-Task Analysis
Task analysis is used to identify the specific knowledge and behaviors necessary to master a skill. In the training world, once it has been determined that training is needed, the steps start with what is called a front-end analysis (FEA). In this process, the criterion is performance of the overall task (job)-in-context. It is analyzed with respect to the standards, conditions of work, and performance level required (Crawford, 1962). Next, these are translated into training objectives to lead to performing the overall, complex, job-task. The educational analogue to this approach is described by Meichenbaum & Biemiller (1998) as the process of "planning and implementing learning settings" (p. 114).

The FEA is then followed by breaking a complex task into smaller, more manageable part-tasks, in order to facilitate early acquisition of the essential psychomotor elements. Assisted by the FEA, it is, in the last analysis, a judgment call by the developer on a case by case basis to define how "complex" the overall task may be and whether parts should all be trained first and then the whole task (see Adams, 1987, for detailed discussion; Hays & Singer, 1989, for discussion as it relates to simulators and part-task trainers). Guidelines are as follows:

For complex tasks, part-task training can be extremely cost-effective:

- Where subtasks are to be performed in sequence, and can be segmented or laid out temporally or spatially,
- Where fractionation, breaking down into parts, which are to be performed simultaneously, or
- Where one or more dimensions of the entire task can be made easier, simplification.
- In many cases, it may be necessary to have an expert in the subject matter to aid in the breakdown of the task into subtasks.
- When part tasks are to be timeshared with other actions, whole task integration must be practiced.
- When relearning of the psychomotor skill is to be accomplished, whole task training should be used.

Observation and Mental Rehearsal
Visual demonstrations have long been acknowledged as one of the most powerful means of transmitting patterns of thought and behavior. Modeled and monitored performance provide vehicles for converting representations into skilled actions. In order to learn new psychomotor skills, the learner must pay attention to the instructions or examples provided.

The method begins with:

- The learner observing the teacher perform a specific task while verbalizing certain statements that relate to the various steps of the task.

- After visually observing the model, the learner then proceeds to work on the task while the teacher instructs him on what to say.
- After the learner is able to do this with the teacher's help, the learner is then instructed to go through the same activity again while verbalizing overtly the comments modeled by the teacher.
- The procedure is then extended until the learner is able to complete the task without assistance.

Mental practice is a cognitive strategy used to acquire, rehearse, or enhance a physical skill. It is the cognitive rehearsal of a task prior to performance (Driskell, Copper, & Moran, 1994). Those who engage in mental practice usually employ self-talk or inner speech and some form of imagery to guide themselves through new or difficult tasks. This approach is used frequently in sports, whether to visualize and rehearse hitting a baseball, or practice shooting foul shots in basketball, or to imagine meeting the tennis ball with a smooth and proper swing.

Typically, in working with a sports psychologist, the basketball athlete (Carter & Kelly, 1997):

- Imagines perfect performance of all the components involved in the task of focus, say shooting 25 foul shots.
- Next, the sport psychologist guides the learner with imagery instructions. The learner, with eyes closed, begins to visualize the context for the upcoming event, the basket, the rim, the entire room, feeling the ball, its texture, and gracefully tossing the ball toward the center of the basket, aided by a thin strong line connecting the ball to the basket. The instructions may or may not contain suggestions regarding confidence, relaxation, or other motivational approaches.
- Next, the learner cognitively practices rehearsing the upcoming event.
- Finally, she or he performs the task live (see Carter & Kelly, 1997, for more specifics of this type of example).

When conducting mental practice, the learner must take certain aspects into consideration for the efficacy of their practice. A meta-analysis by Driskell, Copper, & Moran (1994) found that certain conditions allowed for mental practice to be more effective:

- Mental practice is effective for both cognitive and physical tasks; however, the effect is stronger for tasks that include cognitive elements. They also found that the more a task includes strength and coordination, the less effective is mental practice.
- Another aspect to consider when performing mental practice is the retention interval. Driskell et al. (1994) found that the longer the delay

between practice and performance, the weaker the effects of mental practice on performance.

- The meta-analysis also indicated that there is no difference in the effectiveness of mental practice used by novice or experienced learners; therefore, suggesting that it can benefit all levels of learners. However, when looking at the type of task, novice subjects had stronger effects of mental practice when using it for cognitive tasks than for physical tasks. Experienced learners benefit equally well from mental task, regardless of task type. This finding is also supported in the review by Murphy and Martin (2002).
- The number of times an individual practices does not predict the effect of mental practice on performance.
- When the overall length of the mental practice intervention increases, the beneficial effects on performance decreases. In other words, mental practice is beneficial to one's performance, however, the longer someone mentally practices, the less beneficial it becomes. Therefore, the learner does not want to overdo how much mental practice is used.

Similar to mental practice, Meichenbaum's "cognitive self-guidance" (Meichenbaum, 1977) is a training program designed to improve task performance and develop self-control through training in the comprehension of the tasks, spontaneous reproduction of verbal mediators, and the use of mediators in controlling nonverbal behaviors such as psychomotor activities.

The method begins with:

- The learner observing the teacher perform a specific task while verbalizing certain statements that relate to the various steps of the task.
- After observing the model, the learner then proceeds to work on the task while the teacher instructs him on what to say.
- After the learner is able to do this with the teacher's help, the learner is then instructed to go through the same activity again while verbalizing overtly the comments modeled by the teacher.
- The procedure is then extended until the learner is able to complete the task without assistance.

As a bridge between the Acquisition Phase and Automaticity, we present a detailed example of part-task learning and integration. Several part-tasks comprise the process of learning to fire an army rifle (McGuigan & MacCaslin, 1954). Following the steps outlined above in the Acquisition Phase, the learner/trainee would learn the meaning of the basic elements: postures, the sling, rifle sights, loading and unloading the rifle, breath control, and trigger squeeze, and to associate them with the appropriate motor requirements. She or he would be given a visual demonstration of the overall sequence as an advanced organizer.

In sequence, the trainee must learn:

(1) To assume certain well-defined postures for firing in the standing, kneeling, sitting, and prone positions;

(2) Either to wrap ('hasty sling') or loop ('loop sling') the rifle sling about his arm as the position demands, to give him greater stability;

(3) To move the slight-adjustment to alter the demands, to give him greater stability;

(4) To move the sight-adjustment to alter the strike of the bullet;

(5) To load and unload the weapon;

(6) To align his sights on the target to obtain the proper 'sight picture';

(7) To control his breathing – to take a breath and hold it until he has fired;

(8) To squeeze the trigger gradually (to avoid stimuli to which an anticipatory startle or flinching response might be anchored).

The key is that the learner must practice these part-tasks to criterion in order to demonstrate "mastery". The level of mastery will vary depending upon the amount of resources available, and the judgment that "x-number of errorless trials" are sufficient. This is not a trivial decision since each succeeding level comes at an increase in cost of time, dollars, and other resources.

Where tasks are sequential like these in firing the rifle, the "progressive" part-task method is recommended (Romiszowski, 1999, p. 472). It involves training on step 1, then 1 and step 2, then 1, 2, and add 3, etc. and lastly, the entire task. van Merrienboer,, Kirschner, and Kester's (2003) example of scaffolding using differentiated "task classes" is similar to the progressive part-task instructional procedure. So, what we have is a relatively seamless transition from the acquisition of basic elements into practicing for automaticity greater and greater numbers of part-task integration until the whole sequence is automated. After s/he has learned to do these part-tasks and integrated them with a slow fire instructional criterion, s/he must learn to adapt the same techniques to sustained (rapid) fire. Then, near-term transfer would occur with practice to a criterion under sustained fire.

Automaticity Process

Table 3.3. Automaticity Process of the Psychomotor Domain

Process Requirements	Acquisition	Automaticity	Transfer: Near term	Transfer: Far term
PSYCHOMOTOR *physical actions *perceptual acuity	Learning basic procedures (e.g., letter indentation on keyboard); Practicing the elements of the basics (e.g., typing letters, etc.)	Repetitive or automated skills (e.g., practicing typing procedures for automaticity; practicing competitive running)	Strategy or planning skills (e.g., playing football, defensive driving)	Inventing a new strategy or skill (e.g., use of the curve ball in baseball)

The keys during this phase are:

o   **Learner practices repetitively.**
o   **The learner eliminates distractors through attention focus training.**
o   **All practice is aided by distributing this over time and by part-task.**
o   **Instructor uses forced pacing for practice on continuous tasks.**
o   **Knowledge of results (both process and outcome) is given, including**
o   **Observational feedback (watching expert); with**
o   **Involving the learner in the modeling process early in learning to facilitate understanding of how the skill is to be performed.**
o   **Increasing the number of dimensions (pressures, muscular tensions, and external features of the movement) to eventually simulate overall task.**
o   **Overlearning is used to enhance retention.**

Types of Practice
As was seen in the rifle-firing example above, an important factor in skill acquisition during the Automaticity stage is practice; and the practice mode should be consistent with the part-task strategy suggested for the Acquisition phase. All learning trials on one part-task (whether separate or progressive) are completed before practice on another part-task is undertaken. The practice is therefore distributed by part-task. Practice should also be distributed over time in order to affect stronger learning. One should not attempt to accomplish the learning in one learning session. While it

may lead to faster learning if tested immediately, massed training does not result in effective retention and transfer (see Rosenbaum et al., 2001, for discussion).

Many psychomotor activities require the learner to selectively attend to and concentrate on relevant cues in their environment while disregarding irrelevant ones (the distractors). This allows the learner to accomplish the goal of an open or closed task. During the learning process, there are many outside factors, such as auditory and visual distractors, that can interfere with the attention of the learner and moving toward automaticity of a motor skill. Singer, Cauraugh, Murphey, Chen, and Lidor (1991b) suggested that attentional-focus training programs assist in improving attention and focus and disregarding potentional distractors. This, in turn, results in more effective performances (Singer, Cauraugh, Murphey, Chen, & Lidor, 1991b; Singer, Cauraugh, Tennant, Murphey, Chen, & Lidor, 1991a). Some key steps in the attentional-focus training programs include:

- **Relaxation**: The learner practices proper breathing patterns necessary for his or her best performance and to repeat the same pattern each time. Prior to performance, it is recommended to take slow, deep breaths through the nose, holding the breath, and exhaling through the mouth.
- **Visualization**: The learner identifies the most important movement components to be executed precisely in the proper sequence. They are instructed to see, imagine, and feel himself or herself executing the task.
- **Focusing attention**: The learner is instructed to focus his or her attention on relevant cues during the practice of the task. He or she is instructed to "feel committed to the task and to direct all of their attention to the focal point selected" (Singer, Cauraugh, Murphey, Chen, & Lidor, 1991b, p. 60).
- **Refocusing attention after distraction**: If irrelevant cues distract the learner, the learner is encouraged to immediately refocus on the target. If distractors result in a poor performance, the learner is instructed to disregard the previous performance and to focus their attention on the next trial.

The reader will note the similarity in operations with the Carter and Kelly (1997) imagery procedures described earlier in the Acquisition discussion. Murphy and Martin (2002) also describe a similar set of procedures as a combination of Motivation general-mastery (MG-M) and Cognitive-specific (CS) imagery, where the athlete images mastery and coping, "…focused during sport competition" (p. 419), and also rehearses her or his specific skills, such as soccer kicks or dismounts from a pommel horse. The added feature with attention focus training is that it takes place during practice and performance of the targeted task.

Another example of a training procedure, which encompasses the learning process from Acquisition through Near Term Transfer is seen in learning how to copy Morse code (Wisher et al., 1995). A student performs this task on a standard computer keyboard.

- Basic skills are demonstrated to the student, occurring in the Acquisition Stage.
- Cognitive associations are made to the alphabetic character elements
- Then the student moves into the Automaticity Stage. In Morse code training, instruction is given six hours a day until a single block is copied at an accuracy of 96%. The student practices the task repeatedly until they reached 96% accuracy. The task is then adjusted to the new, learned skills. It is more difficult, and practice is needed again to acquire the additional skills.
- The progressive part task method is used, adding more and more of the target characters to the knowledge base starting with easy and moving towards more difficult tasks (see Clawson, Healy, Ericsson, & Bourne, 2001).
- Integration of the skills takes place in the Near Term Transfer stage. Here the student is required, with forced pacing, to apply the learned copying technique to presentations at faster speeds. Thus, at the more advanced levels of learning to copy Morse code, the presentation speed for the student is raised. Again, repetitive practice occurs with forced pacing. At the 70-character per minute speed, the new strategy or secondary acquisition kicks in. This integration and transfer continues until complete and accurate automaticity of the entire task is reached, the maximum required presentation speed coupled with excellent copying accuracy.
- This instructional design illustrates adaptive, part-task training followed by integration with a heavy emphasis on practice, in which the training schedule is adapted to the rate of the student's progress.
- Lastly, once the criterion for learning has been reached, continued practice, called over-learning, can be very important, if time permits, to enhance retention.

Knowledge of Results
Knowledge of results (both process and outcome) provides the most effective form of information given during the Automaticity stage in learning a Closed skill. It is recommended to use kinematic feedback as well as outcome knowledge of results in order to facilitate psychomotor learning. Kinematic feedback involves giving the student feedback of his particular segments of motions. This can be accomplished directly by the instructor drawing the student's attention to his sequence of moves, or by showing the student how his moves compare to that of the ideal movement by superimposing his moves over that of the ideal and what the feedback from the moves feel like. Finally, videotaping the students' movements and critically commenting on the trainees' specific movements sequence may also be used. It is provided as the student is learning to make the movement (Carroll & Bandura,

1990). The latter method is a standard one used when training athletic skills (Adams, 1987).

The student should be aware of how well s/he is performing during a task and what changes she or he can make. Students should also always know the expected outcomes and have both short-term and long-term objectives. For example, when learning to play basketball, a short-term objective could be mastering how to successfully shoot a foul shot, and a long-term objective could be shooting free throws with accuracy greater than 70%. Note that both of these represent part-tasks to be followed by integrating and transferring them into the complex task of playing a basketball game.

Observational feedback is also valuable as a corollary to the kinematic feedback. It has value in both the Acquisition stage and Automaticity stage. Briefly, the student observes a model performing the motions or he or she watches a video or film of an expert performing the motions. Then the student, drawing upon a cognitive representation, reproduces the motions.

Psychomotor learning is facilitated during both the Acquisition stage and Automaticity stage by providing an increased number of dimensions to simulate the overall task. So for example, in a movement related task requiring a certain amount of pressure for criterion performance, it would be useful during training to provide the dimensions of pressures, muscular tensions, and external features of the movement that are not visual (Adams, 1984). Virtual reality (VR) training using a glove with sensors is one technique that is under development and attends to these issues (see Seidel & Chatelier, 1997 for a discussion of VR issues).

Transfer Process: Near Term

Table 3.4. Near Term Transfer Process of the Psychomotor Domain

Process Requirements	Acquisition	Automaticity	Transfer: Near term	Transfer: Far term
PSYCHOMOTOR *physical actions *perceptual acuity	Learning basic procedures (e.g., letter indentation on keyboard); Practicing the elements of the basics (e.g., typing letters, etc.)	Repetitive or automated skills (e.g., practicing typing procedures for automaticity; practicing competitive running)	Strategy or planning skills (e.g., playing football, defensive driving)	Inventing a new strategy or skill (e.g., use of the curve ball in baseball)

Transfer of schemas or principles is accomplished by:

- **The use of numerous and varied examples and opportunities for practice;**
- **Maintaining short time intervals between practicing the numerous and varied examples and application to the transfer task;**
- **Making the practice as interesting as possible to maintain motivation with advanced learners;**
- **Involving the learner in the modeling process to facilitate understanding of how the skill is to be performed.**

Near Term Transfer involves the application of principles or strategies within a domain. Analogous to the strategy of providing multiple contexts to aid transfer in cognitive learning, when a task involves a sequence of movements to be performed in a variety of conditions, training, transfer, and retention on this task can be facilitated by including these variations in the training itself (see Salas & Cannon-Bowers, 2001). This approach aids in abstracting the rule or schema to be learned. For example in an aircraft tracking and positioning task, an air traffic controller must pay attention to the varying numbers of aircraft entering or leaving the target airspace, the changing wind and weather conditions, etc. How she or he responds must involve flexibility.

This type of transfer is also noted in the description above of Morse code training process at the higher criterion levels for expert copying. It can be further understood by examining in some detail the model proposed by Wisher et al. (1995) to account for the transition between Automaticity to Transfer in developing the skill of copying Morse code.

1. Learn the basic elements; i.e., memorizing the dots and dashes for the characters, listening, and paying attention to initial groups of them at a slow speed, required for learning to copy Morse code (Acquisition Phase).
2. With practice (done in the Automaticity Phase), response execution becomes autonomous, proceeding without the need for attention.
3. Attention shifts between the element activation (sensory input) and character selection processes.
   Example: At this point, the learner gets the sensory input (listens), and then shifts attention to recognizing the character by selecting it from the already memorized list of characters.
   The feeding of information from the sensory store (element activation) to the character recognition system starts as soon as attention shifts from the selection of the previous character.
4. Element activation from the sensory store stops after a fixed period of time for a given subject.

5.   Character selection decides on a character identity based upon activated information only. Essentially, it is a cognitive identification phase following the auditory reception of information.

All of this proceeds separately from the autonomous overt response execution; and to the extent that the learner has become a skilled copier, transfer across differing groups of characters at various speeds is successful. Further transfer can occur in the work environment where more noise in the signal is present and there is variability in speeds for incoming codes, in contrast to the learning environment.

Cognitive Process Model
This process of shifting attention between sensory and character selection, while automating the motor response function allows the copier to seemingly fall behind the speed at which characters are presented. This is called "copying behind." It emphasizes the use of storage buffers for the various kinds of information, sensory (for auditory reception), naming (for character recognition), and motor responding (motor organization), and the development of automaticity in response execution. The student is then able to withhold responding in a motor buffer until it is most convenient or to develop a rhythmic output, which matches the average rate of stimulus presentation yet is independent of its fluctuations. These processes are illustrated in the following figure reproduced from Wisher et al. (1995). This figure also illustrates how the cognitive and psychomotor domains interrelate when learning Morse code. Later, in Section II, we discuss in a general framework how this interrelatedness might happen.

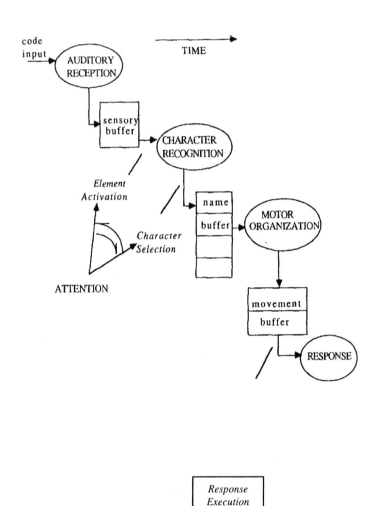

Figure 3.1. Proposed cognitive process model for skilled Morse code

This process is proposed to account analogously for developing expertise in typing. Note that the training process is similar. The learner concentrates first on learning the elements, the letters and numbers, and matches them to the keyboard (Acquisition). Then she or he moves to progressive part-task grouping of elements and practicing typing at faster and faster speeds (Automaticity). The student then accomplishes transfer in much the same manner as the code copier, except that the groups of characters have a context -- words, sentences, and perhaps even short paragraphs (for the most expert typists).

Transfer Process: Far Term

Table 3.5. Far Term Transfer Process of the Psychomotor Domain

Process Requirements	Acquisition	Automaticity	Transfer: Near term	Transfer: Far term
PSYCHOMOTOR *physical actions *perceptual acuity	Learning basic procedures (e.g., letter indentation on keyboard); Practicing the elements of the basics (e.g., typing letters, etc.)	Repetitive or automated skills (e.g., practicing typing procedures for automaticity; practicing competitive running)	Strategy or planning skills (e.g., playing football, defensive driving)	Inventing a new strategy or skill (e.g., use of the curve ball in baseball)

In this phase, transfer is accomplished by:

- **Encouraging the development of meta-cognitive strategies;**
- **Self-monitoring; with**
- **A combination of self-talk and imagery.**

Carrying the code copying and typing examples further, we propose that learning to be aware of the need to shift strategies when reaching a plateau in any complex task will result in a meta-cognitive strategy that will lead to far-term transfer. If we imagine learning to play the piano while reading the notes from a sheet of music, the same strategy would seem relevant. To go beyond reading isolated notes to reading measures and larger musical phrasings, would seem to demand the same adaptive shift. In this case it might be seen in reading ahead while playing a measure or so behind. The analogy falls short in that the visual stimulus is always present in this case, whereas the code copying stimulus is temporary. If we consider typing, learning from dictation would be a closer analogy.

Another instructional strategy recommended to develop meta-cognition is the use of a combination of self-talk and imagery. It is reflected in Gallwey's approach (1974) to practicing "inner tennis" or other imagined practice (Romiszowski, 1999).

Féry and Morizot (2000) contended that the motor system can program closed skills more easily when one can represent efficiently the kinesthetic image of its later excecution. Rushall and Lippman (1998) suggested that imagery is implemented in different phases during physical performance: During skill development and learning, as suggested in the Acquisition Phase of this chapter, and during transfer during competition performance preparation. As Romiszowski notes, the player engages in an "inner game", of mental practice against imaginary obstacles to overcome "...lapses in concentration, nervousness, self-doubts, and self-condemnation" (p. 478). Druckman and Swetts (1988) describe a combination cognitive-behavioral training program, which uses both relaxation to hold down one's arousal level coupled with positive self-talk. This meta-cognitive strategy is the development of a self-monitoring, success model internally as the basis for transfer.

Murphy and Martin (2002) provide an excellent review of imagery applied to sports, elaborating on the value and interpretation of types of imagery strategies. They present a useful taxonomy of five types of mental practice: cognitive specific (imagery rehearsal of specific skills), cognitive general (strategies related to plans for a competitive event), motivational specific (goal-oriented, winning an event, getting kudos, receiving a medal, etc.), motivational general-mastery (being mentally tough, confident and focused during competition), and motivational general-arousal (relaxation, anxiety, stress reduction, and arousal). Depending on the approach of the instructor, the specific task, and the needs of the athlete, combinations of the cognitive and motivational strategies could be used in all four phases of learning.

SECTION II:

SUPPORTING RESEARCH

A person performs an action because they want to produce a particular effect. In most psychological usage, action also implies a preceding intention. Typically, we want or intend to achieve a special goal, and this intention drives the generation of action. Also, actions can be defined as what the mind does to the body and thoughts alone are not sufficient for action. Therefore, from this perspective, imagined movement is not considered an action. Muscular movement, however, is a necessary but not a sufficient condition for action. If a person does not move, they have not performed an action. Thus, the term "action" implies some psychological elements in addition to physical movement. Learning to perform an action has been variously called developing psychomotor skill, perceptual-motor skill or motor skill. Gagne's (1977) five domains of learning include motor skills as one of its domains (The others are verbal information, intellectual skills, cognitive strategies, and attitudes.). Motor skills are defined as movement oriented and represented by coordination of responses to situational cues. Most behaviors involve an interaction of at least four components: psychomotor, cognitive, perceptual and affective. Instruction should therefore (in agreement with Gagne) integrate these processes and skills.

Rosenbaum et al. (2001), on the other hand, avoid this distinction by asserting that any skill means "…an ability that allows a goal to be achieved within some domain with increasing likelihood as a result of practice" (p. 454). A skill, which is "intellectual" for them, has a goal, which is symbolic. A "perceptual motor skill" is one whose goal is not symbolic. Therefore, solving mathematics problems have symbolic goals, while playing a violin, typing, or playing tennis are examples of non-symbolic efforts. Both skills involve actions towards achieving a goal. Once again we are reminded as we were in the Introduction to this chapter that there is no unanimity on a definition of "psychomotor" domain.

Psychomotor Learning: Distinction between Skill and Ability

Singer's (1975) research in psychomotor learning expresses the importance in distinguishing between skills and abilities. Abilities and skills describe different behaviors and there is much more agreement among testing specialists regarding the way to measure a particular skill or knowledge about some subject matter than there is regarding how to evaluate cognitive or psychomotor abilities. Ability is thought to be something that is general and enduring, for example balance is an ability. The term skill is usually used to denote the act or task that is performed or the level of proficiency attained in the performance of a motor task (e.g., Adams, 1987). Skills are easy to observe and measure and there are many more skills than there are abilities. However, the designation of abilities is more conceptual in nature. Abilities are inferred from general analysis and subjective appraisal or statistical techniques, such as correlational and factor-analytic models. For example, when a number of different test scores correlate well together, the inference is that there is something common among them. This underlying characteristic is termed ability. Thus the presence of an ability to a high degree increases an individual's probability to perform well in the tasks to which the ability contributes.

Ability is not directly measurable and that which is often referred to as an ability score is invariably a score registered on a specific paper and pencil or performance test. Many abilities contribute to successful performance execution of tasks. Fleishman (1964), through factor analysis, identified eleven abilities, which underlie achievement in many motor tasks:

1. Control precision: Primarily involves highly controlled large muscle movements.
2. Multi-limb coordination: Simultaneous coordination of the movements of a number of limbs.
3. Response orientation: Selection of right response (visual-discrimination), irrespective of precision and coordination.
4. Reaction time: Speed of response to a stimulus.
5. Rate control: Continuous anticipatory motor adjustments to changing situational cues (speed, direction).
6. Speed of arm movement: Speed where accuracy is not important.

7. Manual dexterity: Manipulation of large objects under speed conditions.
8. Finger dexterity: Manipulation of tiny objects with precision and control.
9. Arm-hand steadiness: Control of movements, while motionless or in motion.
10. Wrist-Finger speed: Tapping activity
11. Aiming: Printed tests requiring pencil accuracy and speed

Skills are developed through constantly well-guided and informative practice, resulting in selective perception and reactions to appropriate stimuli. It can refer to a particular act performed or the manner in which it is executed. Every skill reflects the need for varying degrees of physical, cognitive, motor, and emotional involvement. Skill usually refers to a highly developed specific sequence of responses and as demonstrated by performance is an indication of that which has been learned.

Singer (1975) also stressed that the process of learning, of skill acquisition, reveals a number of consistencies among learners.

1. In athletics, a given body build has been found to be related to excellence in particular athletic endeavors.
2. Enriched and varied early "learnerhood" experiences is a second factor leading to the probability of success in a wide range of undertakings.
3. Specific skills, once learned, will transfer over to situations in which these skills are used.
4. Aspects of personality relate to task achievement in some ways, although clear-cut patterns are often difficult to establish.
5. General motor abilities, as influenced by heredity and environmental variables, will certainly have a bearing on the learner's potential for successful achievement in any endeavor.
6. Physical measures needed for task success (e.g., adequate strength, flexibility, and endurance) must be present.
7. Sense acuity (e.g., kinesthetic, visual, and verbal cues) is important prior to, during, and following an act.
8. Following the reception of information through the senses, perceptual operations typically precede motor activity.
9. Intelligence, which is usually measured by academic achievement or IQ in the research, is positively but lowly related to physical characteristics and motor skills in the normal population of students.
10. Emotions (e.g., anxiety, stress, tension, and the effect of various motivational procedures) are a part of most motor activities.
11. The level of aspiration, or goals, established by an individual when he undertakes a motor task will greatly determine the level one sets for himself.
12. A person's expectancy attitudes are related to task performance. High expectations positively affect performance and low expectations negatively affect performance.

The task itself may be fear inducing because of its very nature, as is the case with gymnastics, jumping on a trampoline, diving, etc., and requires safety precautions. Military, vocational, and driving skills have similar elements and fear that causes anxiety is a deterrent to the learning process.

13. With regard to occupational choices, athletic endeavors, and task performances in general, male and female comparisons lead to interesting observations. Because of certain physiological, anatomical, and personality differences, performances on certain tasks are favored for one sex over the other.
14. Various kinds of motor skill are affected in dissimilar fashion by the aging process.

Both of these detailed analyses, Fleishman's (1964) and Singer's (1975), leave us with the problem of trying to synthesize the approaches into a reasonable classification scheme.

Taxonomies of Motor Skills

A taxonomy is a system of classifying motor skills in terms of characteristics of the movement involved, characteristics of the movement involved, characteristics of the environment in which the skill is performed, the purpose of the skill, and the type of implement used. A taxonomy can provide a better understanding of both commonalities and differences among motor skills across several dimensions, and a recognition of requirements either similar or unique, involved in performance.

The environments or conditions in which psychomotor skills are performed may be fixed, stable, or moving. Gentile (1977) believed the nature of the performance environment, by virtue of its regulatory function, determines the nature of the successful pattern of movement that will be developed as a result of practice of a particular motor skill. He developed a composite taxonomy based upon the consideration of both the performer and the performance environment. Gilchrist and Gruber (1984) also assert taxonomies in the psychomotor domain should delineate the nature of skills to be acquired whether fine, gross; open, closed; discrete, serial, continuous. These skills are based in part on characteristics of the performance context. Fine motor skills involve neuromuscular coordination that are usually precision oriented and involve hand-eye coordination. Some examples of fine motor skills are playing a piano, threading a needle, learning Morse code, and typing. A gross motor skill involves contractions and usage of the large muscles of the body and the whole body is usually in movement (playing a sport). Open skills are those in which the environment is unstable, changeable, and moving. The objective in open skills is to develop a variety or repertoire of movements within a particular class of movement to enable the performer to respond to the changing requirements.

Closed skills are those in which the performance environment is stable, fixed, repetitive, and unchanging between movement selection, initiation, and completion. In closed skills, the goal is to be able to repeat a specific skill as consistently as possible, to habituate skill performance. A continuous task involves a series of adjustments of flowing movements usually without an acknowledged termination point in time or specified movement. Discrete tasks contain one unit or a series of separate units with a fixed beginning or end.

Many instructors of physical skills accept, almost without question, that the levels of student accomplishment are categorized as beginning, intermediate, and advanced without giving attention to the identification of the characteristics or limitations of these levels. Adler (1981) provides a significant exception to this by asserting three identifiable stages of psychomotor development. He states these levels of development can be more suitably and usefully defined by stages of skill acquisition: "the concept stage," "the adaptation stage," and "the automation stage." He also illustrates how each can be recognized.

In the concept stage, learners first become aware of what it is they are trying to accomplish in the whole and begin to get some sense of what will be needed to perform even the rudiments of the whole task. Initial concept formation relies heavily on visual information and active demonstrations of performance. Verbal descriptions seem to be least efficacious in communicating the demands of what is essentially physical information. The second aspect of concept formation is actual accomplishment of the entire task. Concept formation is not complete until the learner knows what if feels like to perform the skill. Reliance on vision is still the most efficient strategy; however, limited verbal assistance has value in this aspect as well.

The concept stage is completed and the adaptation stage begins when the learner is capable of performing the entire skill. In the adaptation stage, performance is adjusted to bring it closer to some criterion or form of accuracy. The training process includes shaping; the learner is brought successfully closer to the ideal performance. Adler (1981) stresses the differences between open and closed skills in the adaptation stage. The objective in open skills is to develop a variety or repertoire of movements within a particular class of movement to enable the performer to respond to the changing requirements. For example, the tennis forehand drive must be used in response to balls which travel at different speeds, levels, directions, and spin. In closed skills, the goal is to be able to repeat a specific skill as consistently as possible, to habituate skill performance. For example, the baseball pitcher must learn to pitch with a consistent rhythm and throw to a designated spot with repetitive accuracy. Regardless of the type of skill, the teacher can assist by focusing the learner's attention on aspects of the skill that require correction or adaptation. There is no emphasis placed on particular style requirements but it is stressed that attention should be focused on a part of the task.

The automation stage is reached when the learner can perform without conscious attention to the movement. The attention of the learner is diverted away form the movement and the changes in performance are noted. For example, the tennis player hits numbered tennis balls and is asked to identify the numbers. Attention is directed towards identifying the numbers and not towards swinging the racket. Once a skill is automated, learning doesn't stop. At this point the student needs to practice extensively to enhance memory. This is sometimes referred to as over-learning and is important to retention.

There is no precise point between the three stages that defines advancement from one stage to the next. There is usually some overlap and often times some fluctuation between stages. However, it is possible for the teacher to specify a desired performance of the learner and arrange the training so that certain performance levels will be developed and exhibited. The instructor must also work at making practice as interesting as possible so that advanced learners will continue to practice.

Romiszowski (1999) proposes a similar, general process of psychomotor skill learning and instruction as well, but with five stages, that seems consistent with our model of learning as it applies principally to closed skill development. Stage 1 involves acquiring knowledge of what should be done, to what purpose, in what sequence, and by what means (acquisition). Stage 2 is the execution of the actions in a step-by-step manner, for each of the steps of the operation. The analogy is for his first two stages to encompass our Acquisition Phase. The next stage, Stage 3, involves transfer of control from the eyes to the other senses or to kinesthetic control through muscular coordination. Stage 4 is the automatization of the skill. His third and fourth stages approximate what we call the Automaticity Phase. Romizsowski's final stage is the generalization of the skill to a continually greater range of application situations (near term transfer). His model suggests three basic steps in the overall instructional process. Step 1: Imparting the knowledge content; Step 2: Imparting the basics skill; and Step 3: Developing proficiency. Our approach also projects recycling from automatic to cognitive involvement in an open type of task, when novel situations or new applications are encountered. This is especially evident in the example of the developing tennis player as she or he moves to a higher level of competition.

An important characteristic of this learning process implied by the above taxonomic approaches is that both cognitive and motor components are used in varying degrees during the proposed stages. We offer in Figure 3.1, and discuss at the end of this chapter, a notional way of capturing these shifts consistent with the above as well as mapping these stages onto our own Acquisition, Automaticity, Near Term Transfer, and Far Term Transfer phases. Qualifications to this transfer process moving to complete automization must be considered. When a task is characterized as being open (see below), uncertainty and variations in the task demands from differing environmental conditions may require increased cognitive involvement; and therefore, the process will involve a recycling through the previous stages. Ackerman and Cianciolo (2000) discuss this issue in relation to an air traffic controller task (TRACON). Directing a plane on where to land or what air space to move to because changing, imposed conditions (e.g., winds, or crowded air space) may demand heightened information processing beyond the simpler, Closed task of directing a plane to land on runway x or y based on known characteristics of the aircraft and the runway length. In their review, Druckman and Bjork (1994) report similar problems when a mapping task was learned to the point of automaticity. Negative transfer occurred when changes in responses were required.

Acquisition Process of Psychomotor Skills

Motor skills are developed through constantly well-guided and informative practice, resulting in selective perception and reactions to appropriate stimuli (Singer, 1975). When demonstrated by performance, they are an indication of what has been learned. Therefore, motor skills often begin as cognitive processes that are performed in a physical context. This is illustrated in Figure 3.1. The availability and usage of necessary psychological and physiological factors are important determinants in the acquisition of psychomotor skills. Some necessary psychological factors include motivation, attention, feedback, and retention. Vision, hearing, kinesthesia, and fatigue are examples of a few of the physical factors that affect the acquisition and performance of a skill.

Psychological Factors
According to Bandura's (1986) social cognitive theory of observational learning, information conveyed by a modeled performance is extracted through selective attention to critical features and transformed into a cognitive representation of the actions by symbolic coding and cognitive rehearsal. Modeled and monitored performance provides vehicles for converting representations into skilled actions. In order to learn new psychomotor skills, the learner must pay attention to the instructions or examples provided. Mental practice is one of the cognitive strategies used to acquire, rehearse, or enhance a physical skill. Those who engage in mental practice usually employ Vygotsky's (1978, 1997) self talk or inner speech, and can be trained to use both relaxation to control level of arousal (see Chapter 4 of this volume) and positive self-talk (Druckman & Swetts, 1988) to guide themselves through new or difficult tasks. Similarly, Meichenbaum's "cognitive self-guidance" (Meichenbaum, 1977) is a training program designed to improve task performance and develop self-control through training in the comprehension of the tasks, spontaneous reproduction of verbal mediators, and the use of mediators in controlling nonverbal behaviors such as psychomotor activities.

Driskell, Copper, and Moran (1994) conducted a meta-analysis of the literature on mental practice to determine the effect of mental practice on performance and to identify conditions under which mental practice is most effective. They found that mental practice has a positive effect on performance. The effectiveness of mental practice is moderated by the type of task, the retention interval between mental practice and performance, and the length of duration of the mental practice intervention. Different types of mental practice also come into play. In a study by Féry (2003), it was found that using mental practice to initially acquire a task (e.g.

the Acquisition phase), visual imagery is better for tasks that emphasize form while kinesthetic imagery is better for those tasks that emphasize timing for minute coordination of the two hands. However, the interpretation is not unambiguous. Unfortunately, in this study the task was short (22 minutes), contrived as opposed to natural, and the controls over isolating visual imagery from kinesthetic seemed inexact. Jarus and Ratzon (2000) conducted a study to determine the effect of age in participants' abilities to use mental practice. They found that mental practice in the acquisition phase of a "bimanual coordination task" was beneficial for children and older adults. In the retention phase (i.e. Automaticity phase) the benefit was confined to older adults. Adults did not differ in their performance when using mental-physical practice and physical-only practice. Jarus and Ratzon concluded that individuals of all ages, children, adults, and older adults, may benefit from mental practice.

It is assumed repeated exposures to a model results in the development of an accurate cognitive representation of the modeled performance. It is also typical that one's experience gained through repeated exposures prior to task performance often takes the form of visual observation (Bandura, 1977, 1986) or the presentation of visual and auditory models (Lee, Wishart, Cunningham, & Carnahan, 1997). Visual demonstrations are considered to be powerful tools used by physical educators and coaches to convey large amounts of skill-related information to learners in a short period of time. Usually a correct or mastery model is incorporated to teach children a new sport skill. Auditory models are thought to be especially useful in tasks requiring timing rhythms, such as playing instruments, and typing. A practical example of using modeled auditory information is the Suzuki method for teaching children to play the violin (Suzuki, 1969). In this method, children are asked to reproduce a musical score after being exposed repeatedly to a recorded piece of music. It was reported that repeated exposure to the music facilitated the children's ability to successfully develop a memory representation to use as a reference from which to evaluate and subsequently correct their own performance.

Fleishman and Rich (1963) believed that initial concept formation relies heavily upon visual information. Verbal descriptions seem to be the least effective in communicating the demands of what is essentially physical information. Visual demonstrations have long been acknowledged as one of the most powerful means of transmitting patterns of thought and behavior (Bandura, 1986). It was postulated that learning occurs through observation because observers are engaged in cognitive activity similar to that of the model during their exposure to the model's performance. Bandura (1986) and Bandura, Jeffery, and Bachicha (1974) proposed when observers are exposed to a model, they extract generalities or rules relating to performance of the task rather than specific stimulus-response associations. They combine those rules to form a cognitive representation that influences their performance in two ways. First, the representation provides an approximation of the task that is used to guide their initial attempts. Second, continued exposure to the model results in the development of error detection and correction mechanisms that the observers can use to evaluate the adequacy of their own performance (see also

Adams, 1971; Schmidt, 1975). Carroll and Bandura (1987) conducted an experiment that examined the role of two forms of visual guidance in facilitating the translation of cognitive representations into action. In it, the subjects matched a modeled action pattern either concurrently with the model or after the model was displayed. The results revealed that observational learning is greatly facilitated by opportunities to structure the appropriate action pattern by visually coordinating one's performances with either the modeled actions or a retained conception of them.

In the social cognitive theory, the acquisition of modeled patterns of behavior is believed to be governed by four constituent processes: (1) Information is conveyed by modeled performances about the dynamic structure of action patterns; (2) This information is extracted through selective attention to spatial and temporal features; (3) It is then transformed into a cognitive representation by symbolic coding and cognitive rehearsal; (4) The cognitive representation both guides the production of skilled action and provides a standard against which to make corrective adjustments in performance. These attentional and representational processes determine acquisition and retention of cognitive representations. A conception-matching process governs the translation of representations into action. Monitored performance then provides the necessary information for detecting and correcting mismatches between conception and action. Finally, motivational processes facilitate acquisition of cognitive representations through their effect on the processes of attention and retention and regulate performance by motivating observers to execute what they have learned observationally. This generic position is consistent with our characterization of the psychomotor task-taxonomy described in both the introductory chart and Figure 3.1.

In recent years, motor learning theorists have begun to question whether a correct/mastery model is the only type of model beneficial for observational learning of a motor skill (Lee & White, 1990; Pollock & Lee, 1997). The collective results of these studies suggest that involving an observer, who is learning a skill, in the cognitive activities of a model, actually facilitates the observer's early learning of a skill. Proponents of learning models have suggested that correct/mastery models promote imitation as opposed to an understanding of how the skill is to be performed. This is due to the fact that correct models provide little or no error information for the observer to process. In contrast, learning models are believed to involve the observer in problem-solving activities, which develop, among other things, error recognition and correction abilities (Lee & White, 1990; Seidel & Hunter, 1970). The whole area of research on simulation is designed to accomplish this. It permits, as Romizsowski (1999) notes, "integrating the performer and the task" (p. 476).

Automaticity Process

An accurate cognitive representation is just one of the requirements for acquiring and reproducing an action. It is important that modeled actions are first organized cognitively and then translated into action. This point of view is shown by the "Cccc and Cccm" Sections of Figure 3.2. The various cells refer to varying degrees of cognitive (c) or motor (m) control over the performance of a targeted psychomotor task. By repeatedly showing the learner the modeled actions, the instructor increases the likelihood that the learner will develop greater accuracy of both her or his cognitive representation and the behavioral production of the appropriate actions or action patterns (Bandura et al., 1974, 1987, 1990). These researchers also found that practicing the expert's model actions during learning also gives the learner an opportunity to rehearse the conversion of the cognitive images into action. Carrying out these behaviors not only helps to refine the more motor aspects of modeled action this activity also aids in increasing refine the more motor aspects of modeled action this activity also aids in increasing the convergence between the cognitive imaging and the performance. In addition, motor rehearsal can enhance cognitive representation, even when conditions are not the best for developing good images (i.e., with a delay in self-monitoring), as well as increase accuracy of reproducing the action sequence and structure (Carroll & Bandura, 1985).

Changes in motor skill form, are not sufficient by themselves to infer the presence or absence of observational learning because, as Carroll and Bandura (1990) state, "people do not always enact everything they learn" (p. 85). Carroll and Bandura attempted to describe the quality of the cognitive representation believed to guide motor reproduction in a series of experiments using only correct models (i.e., 1985, 1987, 1990). In addition to reproducing the movement physically, the adult subjects were asked to arrange randomly ordered photographs depicting each of the movement components into the correct sequence. The accuracy of the cognitive representation was scored according to the number of pictures placed in the correct sequence. On the basis of the high correlation between the pictorial-arrangement test and motor reproduction form scores, Carroll and Bandura (1987, 1990) concluded that the more accurate the cognitive representation, the more accurate the reproduction of the movement sequence.

In learning environmental regulatory features of a motor skill, the important question is whether or not the acquisition and knowledge of regulatory features of a skill is explicit or implicit knowledge and acquired in such a way that we can or cannot explain it. "Explicit knowledge" is operationally defined as information we can verbally describe, or in some other way give evidence that we are consciously aware of the information. "Implicit knowledge" is knowledge that is difficult and sometimes impossible to verbalize (Sternberg, 1988). The research of Shanks and Johnstone (1999), however, implies strongly that if you provide a proper measuring instrument, all learning can be shown to be explicit. The cognitive teaching strategy refers to the *responsible, active learner* who is in *control* of the learning process and *constructs knowledge* in terms of *prior knowledge* and *multiple perspectives* (Fosnot, 1992). This interpretation is also shared by Garrison (1992) and Lord and Levy (1994).

Some of the important factors involved in psychomotor skill automaticity have been found to include instructional techniques involving task analysis, guided practice, and knowledge of results. Task analysis involves identifying the specific knowledge and behaviors necessary to master a skill. An appropriate reinforcer should be consistently provided and progress should be monitored when reinforcing a task. As noted earlier in the discussion of Acquisition strategies, in the training world, once it has been determined that training is needed, the steps start with what is called a front-end analysis (FEA). In this process, the criterion is performance of the overall task (job)-in-context. It is analyzed with respect to the standards, conditions of work, and performance level required (Crawford, 1962). Next, these are translated into training objectives to lead to performing the overall, complex, job-task.

Three general approaches to task analysis were identified by Jonassen, Hannum, and Tessmer (1989), as behavioral analysis, subject matter analysis, and information processing analysis. Behavior analysis requires identifying specific behaviors necessary to perform a complex task. Subject matter analysis involves breaking down a task into specific topics, concepts, and principles and information processing analysis involves identifying the cognitive processes involved in a task.

A word is in order about part-task verses whole-task training. The literature is not unambiguous on this matter. Some researchers (e.g., Romiszowski, 1999) favor whole-task practice; however, one of the classic citations is the McGuigan and McCaslin study (1954). This experiment presented the whole-task group with an overview advanced organizer before learning to fire the rifle, whereas the part-task group was not given that advantage. Therefore, the outcome is contaminated with an extraneous condition. Adams (1987) in his review presents a strong case for efficient psychomotor training using a part-task approach with complex tasks when they can be segmented, or otherwise readily parsed. We generally subscribe to his conclusions as is seen in our suggested strategies, although we do recommend, as does Romiszowski (1999), the progressive part method where feasible. Moreover, following our recommended functional spiral approach from Chapter 1, there is a representation with advanced organizers of the goal or final task from the outset of training. So, strictly speaking, the answer is never either or, whole verses part-task training.

Shasby (1984) revealed the key to effective and efficient acquisition and performance of movement skills lies in the learner's ability to focus his or her attention on selected aspects of the movement task at the appropriate time during learning and performance. He also advocates techniques, such as verbal mediation and self-talk, that have short and long term benefits for the learning process should be employed. Verbal mediation is a technique that can be effectively used to direct attention to the task at hand. It embodies perceptual-motor processes that illustrate the relationships amongst four processes: (1) input; information about the situation and the task, (2) processing; analysis of input data, (3) output; movement execution, and (4) feedback information that becomes a new source of input data for future action plans.

Types of Practice

Another important factor in skill acquisition is practice. A skill can be practiced continuously (massed) or with breaks in between practice sessions (distributed). Research evidence supports the conclusion that distributed practice often leads to better performance than massed practice (Lee & Genovese, 1988). One example comes from Shea and Morgan's (1979) study, in which one group of subjects learned three different spatial patterns under a drill-type schedule, whereby all learning trials on one pattern were completed before practice on another pattern was undertaken. A second group of subjects learned all three patterns at once, in which trials on the task variations were conducted in an unsystematic order. The distributed practice conditions facilitated acquisition and the random practice conditions were detrimental to performance.

During the Automaticity phase, outside distractors can also influence the learning process. Singer, Cauraugh, Tennant, Murphey, Chen, and Lidor (1991a) reviewed concepts and research on the influence of visual and auditory distractors on attentional processes in relation to an individual's performance in sports. They suggested that attentional training programs were effective in improving attentional focus, disregarding potentional distractors, and increasing more effective performances. These programs included techniques in relaxation, visualization, and focus. Singer, Cauraugh, Murphey, Chen, and Lidor (1991b) further studied an attentional-focus training program and found that those who participated in the program were more accurate and consistent early and later in learning. In addition, they found that those groups that were exposed to distractors and underwent the attentional-focus training displayed less absolute constant error and total variability across different trials of a motor task.

While difficult to compare directly, the research by Beilock, Carr, MacMahon, and Starkes (2002) on the effects of distractors does show a difference in performance between experts and novices. The experts were not affected by having to attend to a secondary cognitive monitoring task while performing the primary sensori-motor task (putting, or dribbling a soccer ball). The attained state of automaticity in the experts permitted this while the novice suffered. Another point of difference, acknowledged incidentally by Singer, et al. (1991b), is that their own work purposely focused on the learner only paying attention to the primary task while ignoring the distractor. Another difference is the fact that Beilock, et al. used tasks, which appeared to be more naturally representative, whereas Singer, et al. used tasks, which were more contrived. This may make the comparisons more ambiguous and certainly suggests more research to clarify the issues of automaticity and attention-splitting effects.

In the late 1980s and early 1990s, Singer and his associates (1988; Singer, Lidor, & Cauraugh, 1993) argued that instructing learners to be consciously aware of their body movements during the execution of a skill might not be very effective. Based on anecdotal evidence (Gallwey, 1974; 1981), which suggested that expert performers typically do not think about the details of their actions when executing a skill, Singer (1988; Singer, Lidor, & Cauraugh, 1993) argued that one way to help beginners attain such a state of automaticity might be to use instructional approaches that distract learners from their own movements.

When performing a motor action, the learners' attention is often directed to various aspects of the movement pattern, such as the spatial and temporal coordination between movements of the limbs, trunk, or head. That is, the instructions (or feedback) given to learners often direct their attention to their own body movements. It has long been assumed that making learners aware of what they are doing is a necessary condition for successful performance (Adams, 1971). This finding is important in identifying practice conditions that optimize motor skill learning. Research that has shown some potential involves the manipulation of augmented information (e.g., knowledge of results (KR), concurrent feedback, and auditory and visual models). Knowledge of when to give KR, the type of KR to be given, the preciseness of the KR given, and how often the KR is given are important to the acquisition of a skill. Often this is attempted by manipulating extrinsic feedback, especially knowledge of results, presented after completing the task or concurrent feedback presented during the task. It is also popular to present augmented information prior to initiating the movement. Research reviewed by Adams (1987) supports the conclusion that kinematic (feedback during movement) knowledge of results is more important than simply providing outcome knowledge of results.

Knowledge of results

Knowledge of results (feedback) is considered to be the most effective form of information provided during the automaticity of a closed skill. This information may be provided while the student is executing the task or once the task is complete. Providing students with knowledge of their performance and results are effective mechanisms for providing feedback in the Acquisition stage. When subjects must learn a desired response, acquisition is impossible without some form of knowledge of results. The student should be aware of how well she or he is performing a task and what changes they can make. They should also always know the expected outcomes and have both short-term and long-term objectives. For example, when learning to play basketball a short-term objective could be mastering how to successfully shoot a foul shot, and a long-term objective could be shooting free throws with accuracy greater than 70%.

Adams (1971) studied knowledge of results as information regarding the outcome of movement. He developed a theory of motor learning that states during the course of practice with knowledge of results, the learner develops a composite representation of feedback qualities of the correct movement that he calls the perceptual trace. In simple movements, the learner uses the outcome information in knowledge of results and associates it to centrally stored representations of both previous sensory feedback and response execution information to update the perceptual and memory traces.

The knowledge of performance and the learning of a closed motor skill was tested using a group of subjects who were given knowledge of performance and knowledge of results and another group that was given knowledge of results and verbal encouragement following each basketball shooting trial with the non-dominant hand (Wallace & Hagler, 1979). The group receiving knowledge of performance during the learning trials reached a higher performance level during verbal withdrawal trials than the group that did not receive knowledge of performance. This is what we discussed above as kinamatic KR. There was also a strong trend for knowledge of performance subjects to reach a higher performance level at the end of acquisition and to continue to improve after knowledge of performance was withdrawn.

Transfer (Near Term and Far Term) Process

As we have outlined our approach to the processes of learning, the learner moves from Acquisition, through Automaticity, and on to Transfer, proceeding from the concrete to the abstract. In fact, in Far Term Transfer, the highest level of schema development, the learner is developing meta-domain principles. From our perspective this takes on the cognitive level of information processing, including meta-cognition and other self-regulating skills. It is difficult to grasp the meaning of such abstraction in psychomotor terms; therefore, we present our research discussion without separating Near Term from Far Term Transfer. We also remind the reader that the detailed discussion of such abstract, cognitive functioning is presented in Chapter 2 under Far Term Transfer.

Transfer is an integral part of life and learning. People draw upon previously learned information and skills in order to deal with the new situations they encounter. The previously learned information may facilitate or hinder the learning of new information and skills. Various transfer theories look at different mental processes to account for the phenomenon of transfer. Some have identified several types of transfer effects that include positive, negative, vertical, lateral, specific, and general transfer (see Druckman & Bjork, 1994; Salas & Cannon-Bowers, 2001, for reviews).

Generically, positive transfer occurs when learning in one situation facilitates learning in a second situation. For example, in the case of psychomotor learning, learning how to hit a ball when playing racquetball may aid in learning how to hit a ball when playing tennis. However, learning how to play racquetball may also result in negative transfer effect and hinder one's ability to play tennis because a short racquetball racquet may accustom learners to positioning themselves too close to the ball when playing tennis with a longer racquet. Vertical transfer refers to situations in which the learner acquires new knowledge and skills by building on more information and procedures. This is also called the integration of part-task learning. The skill tasks in subject areas build upon one another in a hierarchal fashion and one skill must be learned prior to moving on to the next. Before learning how to properly hit a ball in baseball one must first learn how to hold and swing a bat as well as the correct stance. Lateral transfer occurs when knowledge of the first topic is not essential to learning the second one but is helpful in learning it just the same. Running track is not essential to learning how to play a wide receiver position in football; however, the knowledge and skills for running track may increase speed and ability for football. Some wide receivers, such as Bob Hayes of the Dallas Cowboys professional football team, were able to capitalize on their track experience. However, we know of no studies, which directly tested this.

Transfer and Functional Context
This perspective could also be seen as a corollary to the functional context position described in the Introduction. Reinforcing once again the notion of interdependence of domains, the reader will recall the discussion in Chapter 2 on Near and Far Term Transfer. The reader should see the relevance of both perspectives for dealing with psychomotor learning.

A number of factors influence the probability that information or skills learned in one situation will transfer to another situation. The extent to which the information is learned thoroughly and in a way that is meaningful affects the probability that it is transferred to a new situation. The more similar the two situations are perceived to be by the learner in stimuli or responses, the more likely it is that what is learned in one situation will be applied to another situation. The transfer of principles is contingent on the learner being able to separate the general rules from the specific context in which they are initially learned. Numerous and varied examples and opportunities for practice increase the extent to which information and skills will be applied in new situations (Seidel & Hunter, 1970; Sweller, 1989; Sweller et al., 1998). In the Seidel and Hunter (1970) example students learned how to construct computer programs. During the learning stages the students were required to construct increasingly complex computer programs, either within a single context (such as dealing with inventory problems) or they were given a variety of contexts for the examples. The variety of context led to superior performance on a transfer criterion requiring synthesizing all previous learning in writing the test computer programs. This superiority was maintained regardless of similarity or dissimilarity to the contexts presented during learning. A spirally generated curriculum as described in the Introduction to this book also aids this schema-building process. As noted earlier, to facilitate this, prerequisite skills should be practiced until they are learned to the point of automaticity; and the probability of transfer decreases as the time interval between the original task and the transfer task increases (Salas & Cannon-Bowers, 2001). Druckman and Bjork (1994) provide a comprehensive review of conditions favorable or unfavorable for transfer and the empirical evidence is fairly clear that "...the usefulness of teaching abstract concepts to facilitate transfer has been shown in a number of subsequent studies" (p. 38).

Singer (1988) determined attempting to perform a movement skill as if it were automatic did not appear to be plausible for beginners. He developed his five-step approach as a compromise between "awareness" and "nonawareness" strategies. The five steps include: (1) readying-attaining an optimal emotional state, thinking positively; (2) imagining-going through the motion mentally, "feeling" the movement; (3) focusing-concentrating on one relevant cue (e.g., the seams of a tennis ball, the dimples of a golf ball, the target) and thinking only of this cue to block out all other thoughts; (4) executing the movement, while not thinking about the act itself or the possible outcome; and (5) evaluating-assessing the outcome and planning adjustments for the next trial, if time permits (Singer, 1988). Thus, although "awareness" components are used in this approach by having the performer mentally imagine the act before executing it, the important point in the present context is that external cues are used to prevent the performer from focusing on what he or she is doing during movement execution.

The study of learning includes grasping knowledge of the factors that contribute to changes in behavior, understanding the learning process and the acquisition of skill, and examining environmental changes and how they might facilitate or impede learning (Singer, 1975). One of the first and most influential schools of thought affecting research on behavior is behaviorism. It is often referred to as stimulus-response (S-R) psychology and the behaviorist teaching strategy refers to the repetition of environmental events (stimulus) and behaviors (responses) until automation occurs. Learning takes place through repetitive trials and correction of errors. When instructing a student in how to properly swing a bat, the instructor will watch his student swing (response) and give him praise (stimulus) each time he does so correctly.

For example, to achieve the action of hitting a baseball, the batter's body and limb movements must spatially and temporally coincide with the spatial and temporal characteristics of the ball's movement. When a baseball player hits a ball, we observe some interesting features about the person's movements and interaction with the environment. At the movement level, we observe a highly coordinated movement pattern as the swing is initiated and carried out. In addition, we observe a perfect interaction between the person and his or her environment, because hitting the ball requires a person to time body and limb movements precisely with the space and time characteristics of a rapidly moving ball. This coupling between ball-movement perception and body or limb action exemplifies a critical characteristic that influences the successful performance of open motor skills requiring the performer to time the initiation and execution of their own movements to act on a moving object. Thus, speed and ball movement are two regulatory features of the environmental context for hitting a moving ball. Non-regulatory features are characteristics that do not influence the movements selected to perform a skill such as ball color (Magill & Hall, 1990). The significance for the open skill is that the environmental conditions are variable (e.g., speed, type of pitch, men on base, etc.) and demand adjustment by the batter.

A Conceptual Framework

We close with a model which we feel captures the concept of overlapping domains and maps coherently the stages of skill development proposed by Gilchrist and Gruber (1984) and Adler (1981) onto our task taxonomy described in Chapter 1 and highlighted at the beginning of this chapter.

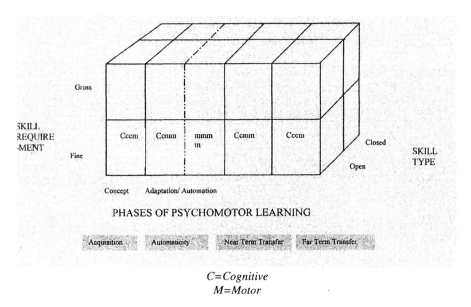

C=Cognitive
M=Motor

Figure 3.2. Mapping the Four Phase Model onto Gilchrist & Gruber's (1984) and Adler's (1981) Stages

As noted in the Introduction to this chapter, one of the difficulties in attempting to establish a domain called Psychomotor is the fact that both cognitive functioning and motor functioning are involved in the skill development process. As noted above, if we consider the possibility that a task consists of four elements, then "Cccc" means it is totally cognitively (c) driven. On the other hand, "Mmmm" would mean that the task is totally automated and motor (m) driven. This is what is intended to be illustrated hypothetically in the figure. The various cells refer to varying degrees of cognitive or motor control over the performance of a hypothetical targeted, open, and fine motor psychomotor task. The fact is that these categories are not independent as the chart would indicate at the beginning of the chapter. This fact is illustrated in Figure 3.2. It represents a modification of two previously suggested models for psychomotor learning. We have incorporated features of the Adler (1981) and Gilchrist and Gruber (1984) models noted above, and have mapped our own proposed process requirements in the shaded areas. In addition, in the cells we illustrate how we see both cognitive and motor skill developments taking place in psychomotor learning.

For example, considering a fine hand-eye coordinated task such as Morse code training or touch typing, the initial stages of learning the elements of the typing tasks such as knowing which keys are where, of learning keyboard, placement of the hands, etc. all represent cognitive skill and Acquisition process requirements. Adler (1981) and Gilchrist and Gruber (1984) called this the concept phase. Moving towards the phase called adaptation by the previously noted authors, and into our proposed Automaticity stage more motor practice is required along with an integration requirement, which shifts the requirements from pure cognitive to a mix of cognitive and motor. Finally, as we move into their automation phase we complete the move to our Automaticity stage and the possibility for transfer to take place. However, the latter will only happen if the task is an open one. It is in this type of task, say learning how to type various formats, integrate graphics of different styles into word processing, etc., where the learner must be prepared for unexpected events. He or she therefore must combine previously learned part-skills in unique ways not necessarily encountered previously. A gross type of skill, which would be open is exemplified by playing tennis, where once again the various part tasks previously mastered must be combined in different ways based upon the conditions of the game. We see therefore the limitations of the cited models in that they do not account for transfer potential. Note how the figure is extended to show the re-entry of cognitive (c) components during transfer.

In a closed task on the other hand, the learner repeats the previously known tasks until completely automated. In other words, the learner continues to practice integration and repetition of the previously acquired part task skills, increasing speed and accuracy until reaching asymptote, such as in an assembly line job. Supporting this point of view, changes from visual stimulus control to proprioceptive cues accompany the automaticity of responses are also reported in the literature (Druckman & Bjork, 1994). This shift is indicated notionally in Figure 3.3.

Taxonomies should also delineate the order of skills to be acquired; other concomitant necessary elements, such as endurance, strength, flexibility; and perhaps most importantly, account for the underlying principles that explain human motor actions. These motor skills, patterns and activities overlap many of those identified in the Psychomotor skill domain in the taxonomy presented in chapter one and include Acquisition, Automaticity, Transfer: Near Term and Transfer: Far Term. They also can be readily mapped onto Figure 3.1 above to illustrate the overlap of processing requirements in the various activities. These are seen as also very similar to Romiszowski's interpretation (1999) presented earlier.

It is also important to reemphasize that the processes do not simply take place linearly. They can recycle as indicated in our discussion based on the changed environmental conditions. For example, in the case of open tasks such as the tennis illustration above, a master at tennis could meet a new expert, whom she or he has not played before, and the old automated strategies don't work. Suddenly, the cognitive domain becomes extremely important until our master tennis player has developed another strategy. Then, she or he can go through the Automaticity phase once again. Regardless of the number of recycles that occur (i.e., with open skills), there is a general shift of influence between the cognitive and motor domain influences as psychomotor skill development takes place and automaticity occurs with increasing, repetitive practice. This shift is illustrated generically in Figure 3.3. The crossover point seen in the figure is likely to occur when the skill is being automated during the Automaticity Stage.

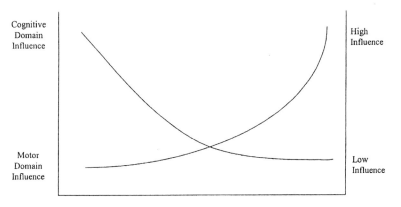

Figure 3.3. Generic Psychomotor Skill Development

In summary, we have attempted to provide the reader with an appreciation for the complexity of attempting to define a domain as independent such as Psychomotor. Simultaneously, we have tried to show the value in applying our taxonomy in selecting useful strategies for aiding the learner to develop psychomotor skills. Although we have concentrated on relating the Cognitive and Psychomotor, it is clear as well that self-confidence of the learner and the influence of peers and other role models also influence the learner. These are dealt with explicitly in Chapter 4, Affective Domain, and Chapter 5, the Interpersonal Domain.

REFERENCES

Ackerman, P. L. & Cianciolo, A. T. (2000). Cognitive, perceptual-speed, and psychomotor determinants of individual differences during skill acquisition. *Journal of Experimental Psychology: Applied, 6*(4), 259-290.

Adams, J. A. (1971). A closed-loop theory of motor learning. *Journal of Motor Behavior, 3*(2), 111-150.

Adams, J. A. (1984). Learning of movement sequences. *Psychological Bulletin, 96*, 3-28.

Adams, J. A. (1987). Historical review and appraisal of research on the learning, retention, and transfer of human motor skills. *Psychological Bulletin, 101*(1), 41-74.

Adler, J. D. (1981). Stages of skill acquisition: A guide for teachers. *Motor Skills: Theory into Practice, 5*(2), 75-80.

Bandura, A. (1977). *Social learning theory.* Oxford, England: Prentice-Hall.

Bandura, A. (1986). *Social foundations of thought and action: A social cognitive theory.* Englewood Cliffs, NJ: Prentice Hall.

Bandura, A., Jeffery, R., & Bachicha, D. L. (1974). Analysis of memory codes and cumulative rehearsal in observational learning. *Journal of Research in Personality, 7*(4), 295-305.

Bargh, J. A. & Chartrand, T. L. (1999). The unbearable automaticity of being. *American Psychologist, 54*(7), 462-479.

Beilock, A. L., Carr, T. H., MacMahon, C., & Starkes, J. L. (2002). When paying attention becomes counterproductive: Impact of divided versus skill-focused attention on novice and experienced performance of sensorimotor skills. *Journal of Experimental Psychology: Applied, 8*(1), 6-16.

Carroll, W. R. & Bandura, A. (1985). Role of timing of visual monitoring and motor rehearsal in observational learning of action patterns. *Journal of Motor Behavior, 17*(3), 269-281.

Carroll, W. R. & Bandura, A. (1987). Translating cognition into action: The role of visual guidance in observational learning. *Journal of Motor Behavior, 19*(3), 385-398.

Carroll, W. R. & Bandura, A. (1990). Representational guidance of action production in observational learning: A causal analysis. *Journal of Motor Behavior, 22*(1), 85-97.

Carter, J. E. & Kelly, A. E. (1997). Using traditional and paradoxical imagery interventions with reactant intramural athletes. *The Sport Psychologist, 11*, 175-189.

Clawson, D. M., Healy, A. F., Ericsson, K. A., & Bourne, L. E. (2001). Retention and transfer of Morse code reception skill by novices: Part-whole training. *Journal of Experimental Psychology, 7*(2), 129-142.

Crawford, M. P. (1962). Concepts of training. In R. M. Gagne (Ed.), *Psychological principles in system development* (pp. 301-341). New York: Holt, Rinehart, and Winston.

Driskell, J. E., Copper, C., & Moran, A. (1994). Does mental practice enhance performance? *Journal of Applied Psychology, 79*(4), 481-492.

Druckman, D. & Bjork, R. A. (Eds.). (1994). *Learning, remembering, believing: Enhancing human performance.* Committee on Techniques for the Enhancement of Human Performance, National Research Council. Washington, D.C.: National Academy Press.

Druckman, D. & Swetts, J. A., (Eds.). (1988). *Enhancing human performance: Issues, theories, and techniques.* Committee on Techniques for the Enhancement of Human Performance, National Research Council. Washington, D.C.: National Academy Press.

Féry, Y. (2003). Differentiating visual and kinesthetic imagery in mental practice. *Canadian Journal of Experimental Psychology, 57*(1), 1-10.

Féry, Y. & Morizot, P. (2000). Kinesthetic and visual image in modeling closed motor skills: The example of the tennis serve. *Perceptual and Motor Skills, 90*, 707-722.

Fleishman, E. A. (1964). *The structure and measurement of physical fitness.* Oxford, England: Prentice-Hall.

Fleishman, E. A. & Rich, S. (1963). Role of kinesthetic and spatial-visual abilities in perceptual-motor learning. *Journal of Experimental Psychology, 66*(1), 6-11.

Fosnot, C. (1992). Constructing constructivism. In T. M. Duffy & D. H. Jonassen (Eds.), *Constructivism and the technology of instruction: A conversation* (pp. 167-176). Hillsdale, NJ: Lawrence Erlbaum Associates.

Gagne, R. M. (1977). *The conditions of learning.* New York: Holt, Rinehart, and Winston.

Gallwey, W. T. (1974). *The inner game of tennis.* New York: Random House.

Gallwey, W. T. (1981). *The inner game of golf.* New York: Random House.

Garrison, D. R. (1992). Critical thinking and self-directed learning in adult education: An analysis of responsibility and control issues. *Adult Education Quarterly, 42*(3), 136-148.

Gentile, A. S. (1977). The effects of symbolic modeling and behavior rehearsal on assertive training with prison inmates. *Dissertation Abstracts International, 38*(1-B).

Gilchrist, J. R. & Gruber, J. J. (1984). Psychomotor Domains. *Motor Skills: Theory into Practice, 7* (1/2), 57-70.

Hays, R. T. & Singer, M. J. (1989). *Simulation fidelity in training system design.* New York: Springer-Verlag.

Jarus, T. & Ratzon, N. Z. (2000). Can you imagine? The effect of mental practice on the acquisition and retention of a motor skill as a function of age. *Occupational Therapy Journal of Research, 20*(3), 163-178.

Jonassen, D. H., Hannum, W. H., & Tessmer, M. (1989). *Handbook of task analysis procedures.* New York: Praeger Publishers.

Lee, T. D. & Genovese, E. D. (1988). Distribution of practice in motor skill acquisition: Learning and performance effects reconsidered. *Research Quarterly for Exercise and Sport, 58*(4), 277-287.

Lee, T. D. & White, M. A. (1990). Influence of an unskilled model's practice schedule on observational motor learning. *Human Movement Science Special Issue: The learning, memory and perception of perceptual-motor skills,* 349-367.

Lee, T. D., Wishart, L. R., Cunningham, S. J., & Carnahan, H. (1997). Modeled timing information during random practice eliminates the contextual interference effect. *Research Quarterly for Exercise and Sport, 68,* 100-105.

Lord, R. G. & Levy, P. E. (1994). Moving from cognition to action: A control theory perspective. *Applied Psychology: An International Review, 43*(3), 335-367.

Magill, R. A. & Hall, K. G. (1990). A review of the contextual interference effect in motor skill acquisition. *Human Movement Science, 9,* 241-289.

McGuigan, F. J. & MasCaslin, E. F. (1954). Whole and part methods in learning a perceptual motor skill. *American Journal of Psychology, 68*(4), 658-661.

Meichenbaum, D. (1977). *Cognitive-behavior modification: An integrated approach.* New York: Plenum.

Meichenbaum, D. & Biemiller, A. (1998) *Nurturing independent learners.* Cambridge, MA: Brookline Books.

Murphy, S. M. & Martin, K. A. (2002). The use of imagery in sport. In T. S. Horn (Ed.), *Advances in sport psychology* (2nd ed.) (pp. 405-439). Champaign, IL: Human Kinetics.

Pollock, B. J. & Lee, T. D. (1997). Dissociated contextual interference effects on children and adults. *Perceptual & Motor Skills, 84*(3, Part 1), 851-858.

Romiszowski, A. (1999). The development of physical skills: Instruction in the psychomotor domain. In C. M. Reigeluth (Ed.), *Instructional-design theories and models: A new paradigm of instructional theory, Volume II* (pp. 457-481). Mahwah, NJ: Lawrence Erlbaum Associates, Publishers.

Rosenbaum, D. A., Carlson, R. A., & Gilmore, R. O. (2001). Acquisition of intellectual and perceptual-motor skills. *Annual Review of Psychology, 52,* 453-470.

Rushall, B. S. & Lippman, L. G. (1998). The role of imagery in physical performance. *International Journal of Sport Psychology, 29*(1), 57-72.

Salas, E. & Cannon-Bowers, J. A. (2001). The science of training: A decade of progress. *Annual Review of Psychology, 52,* 471-499.

Schmidt, R. A. (1975). A schema theory of discrete motor skill learning. *Psychological Review, 82*(4), 225-260.

Schmidt, R. A. & Wrisberg, C. A. (2000). *Motor learning and performance* (2nd ed.). Champaign, IL: Human Kinetics.

Seidel, R. J. & Chatelier, P. K. (1997). *Virtual reality, training's future?: Perspectives on virtual reality and other related emerging technologies.* New York, NY: Plenum Press.

Seidel, R. J. & Hunter, H. G. (1970). The application of theoretical factors in teaching problem-solving by programmed instruction. *International Review of Applied Psychology, 19*(1), 41-81.

Shanks, D. R. & Johnstone, T. (1999). Evaluating the relationship between explicit and implicit knowledge in a sequential reaction time task. *Journal of Experimental Psychology, 25*(6), 1435-1451.

Shasby, G. (1984). Improvement skills through language. *Motor Skills: Theory into Practice, 7*(1/2), 91-96.

Shea, J. B. & Morgan, R. L. (1979). Contextual interference effects on the acquisition, retention, and transfer of a motor skill. *Journal of Experimental Psychology: Human Learning & Memory, 5*(2), 179-187.

Singer, R. N. (1975). Sports psychology. *American Corrective Therapy Journal, 29*(4), 115-120.

Singer, R. N. (1980). *Motor learning and human performance: An application to motor skills and movement behaviors,* Third edition. New York: Macmillan Publishing Co., Inc.

Singer, R. N. (1988). Strategies and metastrategies in learning and performing self-paced athletic skills. *Sport Psychologist, 2*(1), 49-68.

Singer, R. N., Cauraugh, J. H., Murphey, M., Chen, D., & Lidor, R. (1991b). Attentional control, distractors, and motor performance. *Human Performance, 4*(1), 55-69.

Singer, R. N., Cauraugh, J. H., Tennant, L. K., Murphey, M., Chen, D., & Lidor, R. (1991a). Attention and distractors: Considerations for enhancing sport performances. *International Journal of Sport Psychology, 22*(2), 95-114.

Singer, R. N., Lidor, R., & Cauraugh, J. H. (1993). To be aware or not to be aware: what to think about while performing a motor skill. *The Sport Psychologist, 7,* 19-30.

Sternberg, R. J. (1988). *The triarchic mind: A new theory of human intelligence.* New York: Penguin Books.

Suzuki, S. (1969). *Nurtured by love.* New York: Exposition Press.

Sweller, J. (1989). Cognitive technology: Some procedures for facilitating learning and problem solving in mathematics and science. *Journal of Educational Psychology, 81*(4), 457-466.

Sweller, J., van Merrienboer, J. J. G., & Paas, F. G. W. C. (1998). Cognitive architecture and instructional design. *Educational Psychology Review, 10*(3), 251-296.

van Merrienboer, J. J. G., Kirschner, P. A., & Kester, L. (2003). Taking the load off a learner's mind: Instructional design for complex learning. *Educational Psychologist, 38*(1), 5-13.

Vygotsky, L. S. (1978). *Mind in society: The development of higher psychological processes* (M. Cole, V. John-Steiner, S. Scribner, & E. Souberman, Eds.). Cambridge, MA: Harvard University Press.

Vygotsky, L. S. (1997). *Educational psychology* (R. Silverman, Trans.). Boca Raton, FL: St. Lucie Press.

Wallace, S. A. & Hagler, R. W. (1979). Knowledge of performance and the learning of a closed motor skill. *Research Quarterly, 50,* 265-271.

Wisher, R. A., Sabol, M. A., & Kern, R. P. (1995). Modeling acquisition of an advanced skill: The case of Morse code copying. *Instructional Science, 23,* 381-403.

Wrisberg, C. A. (2000). *Study guide for motor learning and performance.* Champaign, IL: Human Kinetics.

CHAPTER 4

AFFECTIVE DOMAIN

Table 4.1. Taxonomy of the Affective Domain

Process Requirements ⟍ Knowledge Domains	Acquisition	Automaticity	Transfer: Near term	Transfer: Far term
	Learning elements of a new knowledge domain (e.g., acquiring nomenclature).	Integrating and applying elements and procedures through extensive repetition (e.g., automating skills)	Developing ability to generalize-apply principles, and strategies (e.g., heuristics) within a domain	Learning to discover new principles in a domain (e.g., creative thinking, problem finding, meta-cognition) and applying them across domains
AFFECTIVE *dealing with oneself (motivations, habits, and self control)	Learning the boundaries of "self"; Acquiring the skill of self-reflection	Conditioned habits and attitudes; approach and avoidance behaviors	Using personal control skills: attention, affective metacognitive skills, volitional skills, self-regulatory skills	Creating "flow" situations in learning, optimal engagement in activities; self-determination theory

In this chapter, we will be highlighting the following learning heuristics as they apply to the learning of affect and the influence of affect on other learning:

- *Classical conditioning is a strong force behind much emotional and attitudinal development.*
- *When intelligence is treated as developmental and not a fixed entity, task-oriented, focused learning behavior is facilitated.*
- *Conversely, treating intelligence as a fixed entity, promotes an ego-involved, threatened approach to learning.*

- *Establishing contingencies between actions and positive feedback results in a sense of control and self-competency in interacting with one's environment.*
- *Positive transfer is facilitated when meta-cognitive skill development is encouraged within a focused, task-oriented learning environment.*

INTRODUCTION

The perspective of affect in learning has at least two parts. One perspective, affective learning, consists of how we learn to express our affect; e.g., learning how to interpret the affective aspects of one's thinking, learning how to be emotionally demonstrative, and at the same time, learning how and when to control such demonstration. This is assumed to be adequately handled by our parents. Or at least it is expected by society that such will be the case. As it turns out, the development of appropriate, emotional expression is much more difficult and complex than it might seem. The failures usually show up first in the principal's office, and if not dealt with adequately at that point, end up both in court and in the clinician's office. Emotion as a topic in psychology has languished for many years between physiology and psychology; but recently took on more importance in the psychological literature as witnessed by the concept "emotional intelligence," given a well-supported equal status with cognitive intelligence (Ciarrochi, Forgas, & Mayer, 2001; Goleman, 1995). This perspective clearly involves learning who we are as individuals. It, therefore, concerns learning the boundaries of "self" as indicated in the chart above for the Acquisition process requirement. Another way of looking at this has been discussed by O'Neil and Drillings (1994) as the difference between an emotional *trait*, or predisposition, as distinct from an emotional *state*, the temporary experience of the emotion.

The second perspective concerns how affect influences learning of traditional domains such as cognitive, psychomotor, and interpersonal subject matters. Both *states* and *traits* have been found to be influential in that regard. For example, as reported by Franken and O'Neil (1994), the results of a meta-analysis of 562 studies in the area of test anxiety over the period from 1952 to 1988 showed that "...test anxiety (particularly worry) causes poor performance and relates inversely to students' self-esteem and directly to their fears of negative valuation, defensiveness, and other forms of anxiety" (p. 204). More recent research suggests, "that the academic performance of highly test-anxious students is affected both directly, by their lack of knowledge, and indirectly, by the cognitive distraction created by task-irrelevant thinking in the test situation itself" (Musch & Broder, 1999, p. 114); and Astleitner (2000) states that "emotions may initiate, terminate, or disrupt information processing" (p. 169). However, Forgas (2001) notes that affect or "...emotional thought can be either intelligent or unintelligent, adaptive or maladaptive" (p. 48), depending on the circumstances. We agree with this general statement and will discuss in Section II what we see as the important conditions for determining the differing effects of affect.

Our concern in this chapter is primarily with the second perspective, although as we will see shortly it is difficult to keep the two perspectives separate. In fact, from the evidence presented by Goleman (1995) and Csikszentmihalyi, Rathunde, & Whalen (1993), we conclude that both are necessary as harmonious parallel systems in the well-adjusted individual. Nonetheless, we will treat affect in this latter context as "motivation;" we apply it when a task is to be learned and/or performed; and our concern is how different types and levels of affect, motivation, and emotion, influence learning.

One of the prime examples given in psychology textbooks about how affective learning takes place is the conditioning example offered by Watson (1959). Watson describes the rather cruel experiment in which a child, Albert, is offered a very soft, cuddly rabbit to play with; and as Albert approaches the animal, an experimenter standing behind Albert hits a hammer against metal causing a loud noise. The immediate result is that Albert shrinks back from the animal and bursts into tears. Following one or two trials, Albert is clearly conditioned to avoid going near the rabbit. Automaticity, Near Term Transfer, and Far Term Transfer were also demonstrated through generalization of Albert's fear, first to other rabbits and animals, and then, to any furry object. Clearly, unintentional, negative, emotional conditioning can take place virtually in one trial. Its persistence in lower organisms has been demonstrated numerous times in the psychological literature, but none more striking than the many experiments of Solomon and his associate on traumatic avoidance learning in the early '50s and '60s (Solomon & Wynne, 1953, 1954). In their studies, Solomon & Wynne showed that aversive conditioning on the part of dogs persisted over hundreds of trials and that the experimenters gave out before the dogs did. In fact, they concluded that some of the changes resulting from the traumatic experience were irreversible. It is our contention, as well as that of others (Forgas, 2001), that Affect is a principal component of all our experiences in everyday life. Therefore, "... affective states are closely linked to any information we store and recall...When in a positive mood, we are significantly more likely to access and recall positive information and information that was first encountered in a previous happy mood state... In contrast, negative mood selectively facilitates the recall of negative information" (Forgas, 2001, p. 50). We cite this as another example of the interrelatedness of all domains; and we emphasize that our charts are not intended to indicate independence of the domains, but to be used as heuristics or guides to emphasize that each domain has its own focus and needs to be addressed separately.

As in the other chapters, we divide the remainder of this chapter into two sections. The first section deals with possible guidance, which the instructional developer may apply. These suggestions are presented in accordance with the four processes described above. Section II provides the psychological research support for the various strategies suggested. It also includes a conceptual framework for Affect drawing upon the literature in an attempt to unify the empirical data and the various positions into a coherent representation. The research section could provide the reader with a more comprehensive understanding of the bases for the strategies suggested. Again, it is not necessary to read the second section in order to apply the strategies suggested in the first section.

Our framework of Affect described in Section II includes levels of energy and differentiates types of energy, task-oriented and threat-avoidance, that a learner may use to acquire proficiency in various learning tasks. The former facilitates a mastery approach, while the latter emphasizes comparative performance (e.g., with my fellow learners, relative grades, etc.). We align the task-oriented energy of Affect with motivation and the threat-avoidance energy with emotion.

SECTION I:

INSTRUCTIONAL GUIDANCE

Introduction

So what affective tools does the learner need in order to develop the necessary task-oriented perspective conducive to maximizing her or his performance in the conceptual framework noted above (and discussed more fully in the later section)?

o   First, parents can help by guiding the new learner to feel secure in who she or he is.
o   Second, schools can help by teaching the new learner how to monitor his or her progress in mastering a curriculum within an encouraging task-oriented context; i.e., an Affective application of meta-cognitive skills.

Taken together, these techniques can help the learner to master the skill of "self reflection" noted in the chart at the start of the chapter. She or he should then be able to track the task demands as separate from personal needs and thereby focus energy in a task-oriented way (motivation) as opposed to an ego-involved manner (emotional).

Guidance Caveats

In describing the features of the curriculum for designing Affective instruction, Martin and Reigeluth (1999) make a distinction between direct and indirect methods. They claim that the former is appropriate for school intervention or instruction and the latter, indirect, intervention is not necessary in the classroom. We would simply assert that if the purpose is to teach understanding and transfer, then schooling should be included. Their use of the term "indirect" seems more to refer to generalizable principles to be learned (i.e., strategies to transfer) rather than to methods of instruction.

Martin and Reigeluth (1999) also discuss possible programs to use and include the teaching of morality and spirituality. This gets us into a tricky area and can be very dangerous. We must be careful about whose morality or spirituality is taught, especially at the expense of others. It is our opinion that this really is the responsibility of parents and spiritual settings, or at least appears to be outside the province of the school system. This caveat also applies to Sternberg's assertion (2001a, 2001b) that we should teach "wisdom" to the learner, said wisdom to be based on the "common good." Who decides what's best for the common good, however -- those with a vested interest in maintaining the status quo, visionaries, or Plato's philosopher kings? While we could agree on a lot of what is appropriate morality for our democratic republic, there are still many differing points of view on a number of issues, which we have seen fit to leave to the family and the churches. In a similar vein, while arguing that technology can never replace teachers, Collinson (2001) tries to present the case that students must be able to depend on teachers for "...help to develop morally as well as intellectually and socially" (p. 8). Yet again, our position is firm that, while a teacher or for that matter, any well-adjusted adult has a societal obligation to uphold laws and pass on general guidance to youngsters, it is the responsibility of parents to build in the moral compass of their children. Surrendering that obligation to the school system can result in serious legal consequences should any problems of conflicting opinions arise.

On the other hand, there are a number of existing programs available concerning values. For example, the Collaborative for Academic, Social, and Emotional Learning (CASEL), offers many programs for strengthening the values of our society that could be used (e.g., conflict resolution, drug prevention, building self-esteem, etc.). See the Remediational Guidance discussion later in this Section.

Acquisition Process

Table 4.2. *Acquisition Process of the Affective Domain*

Process Requirements	Acquisition	Automaticity	Transfer: Near term	Transfer: Far term
AFFECTIVE *dealing with oneself (motivations, habits, and self control)	Learning the boundaries of "self"; Acquiring the skill of self-reflection	Conditioned habits and attitudes; approach and avoidance behaviors	Using personal control skills: attention, affective meta-cognitive skills, volitional skills, self-regulatory skills	Creating "flow" situations in learning, optimal engagement in activities; self-determination theory

The Acquisition Process of the interpersonal domain begins with the parents. The parents initially must provide an environment that supplies first, the moral compass, and next, security and guidance. For the teacher, the first line of instruction is to develop a mastery setting in the classroom, with the focus on task-oriented or motivational energy including all the verbal and non-verbal emphases by the teachers that learning new skills is possible and desirable for all. As a second line of instruction, we propose that the teacher include those approaches needed to reinforce the efforts of the parents. Such approaches deal directly or indirectly with promoting positive emotional states (feeling good about oneself) and decreasing the negative ones (fear, anxiety, anger, sadness).

Parents can be helped by providing access to books and other resources concerning:

- **Exploration of emotional expression,**
- **Listening, communication,**
- **Trust-building, and**
- **Dealing with various emotional problems.**

Teachers can:

- **Establish a mastery environment in the classroom.**
- **Support the discussion of one's feelings in an interpersonal environment.**
- **Promote peer interactions.**
- **Create a secure emotional environment.**
- **Be aware of and appreciate children's different expressive styles.**
- **Provide creative ways for their children to explore, express, and understand their own and others' feelings.**

The details of implementing these approaches are as follows:

Resources for the Parents
Some detailed suggestions to help parents include:

o   Provide resources to the parent to help guide them when faced with a variety of stages and problems. A great Internet resource available to parents is *Parentstages.com: The best of the web for every parenting stage* (http://www.parentstages.com).
o   Provide books and resources to parents that provide advice on how to open up a dialogue, explore feelings, offer advice, and teach values to their children and teens. Some examples include:

- *How to Say it to your Kids: The Right Words to Solve Problems, Soothe Feelings, and Teach Values* by Paul Coleman (2000). This book covers the topics of: adoption, bed-wetting, bullies, death, divorce, drugs, jealousy, HIV/AIDS, money, moving, puppy love, shyness, step-siblings, and more.
- *Hot to Say it to Your Teens: Talking About the Most Important Topics of their Lives* by Richard Heyman (2001). This book covers the topics of: anger, appearance, college, competition, drinking, fitting in, sex, stress, self-control, suicide, and more (this book obviously covers more than acquisition topics; but we place it here because many of the issues relate to primary Affect development).

o   Provide books and resources to parents that help improve parent-child relationships:
   - *Being the Parent you Want to Be: 12 Communication Skills for Effective Parenting* by Gary Screaton Page (1999). This book helps parents speak more effectively, listen more carefully, ask better questions, and be more consistent.
   - *Without Spanking or Spoiling* by Elizabeth Crary (1993). This book provides tips on how to set limits, encourage good behavior, and avoid problems.

o   Provide resources to the parents to aid in developing a connection and building mutual trust:
- *Time-In: When Time-Out Isn't Working* by Jean Illsley Clarke (1998). This book helps parents teach their children how to be competent, to think, and to succeed. It uses four tools: Ask, Act, Attend, and Amend, that can help parents handle any behavior they encounter in children (ages 1 to 12).

Other recommendations can be found in the programs suggested by CASEL (discussed further in this chapter's section on Remediational Guidance).

Establishing the Mastery Environment in the Classroom
- First, establish a classroom environment with mastery as the focus instead of performance in comparison to others.
- Secondly, set the classroom context so that students can "self set" standards towards mastery, which is similar to guidance suggested by Turner et al. (2002) for high-mastery focused classrooms: Emphasize "the meaningfulness of learning, adapting instruction to students' developmental levels, providing teacher support for instructional activities, de-emphasizing ability-related information and emphasizing intrinsic reasons for learning" (p. 90).
- Teachers should speak about learning as an active process; teachers should express strong positive affect about learning and positive expectations for the students. These techniques foster high-mastery oriented classrooms.

- Also, emphasize mastery of the tasks with encouragement to thereby focus the learner on using task-oriented energy. Simultaneously, do not promote learning as a competition between learners. Threats will not motivate a student to exploit his or her talents, although they may work to get the learner to reach a certain minimal requirement. They will not, however, reinforce a task-oriented approach to learning.
- It is also suggested to use techniques for maintaining focus on the task (rather than on self-esteem issues including self-worth) such as teaching positive self-talk.

Teachers are encouraged to provide creative ways for their children to explore, express, and understand their own and others' feelings.
This can be done by:

o Making the curriculum "deliberatively, positively, and reflectively" emotion-centered so the child can understand and appropriately express their emotions. (Hyson, 1994, p. 81). Hyson suggests to:
  - Create a secure emotional environment:
    ▪ Provide an environment that is predictable, accepting of who the students are and how they think and feel, and responsive.
    ▪ Teachers should provide smiles, warm gazes, physical closeness, affectionate touches, and supportive words.
    ▪ Be aware and adapt to changes in the child's emotional needs during the school year.
  - Help children understand their emotions:
    ▪ Enhance concept development, provide experiences for children to observe and express emotions during play with their peers, and be attuned to "prime times" in which one can heighten children's emotional understanding.
    ▪ Emphasize activities that support understanding.
    ▪ Mirror the child's emotional expressions by reflecting, imitating and amplifying his/her emotions.
    ▪ Respond to the children's feelings.
    ▪ Cautiously, help the children label their emotions when they have difficulties describing how they feel.
    ▪ Talk with the children about the causes of their feelings.
  - Teacher models genuine, appropriate emotional responses:
    ▪ Take into consideration the developmental level of the child and the teacher's knowledge of the child's earlier experiences, strengths, and needs.
    ▪ Emotions to be modeled include: joy and pleasure in personal relationships, interest and curiosity in the environment, tolerance for frustration, and pride in hard work.

- Integrate modeling into every kind of activity and interaction, such as the teachers' routine activities, joint activities with children, and teacher-planned opportunities.
- Give the child praise and attention when she or he appropriately reproduces adult behavior.
- Support children's regulation of emotions "to maintain or enhance their positive emotions and to alter their negative emotional states" (Hyson, 1994, p. 147):
  - As the teacher, assume a role (Hyson, 1994):
    o The "smorgasbord host" provides the child with options for different activities and allows him or her to choose what they want to do based off their interests; however, the "smorgasbord host" encourages the child to try new things.
    o The "scaffold" provides support to the children and is physically present and emotionally available them.
    o The "cultural guide" kindly and gently instructs the children how to behave appropriately and in a way that is socially acceptable (i.e., saying please and thank you, excuse me, etc.).
  - Support the discussion of one's feelings in an interpersonal environment.
  - Promote peer interactions. "Children are often less tolerant than adults of unpleasant emotional displays" (Hyson, 1994, p. 153). This way, children can learn from each other.
  - Provide classroom activities, such as pretend play, music, painting, and other creative activities.
- Recognize and honor children's expressive styles:
  - "The more attuned a teacher is to the unique emotional response patterns of young children, the better able she [or he] will be to use this information in building a positive, emotion-centered program" (Hyson, 1994, p. 163).
  - Teachers should make sure that they are able to make accurate judgments about a child's basic emotional expressions and emotion-related behavior before attempting to understand their expressive style.
  - Sit back and observe the children.
    - Take notes;
    - Videotape the children;
    - Use emotion-related scales and checklists.
  - After learning the child's expressive style,
    - Anticipate a child's individual difficulty or enjoyment,
    - Individualize the program to fit children's emotion styles, and

- Respect and honor children's individuality.
o   Unite children's learning with positive emotions:
- Select appropriate, educational experiences that will evoke pleasure and sustained interest and effort in the children. In other words, make learning fun!

More specific suggestions:

o   Harvey and Goudvis (2000) suggest a game to help with providing creative ways for their children to explore, express, and understand their own and others' feelings:
- A feeling word, such as *sad*, is written on a card and pinned on the back of one volunteer student who doesn't know what it says. The child with the card goes to the front of the classroom or the middle of a circle allowing the rest of the children to read the card. The other kids give him or her clues as to how they feel when they are *sad* to help him or her guess the feeling on the card. This game helps kids "clarify their feelings and predict which situations might lead to one feeling or another" (Harvey & Goudvis, 2000, p. 106).
o   Also, help the children express their emotions through drawing. The child can rehearse alternative behaviors on paper in a non-threatening environment. We suggest books including picture exercises to ease the process of talking about feelings. One suggestion is *Draw on Your Emotions* by Margot Sunderland (2000).

Therefore, the first line of instruction is to develop a mastery setting in the classroom, with the focus on task-oriented or motivational energy including all the verbal and non-verbal emphases by the teachers that learning new skills is possible and desirable for all. As a second line of instruction, we propose to include those approaches, which deal directly or indirectly with promoting positive emotional states (feeling good about oneself) and decreasing the negative ones (fear, anxiety, anger, sadness). We call this a second line because it is our position that the primary venue for guiding the learner to develop a strong sense of self is the home environment. It is therefore most important that both lines of instruction be given as early as possible in the educational process, since these opinions of self have multiplicative effects on the growing learner at all later stages of development.

Automaticity Process

Table 4.3. Automaticity Process of the Affective Domain

Process Requirements	Acquisition	Automaticity	Transfer: Near term	Transfer: Far term
AFFECTIVE *dealing with oneself (motivations, habits, and self control)	Learning the boundaries of "self"; Acquiring the skill of self-reflection	Conditioned habits and attitudes; approach and avoidance behaviors	Using personal control skills: attention, affective meta-cognitive skills, volitional skills, self-regulatory skills	Creating "flow" situations in learning, optimal engagement in activities; self-determination theory

In the Automaticity process we examine how to:

- **Reduce fear in instruction,**
- **Reduce envy among classmates,**
- **Avoid anger and aggression during instruction,**
- **Achieve higher sympathy in the classroom, and**
- **Promote pleasure during instruction.**

The particulars for implementing these recommendations are:

- To reduce fear in instruction, follow Astleitner's (2000) suggestions to ensure success in learning:
    o Teach students to accept mistakes as opportunities for learning;
    o Train teachers to induce relaxation;
    o And teach students to be critical, but sustain a positive perspective.
- To reduce envy between students:
    o Encourage comparisons with autobiographical and criterion reference points instead of social standards;
    o Inspire a sense of authenticity and openness;
    o And avoid unequal distributed privileges among students.
- To avoid anger and aggression during instruction:
    o Stimulate the control of anger;
    o Show multiple views of things;
    o Let anger be expressed in a constructive way;

o   And do not show and accept any form of violence.
(See discussion of CASEL database in Remediational Guidance as possible resource for useful programs to implement such strategies. Secondly, see Richard Heyman's book noted earlier, *Hot to say it to your teens: Talking about the most important topics of their lives.* Lastly, Suinn and his associates at Colorado State University (1971, 1998, 2001) have developed and tested an anxiety management program (AMT) for decreasing emotional arousal involving a sequential combination of visualization, relaxation, homework, and gradual development of self-control skills. It has shown to be effective for anxiety and anger reduction.)

- To achieve higher sympathy in a classroom:
  - o   Intensify relationships;
  - o   Instill sensitive interactions;
  - o   Establish cooperative learning structures;
  - o   And implement peer-helping groups.
- Strategies to promote pleasure during instruction include (Astleitner, 2000):
  - o   Enhancing well-being;
  - o   Establishing open learning opportunities;
  - o   Using humor;
  - o   And installing play-like activities.

Finally, the authors also recommend that instructors look for alternatives to using the traditional form of grading. The negative effects of grading range from: diverting attention from learning to a focus on the grade to a concern about lack of ability and failure (see Edwards & Edwards, 1999; Kohn, 1994). We suggest to encourage a focus on the task itself and support the learner's curiosity. In other words, create a mastery environment, where presumably all students can succeed. Creating a mastery-friendly environment encourages the development of good self-regulatory skills and adaptive help-seeking behavior as well. Karebenick's work (2002) is discussed below in the Transfer Phases and elaborates on the research supporting these suggestions. The instructor should balance assessment of process and performance. One facet of this might be to use criterion referenced testing, which permits all learners to achieve 100% when they learn all the objectives related to a lesson. This does indeed promote a mastery approach, a learning task focus, without comparisons to others.

Transfer Process: Near Term

Table 4.3. Near Term Transfer Process of the Affective Domain

Process Requirements	Acquisition	Automaticity	Transfer: Near term	Transfer: Far term
AFFECTIVE *dealing with oneself (motivations, habits, and self control)	Learning the boundaries of "self"; Acquiring the skill of self-reflection	Conditioned habits and attitudes; approach and avoidance behaviors	Using personal control skills: attention, affective meta-cognitive skills, volitional skills, self-regulatory skills	Creating "flow" situations in learning, optimal engagement in activities; self-determination theory

For all the reasons described above concerning the need to aid a child in developing security, a positive sense of self worth, and a productive view towards learning, it is virtually impossible to isolate either Near Term or Far Term Transfer as processes separate from the Acquisition and Automaticity influences of Affect on all learning. Therefore, we present below a description of techniques which can be used to develop a conscious understanding of how Affect can be used to the advantage of the learner; i.e., the development of meta-cognitive strategies for monitoring and self-awareness with the goal of maximizing the learner's potential.

To promote near term transfer:

- **Teach awareness of how Affect influences other domains of learning.**
- **Enhance motivation to learn by providing both extrinsic and intrinsic incentives.**
- **Encourage autonomous help-seeking behaviors.**
- **Use examples from varied and multiple contexts.**

The specifics for accomplishing these are as follows:

- To motivate students to learn "…it is necessary to provide a combination of extrinsic and intrinsic rewards." As Csikzsentmihalyi et al. (1993) note, starting with childhood, "…the immediate external rewards should include recognition, praise, and support from significant others: parents, teachers, and peers" (p. 147).
- We also suggest incorporating the techniques advocated by Turner et al.

(2002) and Karabenick (2002) to encourage autonomous help-seeking behaviors. If done properly, this can become a good tool for far term transfer.

From our own research as well as the review of the Affective development literature by Martin and Reigeluth (1999), it is clear that the following two principles arise again and again and reinforce the notion that all domains can benefit from the application of these heuristics.

1. Use multiple, concrete applications or exercises in order to facilitate the learner's ability to extract the schema or underlying principle, which is the focus of the teaching;
2. Integrate the materials into a spiral curriculum, so that no matter where the student is in his or her development, there will be a coherent, growing curriculum with multiple contexts available from both the presentation materials and practical exercises.

As discussed in Chapter 1, this approach will both aid the learner's appreciation of the functional value of context, and at the same time facilitate the development of the transfer process across domains.

Transfer Process: Far Term

Table 4.4. Far Term Transfer Process of the Affective Domain

Process Requirements	Acquisition	Automaticity	Transfer: Near term	Transfer: Far term
AFFECTIVE *dealing with oneself (motivations, habits, and self control)	Learning the boundaries of "self"; Acquiring the skill of self-reflection	Conditioned habits and attitudes; approach and avoidance behaviors	Using personal control skills: attention, affective meta-cognitive skills, volitional skills, self-regulatory skills	Creating "flow" situations in learning, optimal engagement in activities; self-determination theory

The judicious application of the last two principles above, multiple contexts and spiral curriculum organization, should aid the learner to learn not only what context dependency is, but to enable she or he to develop context-free learning strategies. The teacher can therefore encourage the development of meta-cognitive strategies as we propose here by fostering the development and use of appropriate self-monitoring and self-regulation strategies.

Moreover,

- **To keep challenges optimal for all, individualize the curriculum as much as feasible.**
- **Once again, to instill and maintain motivation (task-oriented energy) reinforce the mastery approach.**

In designing a curriculum for a classroom, one must take into consideration the differences among the students – personality and skill. As feasible, the curriculum should be individualized because what works for one doesn't necessarily work for another. As Csikszentmihalyi & Csikzentmihalyi (1988) note, "why is the same homework boring to some and enjoyable to others? The objective challenges of the task do not account for the differences. Nor does the objective level of skills. They must be looked for in the personality of the students, in their ability to recognize challenges at a level commensurate with their skill, where others only see tiresome obstacles" (Csikszentmihalyi & Csikzentmihalyi, 1988, p. 32).

We also suggest that instructors should include techniques for keeping the exuberance or energy level at the optimal range for type of task. Give pep talks periodically, focus on the ability to achieve, and reinforce this mastery approach with each learner (this is not unlike what coaches do before a game to properly motivate a team). Indeed, as we discussed in Chapter 3 concerning imagery strategies to aid athletes, such as stress management and reduction, mastery techniques can be introduced to assist in focusing (Murphy & Martin, 2002). These techniques can be readily applied to other learning environments.

For example, before tackling a new topic, the learner, with instructor guidance, might:

1. Preplan by listing all the feelings associated with taking on this task;
2. Identify the emotions which might interfere with the new learning;
3. With the teacher's help, develop strategies to replace negative emotional reactions with positive ones, such as positive self-talk and self-affirmation; and
4. Lastly, imagining self-mastery of the task, all of which will aid externally focusing one's energy (motivation) towards successful learning of the new material.

Related to this, Keller's ARCS Motivational Process model (1987a, 1987b) provides a systematic, seven-step approach (Keller, 1997) to designing motivational tactics into instruction. His model asserts, as does Karabenick and others (e.g., Murphy & Martin, 2002), that although the individual is responsible for his or her motivational condition the environment can have a strong impact on both the direction and intensity of an individual's motivation. Because of its generic applicability to instruction, this model yields a clear demonstration of far term transfer. It has been applied to various types of learning environments, "such as classroom instruction, self-paced print, computer-based instruction, and multimedia" (Keller, 1999, p. 39-40).

Possible Strategies to Use Across Processes

The factor analytic survey research of Vermetten, Lodewijks, and Vermunt (2001) is based on goal orientations of the learner and their approach investigated personal belief structures. The research therefore seems particularly relevant for this chapter. Their study resulted in two factors as strategies for learning: a surface strategy and a deep learning strategy.

A surface strategy for learning combined with orientation instructions would be useful during the Acquisition and Automaticity phases, when the learner is acquiring the elements of a new subject matter and automating their initial application. To apply the surface strategy during these phases, while "... teaching ... stress the importance of careful and thorough work and the need for certain amount of cooperation and agreement" (Vermetten et al., 2001, p. 161-167). Also relevant, use: memorizing techniques, and external regulation (teacher led).

Their research provides an insight into the use of a deep learning strategy when instructing for near or far term transfer. During this strategy, there is a shift to self-regulation and critical processing, where the student compares her or his own perspective with an author or the teacher, and draws own conclusions, and concrete processing, where the student personalizes the instruction with examples from own life-experiences, using knowledge outside the study context.

The data suggest that both teaching approaches would benefit from convincing a learner that intellectual skills are developmental and not fixed entities unable to be changed. The hope is that with emphasizing this, students also would be task-oriented and not ego-involved in their approach to learning. The authors admit that some of the elements of surface learning strategy: conscientiousness, compliance, and external regulation, while not conducive to deep learning, "...seem to be important factors for completing a university education" (Vermetten et al., 2001, p. 166). Their work needs to be interpreted in light of the fact that it was accomplished with college level students. Perhaps "versatile approaches" (as they suggest) would indeed be important, especially if we are dealing with K-12 learners learning new subject matter.

Remediational Guidance

The Collaborative for Academic, Social, and Emotional Learning (CASEL) Program Library is an excellent resource for courses at all levels of K-12, Elementary, Middle, and High School. It has developed a guide, which provides educators with the necessary information to choose social and emotional learning programs having a track record of effective implementation, which provide training and technical assistance to teachers and schools, and which have shown to be effective in well-designed evaluations. The staff of CASEL employed a broad, multi-disciplinary, national review panel of experts to incorporate the perspectives of educator/practitioners, researchers, school administrators, etc. in order to develop the database of acceptable courses (Weissberg et al., 2003). These materials can be used to implement the following recommendations (Their website is www.casel.org.).

- Recommend parenting classes so that parents can learn the effects of their approaches to disciplining on their children's emotional conditioning.
- Organize anger management classes for parents and students to learn alternative ways to cope with conflict.
- Conduct conflict resolution cases for students at all levels, K-12.
- Organize courses in self-esteem building.
- Conduct drug prevention courses.

When considering implementing a program to develop a caring community, we advocate that the planning committee examine each program with the following CASEL criteria (Weissberg et al., 2003):

- Is it grounded in theory and research?
- Does it teach students how to apply social and emotional learning skills and ethical values in daily life?
- Does it build connections between students and their school?
- Does it provide developmentally and culturally appropriate instruction?
- Does it help schools coordinate and unify programs?
- Does in enhance school performance by addressing the affective and social dimensions of academic learning?
- Does it involve families and communities as partners?
- Does it establish successful organizational supports and policies?
- Does it provide high-quality staff development and support?
- Does it incorporate continuous evaluation and improvement?

SECTION II:

SUPPORTING RESEARCH

Introduction

Our interest in this chapter is to assess how Affect in learning influences the other domains and how its influence can be marshaled or channeled to improve learning and instruction. One of the complaints about the literature on Affect is the ambiguous and multiple definitions of Affect that influence its development (Linnenbrink & Pintrich, 2002; Martin & Reigeluth, 1999). "The study of affect is broad, and definitions are often varied, leading to some difficulties in interpreting findings in this area" (Linnenbrink & Pintrich, 2002, p. 71). Having given some instructional guidance for the developers of various kinds of "affectively-related" curricula, we hope to clarify the meaning of "Affective domain" with our review of relevant literature, and with a proposed framework presented later in this section.

Acquisition Process

As we noted at the beginning of this chapter, the development of Affect starts with birth (or possibly in utero). In the discussion to follow, we highlight an organizing perspective from Erikson and associative learning research, which would seem to be consistent with this point of view.

Development of Trust

From a clinical perspective, Erikson (1950, 1959) theorized that Affect is the basis for human activity and the primary impetus for growth. He posited eight psychosocial developmental stages from infancy to old stage. At each stage an individual's activities, perceptions, and relationships are organized around the central emotional issue of that stage. The eight stages include: Basic trust vs. basic mistrust; Autonomy vs. shame and doubt; Initiative vs. guilt; Industry vs. inferiority; Identity vs. role confusion; Intimacy vs. isolation; Generativity vs. stagnation; Ego integrity vs. despair. As children move through the stages from infancy through adolescence, they develop more emotional attachments and express their conflicts through their behaviors. At each stage, the child must resolve a conflict and more positive emotions emerge as a result. If the conflicts are not resolved, the child experiences anxiety and develops behavioral and affective problems. Erikson believed that healthy development results from a resolution of each conflict through which the child receives a strong sense of trust and autonomy. His psychodynamic theory is widely accepted and has been expanded on by many other researchers and psychologists. Kroger (2000) has commented on Erikson's point of view in her review. What was influential in her review was the concentration and research on issues of cognitive and personality variables, family communication patterns, and forms of peer interaction as influences in obtaining resolution to the identity question.

Erikson (1950, 1959) suggested that a sense of trust is one of the first accomplishments of infancy and is the first of his stages of psychosocial development. The development of trust is important in the emotional development of a child. Experiences of trust (in home and school) can offer opportunities to strengthen the child's sense of trust and ability to seek new things, explore, and learn. In Erikson's stage of "trust versus mistrust," the child learns that adults can be relied on to meet their physical and emotional needs through repeated experiences. This provides a secure base for the child, which in turn, gives the child confidence. If a healthy balance of "trust versus mistrust" is not achieved, later development is more difficult for the child.

The following review of research on the formation of affective associations implies that an associative learning framework could provide general support for the course of developmental stages outlined by Erikson (1950, 1959). All of this is also consistent with attachment theory and research discussed in Chapter 5.

Learning of Affect through Associations

In their review of associative learning, Wasserman and Miller (1997) take a broad view of forming associations, e.g., causal links, subordinate and super-ordinate relationships, etc. The basic point is that associative learning can take place at all levels and with all types of events. Their concentration in the review is basically on classical conditioning, yet they maintain that the principles apply equally to instrumental conditioning even though the events themselves may differ. They thereby lay the foundation also for the assertion that the rules governing associations in classical and instrumental conditioning may well be very similar for the types of associations that take place in cognitive events as well. They note that since the 1960s the focus of research has changed to "other aspects of cognition" including attention, memory, and information-processing in human beings and animals. The authors also note that the study of associative learning in human beings continues to grow in interest in importance, documented by the recent research in causal perception using the principles of associative theories cited in Wasserman and Miller's article (Allan 1993; Young, 1995). The works of Young and Allan support the argument that contiguity of events modified by contingencies of reinforcement can provide the basis for most associative and predictive learning (whether we wish to introduce the term "causal" or not).

For our purposes here, it is sufficient to note that the paradigm for classical conditioning involves a non-affective stimulus (CS) taking on new emotional meaning because of an association with a strong, naturally-affect producing stimulus (US). The CS precedes the US by a relatively short amount of time. Similarly, discrimination learning or instrumental conditioning is aided by the instrumental response temporally and spatially coinciding with the discriminative stimulus. The responses, which take place as a result of this contingency, are said to be conditioned; and the previously neutral stimuli are called conditioned stimuli (CS).

The research literature has yielded a number of principles by which these contingent associations can be strengthened or weakened or eliminated (Wagner & Rescorla, 1972). The majority of the research has been carried out with animals, and has included some form of external, experimenter-initiated drive to get the animal to be conditioned. So the animal is either made hungry, thirsty, or fearful. Context, occasion setting, generalization, inhibition, and other factors have been studied as influencing the strength of conditioning or association, thus modifying the effects of the primary factor, contiguity.

Wasserman and Miller (1997) present a compelling argument to support the application of these findings to cognitive events in humans. For purposes of this chapter on the Affective Domain, we simply note that positive and negative emotional states and therefore attitudes as well, have their roots in the kinds of associations described in the conditioning paradigm. They occur for sure in early childhood prior to speech development, and from recent research probably before birth.

Seligman and associates (Peterson, Maier, & Seligman, 1993; Seligman, Maier, & Solomon, 1971) developed their theory of learned helplessness as an example of applying contingency theory to humans, in this case having no control over the events surrounding them. For example if there is a history of uncontrollable, aversive events and then subjects are later given control over those events, these organisms may be retarded in learning escape or avoidance responses to negative stimuli. Think about children growing up in abusive or alcoholic homes.

Forgas (2001) speaks of negative affect, "...as an alarm signal, alerting us that the environment is potentially dangerous and...pay close attention to external information" (p. 54). We would characterize this state as ego-involved, and focusing on personal threat, which can be very detrimental to learning. Without getting into the age-old argument of how much of our behavior and temperament is due to genetics and how much is modified by environment, we simply assert that we agree with the general position that we can and do learn affect; and those emotional teachings can be modified. So we can also agree that parents "...transmit a particular biological endowment of physical and psychological potentials..." with some directional push; but that also this does not mean "...that inheritance equals immutability..." (Holland, 1997, p. 17). Following along Holland's theoretical path, a child's unique biological makeup and early experiences lead to initial preferences, attraction toward certain activities and avoidance of others. The fine-tuning of these become interests based on rewards and development of personal satisfaction and go hand in hand with the development of particular skills. It is the interactive and mapping nature of all the components -- heredity, activities, interests, competencies -- with the environmental opportunities of home, school, relations, and friends, which leads to the development of self-concepts and values. It is our thesis that the successful or unsuccessful mapping of the components will influence whether an individual can accept new task challenges in the creative spirit implied by Csikszentmihalyi et al. (1993), or be worried about comparisons with her/his fellow learners and therefore unable to learn effectively. Which of these approaches prevails will determine the positive or negative effect of the individual's Affective development on his or her educational growth.

Automaticity Process

With the formation of early conditionings and the variations in attractions towards activities, the stage is set for mood and attitudes to influence in an automatic manner subsequent learning in the classroom. Carrying forward this notion, different aspects of affect may indeed have different results in the educational process as Forgas advocates (2001). In their analysis of the effect of moods and emotions (which they call affect) on education, Linnenbrink and Pintrich (2002) propose that emotions operate immediately whereas moods are longer lasting and of lesser intensity. They claim that emotions fade overtime and may change into general mood states. We would simply assert that they may not "fade;" rather they persist as an underlying state and tendency to color whatever context in which the learner finds him or herself (see also Forgas, 2001, for further discussion). Linnenbrink and Pintrich (2002) assert further that their focus is on the situational aspects of the students' motivation and affect in classrooms; therefore their goal is to develop their model based on those "affective and motivational processes that are influenced by the context" (p.71). They, therefore, attempt to focus more on affective states rather than on traits. However, our position is that these interact; take the case for example, in learned helplessness. It is clear that the depressed person will have a different perception of the context for solving a challenging problem than the adjusted person. In examining the Linnebrink and Pintrich (2002) review, one thing stands out in the literature above some of the ambiguities in measuring instruments and methods across studies. We should strive as much as possible to create a mastery classroom environment, and where feasible have the learners "self-set" standards towards mastery.

Near Term Transfer Process

One of the consistent findings in this literature, and a lesson that we keep learning again and again, is that: multiple contexts are extremely important to help a student accomplish near term and far term transfer (e.g., Wellman & Gelman, 1992). Jacobson and Spiro (1995) have noted the value of multiple perspectives to develop cognitive flexibility; and Hartley and Bendixen (2001) have discussed the value and limitations of the web-based learning environment because of its intrinsically flexible arrangement, which could be, for the independent-minded student, helpful to "promoting higher order thinking skills" (Hartley & Bendixen, 2001, p. 24). As noted in Section I, the message from the research literature is clear that in the design of all instruction concerning the learning of schemas such as principles, heuristics, algorithms, etc., it is necessary to use multiple, concrete applications or exercises in order to facilitate the learner's ability to extract the underlying principle, and to integrate the materials into a spiral curriculum. As discussed earlier, the judicious application of these two principles should aid the learner's ability to learn both what context dependency is, and to enable the learner to develop context-free learning strategies.

Far Term Transfer Process

Next, some comments are in order concerning the concept of "emotional intelligence" introduced by Goleman (1995), Ciarrochi et al. (2001), and others. The relevance of this work cannot be overstated. For example, Goleman's work lays out a path by which the type of conditioning described earlier (the Watson example) can play a profound role in the emotional development of humans. He describes the problems in predicting successful behavior outside of school by simply using the usual cognitive IQ tests. He stresses the importance of "abilities such as being able to motivate oneself and persist in the face of frustrations; to control impulse and delay gratification; to regulate one's moods and keep distress from swamping the ability to think; to empathize and to hope" (Goleman, 1995, p. 34). The senior author has often said that "intelligence is a very specific entity" and by that he means that we all have very many blind spots and have difficulty in transferring knowledge and/or principles that we have learned in one environment to another seemingly different environment, despite the fact that the principles to be used are the same.

We think Goleman (1995) has described quite articulately the Affective underpinnings for those blind spots. His basic position, with which we are in essential agreement, is that, "Emotional [we would say, Affective, to be generic] life is a domain that, as surely as math or reading, can be handled with greater or lesser skill, and requires its unique set of competencies. And how adept a person is at those is crucial to understanding why one person thrives in life while another, of equal intellect, dead-ends: the emotional aptitude is a *meta-ability*, determining how well we can use whatever other skills we have, including raw intellect" (Goleman, 1995, p. 36). So, learning who we are, that is, self-awareness, can have a profound effect on what we learn and how we perform. The difficulties for us in developing a high degree of affective understanding can occur as a result of emotional conditioning, which happens prior to developing any verbal capacity. And it can be exacerbated by "imprinted traumatic memories" (Goleman, 1995, p. 212). It is heartening to see that Goleman and we agree that psychotherapy can be a form of reeducation for the affective domain.

Motivation
In the motivation literature, researchers have focused on two broad achievement goal constructs, task (also called mastery and learning) and performance (also called ego-) orientation, to explain the reasons why students engage in academic tasks, such as reading. In addition, motivation researchers have recently begun examining multiple patterns of goals students adopt for learning, such as social goals (Wentzel, 1993, 2000) and approach and avoidance states of task and performance orientations (Pintrich, 2000). A task orientation refers to a dedication toward conceptual understanding whereas a performance orientation refers to a focus on outperforming others and demonstrating ability (Dweck, 1986; Pintrich, 2000). Students who have task goals strive to gain insight about content, seek personal challenges, and try to learn useful strategies for self-improvement. In contrast, students who adopt performance goals attempt to outperform others, seek easy tasks, and try to avoid failure (Ames, 1992; Dweck & Leggett, 1988). There is evidence that when students adopt mastery goals, they employ deeper cognitive processing strategies (Nolen, 1988), report higher self-efficacy (Middleton & Midgley, 1997), take academic risks (Clifford, 1991), and maintain effort despite hurdles (Ames & Archer, 1988).

For example, Elliot and Dweck (1988) found that students in a task goal condition sought challenges regardless of level of perceived ability. In an interview study, adolescents were asked why they try to get good grades in school (Wentzel, 1993). Those students who reported having task goals earned significantly higher grades on standardized test scores. Similarly, Wolters (1998) found that task goals significantly predicted course grades. In an experimental study, college students who were given a task-oriented condition of reading to teach others (Benware & Deci, 1984) surpassed students in a performance condition (reading to get a high test score) in conceptual understanding of the text content. These investigations suggest that possessing task goals toward academic learning will lead to achievement.

Students' perceptions of their classroom instruction can have a significant influence over the different motivational goals they adopt (Ames, 1992). Pintrich (2000) reasoned, "goals are assumed to be cognitive representations or knowledge structures which are sensitive to both contextual and internal personal factors. Accordingly, strong classroom contexts or experimental manipulations (where the context defines the situation and appropriate behavior in many ways) can influence individuals to activate different goals than the ones they would normally or chronically access" (p. 102). Task-oriented and performance-oriented goals can be communicated to students through teacher discourse (Turner et al., 1998), task offerings, and evaluation practices (Ames, 1992).

In an observational study, Meece (1991) studied 15 science lessons among five science classrooms. In two classrooms, the majority of students scored high on their possession of task goals whereas in another two classrooms, the majority of students scored very low on their possession of task goals, and the fifth classroom had a mix of goals. After examining the classroom practices, Meece (1991) found that these classrooms had very different qualities. In the classroom that contained students with low task goals, evaluation was salient, tasks were closed with regard to student choice (see also Turner, 1995), and understanding the material was not valued. In contrast, in the classrooms where students indicated high task goals, teachers focused on understanding the material by encouraging personal goals for learning. They emphasized higher-level strategies for concept development.

Accordingly, teachers who emphasize understanding, value effort, and invite students to take risks by challenging themselves appear to increase reading motivation. Ames and Archer (1988) reported that when students perceived their classroom as fostering task goals, they attributed their successes to effort and efficient strategies for learning. In an intervention study, Miller and Meece (1997) found that when teachers encouraged students to complete difficult tasks, gave feedback about progress, and offered opportunities to correct errors, there was a significant decrease in performance goals among students.

Some researchers point to optimal challenge as a strategy for increasing motivation (Clifford, 1991; Csikszentmihalyi, 1975, 1990; Reed, Hagen, Wicker, & Schallert, 1996). Under conditions of optimal challenge, when students' perceived skill levels matched the task difficulty offered in the classroom, students reported cognitive clarity and focused attention (Csikszentmihalyi, 1975). Csikszentmihalyi (1975) described this state as "flow." To describe the state of "flow," one interviewee in Csikszentmihalyi's study (1975) commented, "you are so involved in what you are doing that you aren't thinking of yourself as separate from the activity" (p. 39). Turner and her colleagues (1998) found that students who reported multiple instances of being in "flow" were in high involvement classrooms where teachers emphasized task goals as opposed to low involvement classrooms. High involvement teachers pressed for student understanding, valued mistakes as part of the learning process, and provided feedback rather than evaluation. In contrast, low involvement teachers emphasized procedures and avoidance of error. They fostered more performance-oriented reasons for learning.

After reviewing relevant research, Linnenbrink and Pintrich (2002) conclude that "more general affective states such as moods may be more likely to predict the perception of contextual mastery goals or the adoption of personal mastery goals. In contrast, mood does not seem to be related to performance goals at either the contextual or personal levels" (p. 77). Clearly, setting a classroom and curricular context, which facilitates a mastery approach for goal setting should facilitate learning. Karabenick's work (2002) on help seeking behavior supports this perspective. From other research, mood (what they call, prolonged core affect) has been shown to predict "…one third of the variance in one's momentary affect…" (Yik & Russell, 2001, p. 274). Therefore, we conclude mood can influence affective context, and by extension, motivation.

In response to problems with establishing and maintaining student motivation, Keller (1987a, 1987b) developed the ARCS Motivational Process model described under Strategies earlier in Section I. This model analyzed the motivational needs of the learner and corresponding tactics based on four dimensions of motivation: attention (A), relevance (R), confidence (C), and satisfaction (S). The dimensions were derived from a synthesis of research on human motivation. Keller (1999) suggested that a simplified version of his model provided "an efficient and effective means of supporting educators in improving the motivational aspects of learning environments" (p. 46). He also suggested that his "systematic motivational design can be incorporated into formal instructional design and curriculum development projects, it can serve as a basis for motivationally adaptive computer-based instruction, and it can increase student motivation and performance by improving the student support system in distance learning" (Keller, 1999, p. 46). The generic value of the ARCS model comes from both the technology applications and Keller's stressing its important multicultural aspects. In fact, the ARCS model is being used in different countries across the world, including countries in Asia and Europe (Keller, 1999).

For our purposes here, we note that Keller's approach serves as a means of helping to focus the learner's energy on the task and mastery rather than on personal fears about performance. We discuss these differences more fully later in the chapter when describing our model of efficient learning and performance, taking into account motivation to master a task verses emotional need to avoid threats. In the following discussion, the development of meta-cognitive skills of adaptive self-regulation and help-seeking behaviors, similarly aid the learner to focus on mastery, and would benefit from adding the ARCS approach to accomplish this development.

Self-regulatory skills

The research on self-regulatory skills has revealed a number of dimensions and provided useful suggestions for instructional strategies. One such area is the seeking of help by the learner. As Karabenick (2002) noted, "...seeking help can be an adaptive strategy of self-regulated learners" (p. 2), and is the only one that is inherently social. By providing an engaging learning environment, the teacher can encourage strategic seeking of help, and in turn can help the learner develop good meta-cognitive skills for self-monitoring/regulating her/his development.

Astleitner (2000) suggests "emotionally sound instruction consists of instructional strategies to increase positive and to decrease negative feelings during regular instructional settings" (p. 173). His "prescriptive propositions point out what should be done by teachers during instructing or what kind of strategies should be applied in order to get the desired emotional outcomes from the students" (Astleitner, 2000, p. 173). Astleitner concentrates on five types of feelings: fear, anger, envy, pleasure and sympathy. We do not agree that this should be the heart of the instructional strategy. In promoting a mastery oriented classroom, the instructor is already allowing for an increase in sympathy and pleasure and a reduction in fear, envy, and anger. Our first line of instruction is to create a mastery setting in the classroom and carry with it the verbal and non-verbal position by teachers that the learning of the new skills is possible. Astleinter's (2000) suggestions can be used as a second line of instruction or as remediational affective instructional techniques when there are problems in a certain area of emotion. Similarly, the research by Suinn and associates (2001) cited earlier has found reductions in anxiety and anger with the use of their AMT program with adult populations and suggests that this program can also be used effectively as a remediational technique.

Help-Seeking Behaviors

How the student' s affect influences his or her learning can be seen in the degree and kind of help seeking behavior, which the learner engages in during a learning experience. The literature on the seeking of help by students in a classroom situation reveals a number of categories of intention and conditions under which students will seek help. For example, Karabenick (2002) noted from his research that he could categorize the help seeking behavior as: 1) seeking autonomous help from teachers, called an approach orientation; or 2) the seeking of expedient help, or an avoidance orientation; that is, feeling threatened and therefore wanting to avoid being looked upon negatively. Moreover, as Karabenick notes, the type of contexts, which the teachers set for the classroom, will also influence whether the students tend to take an autonomous approach or an expedient approach to seeking help. That is, when the teachers emphasize mastery goals, then the students are more likely to seek autonomous help; whereas when the teachers emphasize performance goals, the students are more likely to seek expedient types of help. The latter emphasis taps into whatever ego-insecurities and personal threat worries that the student already has. Turner et al. (2002) also supported this in their research on avoidance strategies in mathematics. They believed there to be a relationship between the learning environment and the use of avoidance strategies, claiming that the results of high high-mastery/low avoidance and low-mastery/high avoidance classrooms were correlated with the instructional and motivational discourse of the classrooms. Teachers who supplied high motivational support produced students who would seek autonomous help. This provides support for the instructional guidance, which emphasizes mastery of the tasks with encouragement to thereby focus the learner on using task-oriented energy.

Such an approach would be consistent with promoting optimal performance as noted in our model. Urdan's review (1997) on mastery-orientation reveals similar support. In like manner, Butler (2002) characterizes these types of orientation by the student as his or her "...endorsement of task, ego, and work -- avoidant orientations to learning, respectively" (presentation summary, 2002). Butler's research also supports the importance of context as defined by the teacher as a strong determinant of which kind of help seeking behavior occurs. Said another way, it is necessary to distinguish between dependency-oriented help seeking and adaptive or strategic help seeking which can promote autonomy.

Martin's (2003) discussion on competition and self-attribution are relevant to the proposal we make in our model's distinction between ego and task-orientation, motivation verses emotion, and is also relevant to Karabenick's position on self-regulation, asking questions in a mastery verses performance environment. His research indicates that educators must also be aware of self-handicapping and defensive pessimism strategies employed by their students. Self-handicapping "refers to the choice of impediments or obstacles to successful performance that enable the individual to deflect the cause of failure away from his or her competence and on the acquired impediments" (Martin, 2003, p. 3). (We would suggest that this is quite similar to accepting failure.) Defensive pessimism "is a protective strategy in the sense that cushions the blow of potential failure and sets lower and safer standards against which to be judged" (Martin, 2003, p. 3). These strategies "tend to be a response to factors operating in students' academic lives and underscore the need for educators to recognize the presence of these factors and ways to address them" (Martin, 2003, p. 4). Performance orientation, in which there are concerns about ability, needs to demonstrate competence, and concern about how their performance is perceived by and compared to others, is a predictor of both strategies. Competition produces these concerns. It is recommended that there be a balance between a competitive approach and task-oriented and collaborative strategies, such as cooperative learning and competitive learning (This will be discussed further in Chapter 5.). The strongest predictor of self-handicapping is external attributional orientation. In this circumstance, Martin (2003) suggests "a need to encourage students to attribute outcomes to internal and controllable factors such as effort and strategy" (p. 4). In regards to defensive pessimism, Martin predicts that uncertain personal control is a factor, which can be produced by non-contingent or inconsistent feedback. To enhance perceived control, it is suggested to administer positive reinforcement coupled with KR feedback.

An Organizing Framework

Finally, we will describe an "Affect" framework within which both concepts, emotion and motivation, can be related. Within this framework, we will propose how they both may have a role in learning and performing various tasks. Support for the positions taken in our model is provided in the educational research of Csikszentmihalyi, Rathunde, and Whalen (1993). The concentration of the research of these authors was limited to the study of the development, or lack thereof, of talent by teenagers. Despite the narrowness of their focus, their conclusions are applicable generically to the construct of Affect (motivation and emotion). So for example, they find that time and effort students devote to study depends a great deal on the kind of emotional support they are given by their parents. They also speak of learners having a certain amount of energy (which they call *psychic energy*). "Because it takes attention to make anything happen, it is useful to think of attention as psychic energy. And like other forms of energy, attention is a limited resource..." (Csikszentmihalyi, Rathunde, & Whalen, 1993, p. 11). As we will show in our model later in this section, this energy can be focused on the task at hand or it can be diffused from that task as concerns about personal threat, inadequate performance, and resulting anxiety take over.

Another point emphasized by those authors is consistent with our approach as well. That is, Affect exists as a parallel and equally significant domain to our information processing domains such as cognitive and psychomotor. "Pursuing the analogy between computers and the human brain, the same considerations of clarity and rationality have become the main goals of educators designing school curricula and instruction. But the analogy misses the fact that students, as distinct from computers, will not process information presented to them unless they are motivated to do so... Learning has to be engaging and rewarding for students to learn... Two adverse conditions are especially dangerous: anxiety and boredom" (Csikszentmihalyi et al., 1993, p. 9-10).

Csikszentmilhayi's (1988) concerns in his research have been from the outset to study the "quality of the subjective experience" (p. 7) in the learner when they were intrinsically motivated. We feel that our model should shed some light on that. Further, to help the student maintain the motivating "flow experience," they assert, one must increase the complexity of the activity by developing new skills and taking on new challenges. Happiness, or flow as Csikszentmihalyi et al. call it, can be the motivation to learn. However, in order to continue to achieve "flow," the teacher must constantly challenge and introduce new things. "Flow forces people to stretch themselves, to always take on another challenge, to improve their abilities" (Csikszentmilhayi & Csikszentmilhayi, 1988, p. 30). This is consistent with our spiral curriculum approach proposed in Chapter 1 (illustrated in Figure 1.1). We advocate starting with multiple examples and expanding upon these as the learner works her/his way through the four learning processes in a domain: Acquisition, Automaticity, Near Term Transfer, and Far Term Transfer. As noted above, Keller's ARCS model (1987a, 1987b) similarly adds support for our characterization of

Affect and task-oriented energy (motivation) as being essential for effective and efficient learning.

Next, without opening any discussion of what we would call a parallel neuro-physiological system, such as where in the cortex or neocortex or sub cortex, the underpinnings reside for psychological events (which Goleman, 1995, finds necessary but we do not), we would like to propose a model for psychologically conceptualizing the Affective domain. We call this: a model for learning and performance efficiency.

The model takes into account the level of energy, type of energy, and their relationships to the performance of particular tasks. In this regard, we propose to include activation level theory (Lindsley, 1951; Russell & Feldman, 1999). Russell and Feldman (1999) define "core affect to refer to the most elementary consciously accessible affective feelings (and their neuro-physiological counterparts) that need not be directed at anything" (p. 806). They propose that these feelings vary in intensity and positive or negative states. We find their position consistent with the way we characterize the dimensions of our model. The qualification is that their theory would call an event focus such as on performing a task or activity an instance of "evaluations." The latter structure refers to "feelings directed at a specific target" (Russell & Feldman, 1999, p. 816). We propose to apply the kinds of distinctions these theorists make to our concepts of personal-threat energy, vs. externally oriented energy. We also propose that our approach builds on previous discussions in the clinical literature concerning ego-involvement vs. task-orientation (Wishner, 1955). Dweck and Leggett (1988) broaden the approach to a "cognitive-affective-behavior" model in a social-cognitive context in order to better understand the construct of motivation. As they note, if the learner focuses on performance goals (competence judgments) as opposed to learning goals (competence enhancements), then she or he will fall prey to the helplessness attitude. Seligman and his associates (1971, 1993) have shown the devastating, and pervasive clinical implications of this "learned helplessness" phenomenon. Zillmann's focus (1983) in the clinical literature is on the relationship between arousal or activation and "annoyance" in order to explain the development of aggression. The research he reviewed seemed to support the inference that the severity of the personal threat was directly related to arousal and aggression. With respect to our approach, we would interpret this as illustrating that the effect of personal threat causes diffusion of the learner's energy away from the task at hand. In education, this attitude of feeling threatened gets fed by the personal belief that intelligence is a fixed entity, and the students' affect and behavior are geared to documenting that self-fulfilling prophecy (Osborne, 2001; Steele, 1997). We would say that these people are moved to act by, emotion or personal-threat energy rather than by motivation or task-oriented energy. These performance-oriented learners are more concerned with how well their competence is judged by others than by a mindset that they can learn and master the task at hand.

In a chapter on individual differences in conation (Affect for our purposes), Snow and Jackson (1994) describe the difference between motivation toward mastery verses performance orientation. In the latter case individuals seek to avoid negative judgments and maintain positive views of their abilities. We would characterize this as the difference between working to avoid personal threat verses a task-mastery orientation. In our proposed model, personal threat energy can be understood as the need to perform to reach a goal in order to avoid a loss of personal esteem or ego. In a classical view of affect (e.g. Young, 1943) this would probably be called emotion. Externally oriented energy would be characterized as motivation. In this instance, the learner is oriented; i.e., motivated, to master the task at hand (see also Urdan, 1997).

Recent researchers (Russell & Barrett, 1999; Yik & Russell, 2001) have studied emotions and affect with the goal of establishing the basic number, type, and structural relationships amongst various emotions. From our perspective, whether or not the basic order or separations of emotions are 135 degrees and 35 degrees verses some other spacing combinations around a proposed circle, is not important for the conceptualization we are putting forth here. We wish simply to highlight the agreement between these researchers and our proposed model that both levels of activation and types of Affect can be identified as important in analyzing the Affective domain. The research is clear that types of affective experience can be distributed around some form of a circle. It is our proposal that an inner circle of task-focused energy (see figure 4.1 below) can be characterized as motivation and is facilitated by a mastery approach to learning. This is to be contrasted with a performance approach, which encourages judgments based on comparisons with others and therefore highlights importance of the emotions (or what we would call personal-threat energy) and impedes the process of learning.

The principal premise for the model is that any task has both an optimal level of required energy and a requirement for externally oriented, task-focused energy in order for the task to be learned and performed to the maximum possible effectiveness (i.e., a mastery approach). While requiring motivated orientation towards reaching a goal or solving the task problem, each type of task can tolerate a certain amount of emotional energy and still allow for successful completion of the task. The argument in the model is that the degree of personal threat energy (anxiety-emotion or ego-involvement) diffuses or diminishes the amount of energy that can be focused externally towards the task itself and prevents therefore maximally motivated problem solving or other required performance. Said differently: 'If I'm worried about how people will view me when I don't do it right, then I'm not going to devote my concentration on the work to be done, but rather on my feelings of self-worth' (i.e., a performance approach). Csikszentmihalyi et al. (1993) offer another view of this construct by characterizing the optimal balance of personal characteristics of the learner who can "sustain and enjoy the intensive dialectic that results in the experience of flow [of energy]" (p. 80). As noted above, they speak of the learner who can enjoy the challenge of risking for something new and the work of the task to be mastered, which would enhance one's skill. The authors describe this development as a "flow in consciousness [which] emerges when one perceives a well-calibrated balance between the challenges that an activity poses and the skills with which one can immediately respond" (Csikszentmihalyi et al., 1993, p. 79). We would assert that this is truly the motivated learner, unconcerned about personal-threat.

At one end of these tasks, requiring very a very small level of energy and little tolerance for personal threat energy, we would place the activity sleep. We have all experienced the difficulties in sleeping based upon emotional upsets (anxiety, depression). It is also the case that sleep can be disturbed because we have too much energy devoted towards problems which needed to be solved and has nothing to do with any personal or ego threat. In either case as Figure 4.1 shows, we are outside the optimal limits for the task of sleep. At the other extreme of tasks we would place running track. Clearly, attempting to run a sub-four minute mile demands a tremendous amount of energy; and, we would submit, tolerates a good deal of diffusion of energy. Tasks at interim levels would include, closer to the sleep level, cognitive problem solving; and, closer to the purely physical activity of running, psychomotor skill tasks, each associated with an optimal level of excitement and a certain tolerance for diffusion of energy when attempting to perform a given task at the respected level.

The model can be visualized as a three-dimensional geometric figure. If we consider it to be an inverted cone with the bottom cut off, we can see how the amount of energy required to perform a task increases as we go up the scale from sleep towards purely motor requirements. We propose that the increasing amount of tolerance for diffusion of energy; vis-à-vis, personal threat, is visualized as the widening or increasing diameter of the inverted cone as we move from sleep to motor activity, as illustrated in Figure 4.1.

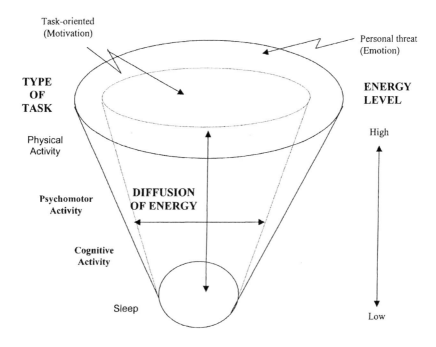

Figure 4.1. A Model for Efficiency of Learning and Performance

It is also important to repeat the point that definitional problems do exist today concerning ambiguities in Affective constructs including values, attitudes, emotions, and self-development. We would hypothesize that the reason for the difficulties in establishing an agreed-upon set of constructs stems at least in part from the fact that researchers label differently, levels of activation and focusing vsverses diffusing of energy (e.g., task oriented verses personal threat) without establishing a scientific basis empirically for these labels. Russell and associates (Russell & Barrett, 1999; Russell & Feldman, 1999; Yik & Russell, 2001) have come as close to clarifying the issues as anyone; and they recognize ambiguities still exist.

It is our hope that providing an overall framework, such as our model, will help to clarify this at least for the practical application of instructional development. The point is also relevant to Martin and Reigeluth's attempts at their own definitions of components and dimensions of Affective development (1999). What is needed is to make the distinction clear between verbal labels and operationally unique dimensions. We need to avoid proliferation of names and attain some degree of parsimony. Thus, intensity levels, our label, could be labeled differently by different researchers or practitioners. The reader needs to determine whether: a "dimension" or "component" is an operationally unique affective state, or rather a label as we have indicated? Additional indirect support for our conceptual framework is provided in the theoretical analysis and review of research on the utility of imagery in sports by Murphy and Martin (2002). They discuss five types of imagery: two types of cognitive, specific and general; and three types of motivational imagery, specific, general, and arousal. In commenting on the value of arousal imagery as an aid to improving an athlete's performance, they note, "…that arousal imagery may not facilitate performance unless it is accompanied by CS [cognitive specific] imagery (i.e., imagery of task performance)" (p. 420). Their review supports the notion that focusing energy on the task (which we call motivation) and ridding oneself of emotional worry about oneself (which we label personal-threat) will lead to superior task performance.

The latest entry into this discussion we found in a review of Emotional Intelligence (EI) literature by Zeidner, Roberts, and Matthews (2002). Their review is very helpful in describing the different varieties of extant theories of EI and the confusing and sparse research available to validate specific theories. These authors were trying to determine whether or not, and how, an EI construct could be scientifically characterized with an aim of answering the practical question: can EI be developed in school. After a comprehensive review of the evidence, pro and con, the authors conclude that the jury is still out concerning the value of EI as a general construct. Moreover, "to what extent we actually need to develop EI as a general construct or instead focus on the development of specific emotional competencies is unclear" (Zeidner, Roberts, & Matthews, 2002, p. 225). They do propose that, "…effective emotional functioning often appears to be situation dependent…" (Zeidner, Roberts, & Matthews, 2002, p. 216). We concur and therefore argue as the authors do for school programs that are targeted toward specific skills for given age levels (We also note that the CASEL approach has attempted to evaluate such programs and list the successes in their database.). Finally, Zeidner et al. (2002) propose that programs should be developed in accordance with careful implementation taking into account the educational, sociocultural, and development context. They also assert, as do we, that regardless of which EI theory the developer subscribes to, the program under development should be subjected to strict empirical validation.

Our discussion in this section has been an attempt to provide some coherence to the many facets of Affect (emotion and motivation) as they relate to influencing the learning of various kinds of tasks across domains. It is our hope that such elaboration can help the developer to put together more meaningful instruction.

Based on our discussion of EI, another issue concerning EI is brought to our attention. To what extent should EI be differentiated from social intelligence? Social intelligence comprises the decoding of social cues, effectiveness of one's social performance, and a social measure with a skill component (Ford & Tisak, 1983). Zeidner et al. (2002) stated that pinpointing which skills do or do not fall within the domain of social intelligence has been difficult. In order for one to form a sense of self; i.e., who they are (EI), they must develop boundaries; and these are learned from the social world surrounding them. This leads us to Chapter 5: the

Interpersonal Domain.

REFERENCES

Allan, L. G. (1993). Human contingency judgments: Rule based or associative? *Psychological Bulletin, 114*, 435-438.

Ames, C. (1992). Classrooms: Goals, structures, and student motivation. *Journal of Educational Psychology, 84(3)*, 261-271.

Ames, C. & Archer, J. (1988). Achievement goals in the classroom: Student's learning strategies and motivation processes. *Journal of Educational Psychology, 80*, 260-267.

Astleitner, H. (2000). Designing emotionally sound instruction: The FEASP approach. *Instructional Science: An International Journal of Learning and Cognition, 28(3)*, 169-198.

Benware, C. & Deci, E. L. (1984). Quality of learning with an active versus passive motivational set. *American Educational Research Journal, 21*, 755-765.

Butler, R. (2002, April). Help-seeking in the classroom: Individual and contextual determinants of help-related attitudes and intentions. Paper presented at the annual convention of the American Educational Research Association, New Orleans, Louisiana.

Ciarrochi, J., Forgas, J. P., & Mayer, J. D. (Eds.). (2001). *Emotional intelligence in everyday life: A scientific inquiry*. Philadelphia, PA: Psychology Press, Taylor & Francis Group.

Clifford, M. M. (1991). Risk taking: Theoretical, empirical, and educational considerations. *Educational Psychologist, 26*, 263-298.

Coleman, P. W. (2000). *How to say it to your kids: The right words to solve problems, soothe feelings, and teach values*. Englewood Cliffs, NJ: Prentice Hall Press.

Collinson, V. (2001). Intellectual, social, and moral development: Why technology cannot replace teachers. *High School Journal, 85(1)*, 35-45.

The Collaborative for Academic, Social, and Emotional Learning Organization. (2000). Retrieved April 29, 2003, from http://www.casel.org.

Crary, E. (1993). *Without spanking or spoiling*. Seattle: Parenting Press, Inc.

Csikszentmihalyi, M. (1975). *Beyond boredom and anxiety*. San Francisco: Jossey-Bass.

Csikszentmihalyi, M. (1990). Literacy and intrinsic motivation. *Daedalus, 119*, 115-140.

Csikszentmilhayi, M. & Csikszentmilhayi., I. S. (1988). *Optimal experience*. New York: Cambridge University Press.

Csiksentmihalyi, M., Rathunde, K., & Whalen, S. (1993). *Talented teenagers*. New York: Cambridge University Press.

Dweck, C. S. (1986). Motivational processes affecting learning. *American Psychologist, 41*, 1040-1048.

Dweck, C. S. & Leggett, E. L. (1988). A social-cognitive approach to motivation and personality. *Psychology Review, 95(2)*, 256-273.

Edwards, C. H. & Edwards, L. (1999). Let's end the grading game. *Clearing House, 72(5)*, 260-263.

Elliot, E. S., & Dweck., C. S. (1988). Goals: An approach to motivation and achievement. *Journal of Personality and Social Psychology, 54*, 5-12.

Erikson, E. H. (1950). *Childhood and society*. New York: Norton.

Erikson, E. H. (1959). *Identity and the life cycle*. New York: Norton.

Ford, M. E. & Tisak, M. (1983). A further search for social intelligence. *Journal of Educational Psychology, 75*, 196-206.

Forgas, J. P. (2001). Affective intelligence: The role of affect in social thinking and behavior. In. J. Ciarrochi, J. P. Forgas, & J. D. Mayer (Eds.), *Emotional intelligence in everyday life: A scientific inquiry* (pp. 46-63). Philadelphia, PA: Psychology Press, Taylor & Francis Group.

Franken, J. & O'Neil, H. F. (1994). Stress induced anxiety of individuals and teams in a simulator environment. In H. F. O'Neil & M. Drillings (Eds.), *Motivation: theory and research* (pp. 201-218). Hillsdale, NJ: Lawrence Erlbaum Association, Inc.

Goleman, D. (1995). *Emotional intelligence*. New York: Bantam Doubleday Dell Publishing Group.

Hartley, K. & Bendixen, L. D. (2001). Educational research in the internet age: Examining the role of individual characteristics. *Educational Researcher, 30(9)*, 22- 26.

Harvey, S. & Goudvis, A. (2000). *Strategies that work: Teaching comprehension to enhance understanding*. York, ME: Stenhouse Publishers.

Heyman, R. (2001). *Hot to say it to your teens: Talking about the most important topics of their lives.* Englewood Cliffs, NJ: Prentice Hall Press.

Holland, J. L. (1997). *Making vocational choices (3rd edition): A theory of vocational personalities and work environment.* Odessa, FL: Psychological Assessment Resources, Inc.

Hyson, M. C. (1994). *Emotional development of young children: Building an emotion-centered curriculum.* New York: Teachers College Press, Teachers College, Columbia University.

Illsley Clarke, J. (1998). *Time-in: When time-out isn't working.* Seattle, WA: Parenting Press, Inc.

Jacobson, M. J. & Spiro, R. J. (1995). Hyper-text learning environments, cognitive flexibility, and the transfer of complex knowledge: An empirical investigation. *Journal of Educational Computing Research, 12,* 301-333.

Karabenick, S. A. (2002, April). Students' help-seeking goals and intentions in large college classes: The effects of context. Paper presented at the annual convention of the American Educational Research Association, New Orleans, Louisiana.

Keller, J. M. (1987a). Strategies for stimulating the motivation to learn. *Performance and Instruction, 26*(8), 1-7.

Keller, J. M. (1987b). The systematic process of motivational design. *Performance and Instruction, 26*(9), 1-8.

Keller, J. M. (1997). Motivational design and multimedia: Beyond the novelty effect. *Strategic Human Resource Development Review, 1*(1), 188-203.

Keller, J. M. (1999). Using the ARCS motivational process in computer-based instruction and distance education. *New Directions for Teaching and Learning, 78,* 39-47.

Kohn, A. (1994). Grading: The issue is not how but why. *Educational Leadership, 52*(2), 38-41.

Kroger, J. (2000). Ego identity status research in the new millennium. *International Journal of Behavioral Development, 24*(2), 145-148.

Lindsley, D. B. (1951). Emotion. In S. S. Stevens (Ed.), *Handbook of experimental psychology* (pp. 473-516). New York: Wiley Publishing.

Linnenbrink, E. A. & Pintrich, P. R. (2002). Achievement goal theory and affect: A symmetrical bi-directional model. *Educational Psychologist, 37*(2), 69-78.

Martin, A. J. (2003). Self-handicapping and defensive pessimism: Predictors and consequences from a self-worth motivation perspective. *Newsletter for Educational Psychologists, 26*(1), 3-4.

Martin, B. L. & Reigeluth, C. M. (1999). Affective education and the affective domain: Implications for instructional-design theories and models. In C. M. Reigeluth (Ed.), *Instructional-design theories and models, Volume II: A new paradigm of instructional theory* (pp. 485-509). Mahwah, NJ: Lawrence Erlbaum Associates, Publishers.

Meece, J. L. (1991). The classroom context and students' motivational goals. In M. L. Maehr & P. Pintrich (Eds.), *Advances in motivation and achievement, Volume 7* (pp. 261-285). Greenwich, CT: JAI Press.

Middleton, M. & Midgley, C. (1997). Avoiding the demonstration of lack of ability: An under explored aspect of goal theory. *Journal of Educational Psychology, 89,* 710-718.

Miller, S. D. & Meece, J. L. (1997). Enhancing elementary students' motivation to read and write: A classroom intervention study. *Journal of Educational Research, 90,* 286-301.

Musch, J. & Broder, A. (1999). Test anxiety versus academic skills: A comparison of two alternative models for predicting performance in a statistics exam. *British Journal of Educational Psychology, 69,* 105-116.

Murphy, S. M. & Martin, K. A. (2002). The use of imagery in sport. In T. S. Horn (Ed.), *Advances in sport psychology* (2nd ed.) (pp. 405-439). Champaign, IL: Human Kinetics.

Nolen, S. (1988). Reasons for studying: Motivational orientations and study strategies. *Cognition and Instruction, 5,* 269-287.

O'Neil, H. F. & Drillings, M. (1994). Introduction to motivation: Theory and research. In H. F. O'Neil & M. Drillings, & (Eds.), *Motivation: Theory and research* (pp. 1-9). Hillsdale, NJ: Lawrence Erlbaum Association, Inc.

Osborne, J. W. (2001). Testing stereotype threat: Does anxiety explain race and SES differences in achievement? *Contemporary Educational Psychology, 26,* 291-310.

Parentstages.com: The best of the web for every parenting stage (2003). Retrieved May 19, 2003, from http://www.parentstages.com.

Peterson, C., Maier, S. F., & Seligman, M. E. P. (1993). *Learned helplessness.* New York: Oxford University Press.

Pintrich, P. R. (2000). An achievement goal theory perspective on issues in motivation terminology, theory, and research. *Contemporary Educational Psychology, 25,* 92-104.

Reed, J. H., Hagen, A. S., Wicker, F. W., & Schallert, D. L. (1996). Involvement as a temporal dynamic: Affective factors in studying for exams. *Journal of Educational Psychology, 88,* 101-109.

Russell, J. A. & Barrett, L. F. (1999). Core affect, prototypical emotional episodes, and other things called emotion: Dissecting the elephant. *Journal of Personality and Social Psychology, 76*(5), 805-819.

Russell, J. A. & Barrett, L. F. (1999). Core affect, prototypical emotional episodes, and other things called emotion: Dissecting the elephant. *Journal of Personality and Social Psychology, 76*(5), 808-819.

Screaton Page, G. (1999). *Being the parent you want to be: 12 Communication skills for effective parenting.* White Plains, NY: Performance Learning Systems, Inc.

Seligman, M. E. P., Maier, S. F., & Solomon, R. L. (1971). Unpredictable and uncontrollable aversive events. In F. R. Bush (Ed.), *Aversive conditioning and learning* (pp. 347-400). New York: Academic Press.

Snow, R. E. & Jackson, D. N. (1994). Individual differences in conation: Selected constructs and measures. In H. F. O'Neil & M. Drillings (Eds.), *Motivation: Theory and research* (pp. 71-99). Hillsdale, NJ: Lawrence Erlbaum Association, Inc.

Solomon, R. L. & Wynne, L. C. (1953). Traumatic avoidance learning: acquisition in normal dogs. *Psychological Monographs, 67*(4), (No. 354), 19.

Solomon, R. L. & Wynne, L. C. (1954). Traumatic avoidance learning: the principles of anxiety conservation and partial irreversibility. *Psychological Review, 61,* 353-385.

Steele, C. M. (1997). A threat in the air: How stereotypes shape intellectual identity and performance. *American Psychologist, 52,* 613-629.

Sternberg, R. J. (2001a). How wise is it to teach for wisdom? A reply to five critiques. *Educational Psychologist, 36*(4), 269-272.

Sternberg, R. J. (2001b). Why schools should teach for wisdom: The balance theory of wisdom in educational settings. *Educational Psychologist, 36*(4), 227-245.

Suinn, R. M. (1998). Anxiety? Anger Management Training. In G. Koocher, J. Norcross, & S. Hill (Eds.), *Psychologists' desk reference* (pp. 318-321). New York: Oxford University Press.

Suinn, R. M. (2001). The terrible twos: Anger and anxiety. *American Psychologist, 56*(1), 27-36.

Suinn, R. M. & Richardson, F. (1971). Anxiety Management Training: A non-specific behavior therapy program for anxiety control. *Behavior Therapy, 2,* 498-512.

Sunderland, M. (2000). *Draw on your emotions.* Chesterfield, Derbyshire: Speechmark Publishing Limited.

Turner, J. C. (1995). The influence of classroom contexts on young children's motivation for literacy. *Reading Research Quarterly, 30,* 410-441.

Turner, J. C., Meyer, D. K., Cox, K. E., Logan, C., DiCintio, M., & Thomas, C. (1998). Involvement in mathematics: Teachers' strategies and students' perceptions. *Journal of Educational Psychology, 90*(4), 730-745.

Turner, J. C., Midgley, C., Meyer, D. K., Gheen, M., Anderman, E. M., Kang, Y., & Patrick, H. (2002). The classroom environment and students' reports of avoidance strategies in mathematics: A multimethod study. *Journal of Educational Psychology, 94*(1), 88-106.

Urdan, T. C. (1997). Achievement goal theory: Past results, future directions. In M. L. Maehr & P. R. Pintrich (Eds.), *Advances in motivation and achievement, Volume 10* (pp. 99-142). Greenwich, CT: Jai Pr., Inc.

Vermetten, Y. J., Lodewijks, H. G., & Vermunt, J. D. (2001). The role of personality traits and goal orientations in strategy use. *Contemporary Educational Psychology, 26*(2), 149-170.

Wagner, A. R. & Rescorla, R. A. (1972). Inhibition in Pavlovian conditioning: Application of a theory. In R. A. Boakes & M. S. Halliday (Eds.), *Inhibition and Learning* (pp. 301-336). London: Academic.

Wasserman, E. A. & Miller, R. R. (1997). What's elementary about associative learning? *Annual Review of Psychology, 48,* 573-607.

Watson, J. B. (1959). *Behaviorism.* Chicago: University of Chicago Press.

Weissberg, R. P., Resnik, J. P., & O'Brien, M. U. (2003, March). Evaluating social and emotional programs. *Educational Leadership*, 46-50.

Wellman, H. M. & Gelman, S. A. (1992). Cognitive development: Foundational theories of core domains. *Annual Review of Psychology, 43*, 337-375.

Wentzel, K. R. (1993). Social and academic goals at school: Motivation and achievement in early adolescence. *Journal of Early Adolescence, 13*, 4-20.

Wentzel, K. R. (2000). What is it that I'm trying to achieve? Classroom goals from a content perspective. *Contemporary Educational Psychology, 25*(1), 105-115.

Wishner, J. (1955). The concept of efficiency in psychological health and psychopathology. *Psychology Review, 62*(1), 69-80.

Wolters, C. A. (1998). Self-regulated learning and college students' regulation of motivation. *Journal of Educational Psychology, 90*(2), 224-235.

Yik, M. S. M. & Russell, J. A. (2001). Predicting the big two of affect from the big five of personality. *Journal of Research in Personality, 35*, 247-277.

Young, M. E. (1995). On the origin of personal causal theories. *Psychology Bulletin Review, 2*, 83-104.

Young, P. T. (1943). *Emotion in man and animal*. New York: Wiley.

Zeidner, M., Roberts, R. D., & Matthews, G. (2002). Can emotional intelligence be schooled? A critical review. *Educational Psychologist, 37*(4), 213-231.

Zillmann, D. (1983). Arousal and aggression. In R. G. Geen & E. Donnerstein (Eds.), *Aggression: Theoretical and empirical reviews, Volume 1* (pp. 75-102). New York: Academic.

CHAPTER 5

INTERPERSONAL DOMAIN

Table 5.1. Taxonomy of the Interpersonal Domain

Process Requirements Knowledge Domains	Acquisition	Automaticity	Transfer: Near term	Transfer: Far term
	Learning elements of a new knowledge domain (e.g., acquiring nomenclature).	Integrating and applying elements and procedures through extensive repetition (i.e., automating skills)	Developing ability to generalize-apply principles, and strategies (e.g., heuristics) within a domain	Learning to discover new principles in a domain (e.g., creative thinking, problem finding, meta-cognition) and applying them across domains
INTERPERSONAL *dealing with others (social habits and skills)	Learning cooperative play; Learning to work in teams; Socialization skills	Conditioned social responses (e.g., socialized behaviors)	Interpersonal control skills (leadership, persuasion, prosocial skills, e.g., management skills)	Applying management skills from one domain to another (e.g., civilian to military life or vice versa)

Unique Heuristics highlighted in this chapter on Interpersonal Development:

o   *Imitative learning (observational) and modeling of authority figures, starting with parents, influences the development of filters and templates, through which the child learns to see her or his world.*
o   *Developmental factors affect observational learning.*

o   *Repeated exposures to modeled behaviors are necessary because of potential complexities and rates of presentation, both of which can decrease attention.*

o   *Whom one associates with (social networks), imposed or by preference, limit the observational patterns to which the individual is repeatedly exposed and therefore, those which will be learned more thoroughly than others.*

o   *Peer learning is a powerful influence in school learning and outside the school environment.*

INTRODUCTION

It is perhaps fitting that we end our study with the Interpersonal Domain. As we have noted in the prior chapters, the domains are not as independent as they at first seem. Interpersonal development can be traced to birth, with the influences of mother (perhaps, nowadays, dad too) including holding, fondling, talking, and emoting to, and with, the newborn. So too, we have the beginning of interactions and interdependence among cognitive, motor, psychomotor, and affective domains (Some would assert that this occurs even earlier with evidence of pre-natal interpersonal influence.).

Gardner (1983, 1993) proposed a theory of multiple intelligences. In Chapter 4, we discussed how we learn who we are as individuals, which Gardner called "intrapersonal intelligence." Ideas are presented on how an individual learns to be emotionally demonstrative and at the same time, learns how and when to control such demonstration in the process of education. This leads us into Chapter 5. With this foundation, an individual next learns how to interact with others and then how to learn from these people. This role of social intelligence is labeled "interpersonal intelligence" by Gardner. It encompasses the understanding of others and acting on that understanding. Others have described this social and emotional development as governing the recognition and management of emotions, along with the development of empathy, and the ability to, "...establish positive relationships, and handle challenging situations effectively" (Weissberg et al., pp. 46-47). In this regard, the CASEL group at the University of Chicago was formally established to "...advance the science and practice of social and emotional learning..." (Weissberg et al., p. 46). They have developed, assembled, and evaluated instructional programs covering empathy, and establishing positive relationships, thereby enabling the student to be successful, not only in academics, but overall to become "...healthy, caring, ethical, and actively involved in their schools and communities" (Weissberg et al., p. 46). The question we answer in this chapter is: how does one acquire these skills?

The social cognitive theory proposed by Bandura (1986, 2001) is supportive of our ideas on the process requirements of the interpersonal domain. He asserts that, "human functioning is explained in terms of a model of a triadic reciprocality in which behavior, cognitive and other personal factors, and environmental events all operate as interacting determinants of each other" (Bandura, 1986, p. 18). One needs the environment and that which composes the environment, as well as their developed self (personal, cognitive, and behavioral), to form new interactions and enjoy the capacity to learn new things.

In order to learn how one develops social skills, we must first learn what they are and why they are important. Social skills have been defined as the cognitive functions and specific verbal and nonverbal behaviors that an individual engages in when interacting with others (Coleman & Lindsay, 1992). Social skills have a significant effect on one's daily life. These skills can vary from problem avoidance, to making choices, to interpreting facial expressions. "Specific skills deemed essential by teachers to succeed in general education settings...include coping skills, work habits, and peer relationships" (Gut & Safran, 2002, p. 88). We remind the reader that these skills do not take place in isolation; rather, they are learned and develop alongside the Affect developments noted in Chapter 4. Based on all these skills, one interacts with others. Social skills start developing when a child is born and continue to develop throughout one's lifespan. "Since age is a critical consideration, a developmental picture of normative social skill development is helpful. A young child of 20 months is able to name and label emotions, and by 2 ½ years, [she or he] is able to understand the causes and consequences of emotions. By age six, a typically developing child has the ability to identify facial expressions (emotions), and by twelve [she or he] can match [his or her] social skills with the demands of the situation" (Gut & Safran, 2002, p. 88). Bradley et al. suggest that when children are young, they function in the role of "reactors to and elicitors of specific environmental inputs." As the children get older, they become "more active in seeking out and constructing environments that suit their needs and proclivities" (Gut & Safran, 2002, p. 1869). As noted, social abilities can be affected by a multitude of factors including "biological, developmental, emotional, familial, cultural/ethnic, economic, and peer group factors" (Gut & Safran, 2002, p. 89). Deficits can occur in these social skills resulting in debilitating effects, which in turn, can result in social rejection and isolation. In brief, social skills are critical in how we interact with those around us and are a result of many factors. Specific to educational effects, the development of pro-social behavior in early childhood has been found to have a strong positive effect on later academic achievement (Caprara et al., 2000).

Again, we will introduce in Section I different types of guidance to aid Interpersonal learning during the Acquisition, Automaticity, Near and Far Term Transfer stages. We conclude in Section II with research to support the suggested strategies.

SECTION I:

POSSIBLE INSTRUCTIONAL GUIDANCE

Acquisition Process

Table 5.2. Acquisition Process of the Interpersonal Domain

Process Requirements	Acquisition	Automaticity	Near Term Transfer	Far Term Transfer
INTERPERSONAL *dealing with others (social habits and skills)	Learning cooperative play; Learning to work in teams; Socialization skills	Conditioned social responses (e.g., socialized behaviors)	Interpersonal control skills (leadership, persuasion, prosocial skills, e.g., management skills)	Applying management skills from one domain to another (e.g., civilian to military life or vice versa)

In this phase, acquisition of social skills is accomplished by the efforts of parents and teachers, through:

o **Making the child's environment conducive to the development of pro-social skills and schemas;**
o **Encouraging unstructured play;**
o **Providing the child with early social experiences with their peers, such as quality daycare, which influence social competence;**
o **And including social skills instruction into the curriculum.**

Since socialization starts at home, it is necessary to make this environment conducive to the development of pro-social skills. Andersen and Chen (2002) have outlined a social-cognitive theory of how significant relationships develop for the individual. They have proposed the concept of the "relational self", which starts its growth within families of origin and continues with non-family members. Basically, how we respond to others "emotionally, motivationally, and behaviorally" are the result of mental representations accumulated over time in our interactions with significant others (parents, siblings, etc.). So, a new person encountered is interpreted based on similarities to representations already established. Transference of the old representations to the new occurs in this manner. Modifications take place based on frequency and intensity of contacts, and from the varied contexts in which these contacts take place. We will discuss this further in Section II. Suffice it to say here that it agrees with our notion of template development starting at home with the child; and it is through this lens that the young child engages her or his educational world. The suggested strategies must take this into account, while attempting to help the learner maximize potential.

Promoting Active and Interactive Learning
We suggest that parents set aside time for unstructured play so that kids can develop social skills. During preschool years, Mastrilli (2003) suggests that children begin to role-play adults in their lives, others in the community, personalities in the media, and animals or animated characters. Creativity is used to develop the characters and scenes of their play. However, as the children play together, other skills begin to develop. "Children begin to express their desires, needs, and interests. They negotiate their roles and communicate as that imitated person or character" (Mastrilli, 2003, p. 12). In other words, their social skills begin to develop. As the children get older and enter elementary school, the play changes to games with set rules that are played with siblings or peers. They learn to be flexible in negotiating, to listen and relate to others, to prioritize, to compromise, and to play together successfully. The strategies for parents suggested by Mastrilli (2003) give the child an opportunity to develop the basic elements of social skills, which allow the development of leadership skills, decision-making abilities, and conflict resolution. These strategies include (Mastrilli, 2003, p. 13):

o   Make time for unstructured play.
o   Limit the amount of inactive play such as, watching television or playing video games.
o   Emphasize the value of play by playing with the child.
o   Provide supervision and guidance, but allow the child to solve problems on their own.
o   Role model appropriate interactions.
o   Give the child suggestions for play ideas or tools to assist in their play based on the child's interests.
o   Provide materials and toys that promote creative play rather than task-specific play.
o   Encourage a wide variety of play, incorporating realistic, dramatic, and imaginary elements.
o   Act out stories with dolls, stuffed animals, puppets, etc.
o   Demonstrate successful responses and conflict resolution in your everyday life.

Prior to attendance in schools, the amount of time spent in out-of-home care and the quality of early home and out-of-home care play an important role in shaping the children's social skills. We suggest that experiences in daycare early in life may influence social competence. These include:

o   Interaction with different children of all ages, genders, and racial and cultural backgrounds under the supervision of caretakers.
o   Foster individual differences.
o   To maximize the value of daycare experience in developing positive peer relationships, start daycare two, or at least one year prior to kindergarten (3-3½ years of age).

The quality of these early experiences reflecting social skills development is later demonstrated in the classroom. This is most likely where deficits and strengths will be noticed. Perhaps one of the most primitive and important skills is to become aware of and appreciate the needs of others.

Learning to Care
Negative behavior towards one another can be helped by encouraging a caring environment through helping children become aware of the feelings and thoughts of others. Borba (2003) offers some solutions to encourage children to respect and care for everyone at home and increase positive behaviors towards others.

o   Identify uncaring behavior and prohibit it.
o   Write out the words and gestures that are not allowed in a "caring contract."
o   Involve everyone in making suggestions for enforcing the rules and goals.
o   Have everyone sign a "caring contract" and make it visible to the family.
o   When the child makes a negative, uncaring comment, have him or her turn it around with a positive statement.
o   Encourage goals of complimenting and encouraging others rather than putting them down.
o   Whenever she or he says a negative comment or a put-down, she or he must put some money into a community jar. When the jar is filled, donate the money to your favorite charity, demonstrating compassion for others.
o   Create "Caring Coupon Books" to encourage acts of caring and service. Coupons can include doing chores for one another, sharing, allowing their sibling to choose the television program or music in the car, etc. Make the book with a variety of coupons and give it to a family member.

Gut & Safran (2002) suggest two useful strategies to further develop social skills in school by incorporating "social skills instruction into the existing curriculum" (p. 89):

o   **Cooperative learning groups**: Cooperative group work connects to thinking through collaborative knowledge building. In this setting, students learn how to search out information on questions generated by the teacher or others in their group and learn techniques for analyzing, interpreting, negotiating, and communicating their information as a team (Adams &

Hamm, 1990). Guthrie & Cox (2001) also suggest this as a strategy as stated in Chapter 2. Their position is that collaboration in instruction would lead to increased engagement in school activities.

o   Gut and Safran (2002) suggest that the class be divided into two groups, which are facilitated by the teacher. The groups "can be used as an avenue to discuss a book read in class or to prepare a product demonstrating the groups' comprehension of key issues and/or themes addressed in a story" (Gut & Safran, 2002, p. 89). Books that include themes of pro-social behaviors can be chosen to further reinforce the social skills. Role-plays are assigned to individual students among the groups to portray the possible reactions of the characters in the stories. Directions are given to the students to act how the student thinks the characters will deal with specific situations. This "will enhance the students' ability to investigate a variety of behavioral strategies and experience the outcome in a safe environment" (Gut & Safran, 2002, p. 89). This structure provides a safe environment for trial and error because it allows the students to ask questions, express opinions, and take risks. The student is individually held accountable but all students are encouraged to bring their talents together to help each other learn. Each student brings unique strengths and experiences to the group and as a result, respect for individual differences can be enhanced.

o   **Social stories**: Social cues involve the child's understanding of, and acceptable response to, social situations. Social stories can be implemented in the classroom to help a child adjust to new social cues and teach them acceptable responses to these social cues. Social stories describe important social information on what is occurring and why. The teacher assists the child in production of a story about various social situations. The story includes statements defining who, what, where, when and why of a specific situation. Explanations of the behaviors and feelings of others are included in the story, as well as statements describing what the character is expected to say and do. Guidance on how to remember what to do in future situations and how to understand them is also included. The stories "facilitate an understanding of the social context and how individuals feel, helping to develop awareness of empathy" (Gut & Safran, 2002, p. 90).

o   Other strategies to acquire social skills during the Acquisition process include the use of:

   o   **Activity Books**: Activity books provide different games to help children learn a variety of social skills such as: sensitivity and formal manners, consideration for others, meeting people, making conversation, teasing, apologizing, table manners, telephone etiquette, gossip, and sleep-over etiquette (e.g., *Manners Matter: Activities to teach young people social skills*, by, Debbie Pincus-Ward (1996)).

   o   **Videos**: Videos provide skits performed by kids and can "illustrate negative, then positive, reactions to real-life situations." The contrast between "how to" and "how not to" stimulates discussion. Such videos concentrate on skills including: introducing yourself, starting a conversation, giving a compliment, following rules, sharing, suggesting an activity, helping a friend in trouble, showing concern for a friend, expressing negative feelings, getting attention appropriately, and asking to borrow things (e.g., *Social skills video skits*, by Berthold Berg, for ages 10-16, see http://www.creativetherapystore.com for ordering details).

o **Problem Solving Books**: *Children's problem solving books* (Crary, 1996a, 1996b, 1996c, 1996d): These books, for ages 3 through 8 years, assist in children learning how to resolve conflicts in their social lives. They help children become more aware of alternatives to and consequences of their various behaviors. The books address problems common to young children, such as sharing, taking turns, feeling lonely, and separation anxiety. Techniques in using these books include: reading the story straight through and discussing or allowing children to determine the course of the stories by deciding the characters' actions.

o **Skill streaming** for Elementary School Children and Adolescents (McGinnis & Goldstein, 1997a, 1997b) (see http://www. creativetherapystore.com for ordering details): This kit provides new strategies and perspectives for teaching pro-social skills. It can be used with many students. There is an elementary school version (grades 2 through 5) and an adolescent version (grades 6 through 12), which include a Handbook, Program Forms Booklet, Skill Cards, and Student Manual.

The elementary school version provides activities for learning the basic interpersonal elements during the Acquisition phase, learning cooperative play and socialization. Whereas, the adolescent version is teaching advanced skills based on the basics, as done in the Automaticity phase, applying conditioned socialization skills, and Near Term Transfer phase, developing leadership and other interpersonal control skills.

The Handbook for *elementary students* shows how to teach skills in five different areas: classroom survival skills, friendship skills, dealing with feelings, alternatives to aggression, and dealing with stress. Specific skills targeted include asking for help, accepting consequences, using self-control, and dealing with pressure. The Handbook for *adolescents* teaches pro-social skills in the following areas: beginning social skills, advanced social skills, dealing with feelings, alternatives to aggression; dealing with stress, and planning skills. Starting a conversation, apologizing, responding to failure, and setting a goal are amongst the specific skills that are targeted in this product.

Project ACHIEVE
In addition to the above suggestions, we recommend implementation of Project ACHIEVE. Dr. Howard Knoff developed Project ACHIEVE for preschool, elementary, and middle school students for the Acquisition and Automaticity of social skills (http://cecp.air.org/teams/greenhouses/projach.pdf). Project ACHIEVE attempts to increase school and staff effectiveness through positive behavioral and academic prevention programs. The project places emphasis on increasing student performance in the areas of: social skills and social-emotional development, conflict resolution and self-management, achievement and academic progress, and positive school climate and safe school practices. Project ACHIEVE, which is also known as the Stop and Think Program, provides opportunities for students to receive recognition and appreciation for making good choices and doing the right thing. This program has received extensive evaluation, has been implemented at 25 locations across the U.S., and is touted as a model program by the Substance Abuse and Mental Health Services Administration of the U.S. Department of Health and Human Services (www.samhsa.gov).

Automaticity Process

Table 5.3. Automaticity Process of the Interpersonal Domain

Process Requirements	Acquisition	Automaticity	Near Term Transfer	Far Term Transfer
INTERPERSONAL *dealing with others (social habits and skills)	Learning cooperative play; Learning to work in teams; Socialization skills	Conditioned social responses (e.g., socialized behaviors)	Interpersonal control skills (leadership, persuasion, prosocial skills, e.g., management skills)	Applying management skills from one domain to another (e.g., civilian to military life or vice versa)

The focus during the Automaticity phase is to:

- **Continue learning,**
- **Practicing, and**
- **Integrating appropriate social skills into the lives of learners, by**
- **Accentuating the skills the individual has.**

Specific suggestions include the use of:

o **Videos:** Videos stimulate discussion and behavior change. They can include performances by kids demonstrating "negative, then positive, reactions to real-life situations." There is a contrast between "how to" and "how not to" behave that will stimulate discussion. The skits can have different themes depending on the individual or classroom needs – such as anger (how to recognize anger and aggression, how to empathize with victims, how to control anger through self-talk, how to find alternatives to aggression, and how to use assertion) (Example: *Anger and Aggression Video Skits*, by Berthold Berg, PhD for ages 10-16, see http://www.creativet herapystore.com for ordering details).

o **Books**: Have books with themes centralized around social skills available to the children during their free time. The books can also be assignments for book reports, class discussions, etc. Examples include: *Charlotte's Web* by E.B. White (1974) (Age 8-12); *Don't be a menace on Sundays!* by Adolph Moser, Ed. D (2002) (Ages 4-12); *Danny, the Angry lion*, by Dorothea Lachner (2000) (ages 3-7); *Stand Tall, MollyLou Melon*, by Patty Lovell (2001) (ages 5-10); *Enemy Pie*, by Derek Munson (2000) (ages 5-10); *Nobody likes me*, by Raoul Krischanitz (1999) (ages 4-10); *Good Friends are hard to find*, by Fred Frankel, Ph.D (1996) (ages 5-12); *Cliques, Phonies, and other Baloney*, by Trevor Romain (1998) (ages 8-14).

o **Interactive guides**: There are many books available to practitioners, teachers, and parents on how to help their children with a variety of social skills and problems. Care should be taken in choosing which books will be used. One suggestion is *The Shy Child: Helping Children Triumph Over Shyness* (Ward, 2000). Shyness is common in children and adults and can sometimes hinder a child's development. Ward offers a guide with step-by-step solutions for parents and children on how to deal with the problems of shyness. The book discusses the signs of shyness from infancy to adolescence, how the shy child responds physically and mentally to stress, how the child's artwork reveals his or her emotions, how drawing together can reinforce trust and understanding, why shy children are vulnerable to bullies and how to intervene, and how to teach the child to cope with anxiety-producing situations. The author suggests that scriptwriting, rewriting, role-playing, and rehearsing are important tools for the shy child.

Reinforcement procedures can effectively address a wide array of behaviors and/or problems in children and adolescents, including hyperactivity, aggression, disruptive classroom behavior, as well as other behaviors. Using positive reinforcement is a technique to continue reproduction of appropriate social skills. This can be done in a variety of ways. Poster boards with charts in which children receive smiling or frowning stickers, as a result of demonstrating various behaviors, can be displayed at home or in a classroom. Praise given to children in the classroom in the presence of classmates can be helpful. Many different positive reinforcements have been experimented with and found successful over the years. A good source for many of the classic studies and experimental points of view can be found in Honig (1966). Many different kinds of tokens, variations in the use of verbal praise, and distribution of the reinforcement over time are all discussed in the context of experiments used to show the value of reinforcement.

Transfer Process: Near Term

Table 5.4. Near Term Transfer Process of the Interpersonal Domain

Process Requirements	Acquisition	Automaticity	Near Term Transfer	Far Term Transfer
INTERPERSONAL *dealing with others (social habits and skills)	Learning cooperative play; Learning to work in teams; Socialization skills	Conditioned social responses (e.g., socialized behaviors)	Interpersonal control skills (leadership, persuasion, prosocial skills, e.g., management skills)	Applying management skills from one domain to another (e.g., civilian to military life or vice versa)

Key areas here are developing awareness and learning social skills of:

- **Leadership and persuasion by**
- **Observation of positive role models through various media,**
- **Imitating behaviors, and**
- **Integrating these developments into everyday life.**

Educators and trainers should take the following as an example for learning techniques in the social realm. The following focuses on Near Term Transfer by using television shows to persuade people to change the ways they view a given social issue or problem. In other words, folks around the world have developed social skills within their own cultures, such that they are aware of AIDS, for example, but not how to deal with it in a new light and with new techniques. Bandura's model (1986, 2001), which is discussed in the Supporting Research Section, is the basis for these techniques: One can learn by watching and mimicking another's behavior. Currently, Bandura's model is being integrated through modern technologies such as radio and television into everyday life to promote solutions to some of the world's everyday problems. Smith (2002) summarized how television and radio shows all over the world, from Tanzania to Mexico to China, have been using Albert Bandura's social cognitive theory as their foundation to benefit millions of people. The themes of the shows are centered on problems that the home country faces, such as AIDS, unwanted pregnancies, literacy, environment, population size, and gender issues. The shows feature characters that model ways to improve their lives and connect the viewers with real-life services in their communities with the ultimate goal being to foster the viewers' self-efficacy. The shows contain "crafted characters" who include "positive role models whose behavior results in good things, negative role models whose behavior has adverse effects, and transitional models who start out negatively but turn into positive role models by the end" (Smith, 2002, p. 31-32). This is an example of how one can learn through the actions and consequences of others' experience by modeling. It also emphasizes how important the roles of local cultures and society are for this modeling to be effective.

We have discussed the use of videos in the Acquisition and Automaticity phases of interpersonal development. This form of instruction is relevant, once again, during Near and Far Term Transfer. This strategy, similar to the television shows above, may help students gain insights in dealing with problems that they may face. Hebert and Speirs Neumeister (2002) propose strategies in guided viewing of film that may help with problems faced by young gifted students. We believe that videos can be helpful to children of all ages and intellectual levels. Videos can help can assist the child to "reach self-understanding and consider ways of developing relationships with others" (Hebert & Speirs Neumeister, 2002, p. 17). The film provides metaphors that help the child understand what is bothering them and in turn, allows them to see their issues in a different, more positive light. They witness alternate solutions to their problems through the films.

Hebert and Speirs Neumeister (2002) supply guidelines for film viewing:

o The teacher should familiarize themselves with the content of the film and how it reflects the emotions, attitudes, and children's beliefs;
o Create a menu of discussion questions;
o Introduce the film to the child or children and make reference to the situations occurring in the film;
o Assist the learners in understanding the movie and it's characters relative to their own experiences through discussion.
o Respond to the learner's comments and questions with concern and empathy, recognizing their contribution and with acceptance of their emotions;
o "Design follow-up activities that allow children to process through their feelings" (Hebert & Speirs Neumeister, 2002, p. 18). Activities suggested include artistic projects, writing activities, role-playing, and creative problem solving.

Films suggested by Hebert and Speirs Neumeister (2002) for viewing include:

o *Matilda* (De Vito, Shamberg, Sher, & Dahl, 1996), a film focusing on how children's intellectual abilities should be appreciated and nurtured;

o *The Sand Lot* (Gilmore, de la Torre, & Evans, 1993), a film centering around the themes of father-son relationships, non-athleticism, and peer group acceptance;

o *My Girl* (Glazer & Zieff, 1991), a film touching on the topics of choosing friends, a parent's remarriage, appreciating intelligence in young females, using one's imagination and creativity, and dealing with the loss of loved ones;

o *Wide Awake* (Woods, Konrad, & Shyamalan, 1997), a film that focuses on a boy's struggle to understand mortality and the after life, as well as adolescent issues including the discovery of the opposite sex, coping with a school bully, acknowledging fears, and developing empathy for those kids not appreciated by their peer group;

o *Annie O.* (McClary, 1995), a film that addresses gender related issues with upper elementary school students;

o and *Searching for Bobby Fischer* (Rudin, Wisnievitz, Hohrberg, & Zaillian, 1993), a film that focuses on the role of a mentor in talent development, keeping competition in perspective, dealing with parental expectations, and maintaining a healthy balance of enjoyable activities throughout childhood.

Transfer Process: Far Term

Table 5.5. Far Term Transfer Process of the Interpersonal Domain

Process Requirements	Acquisition	Automaticity	Near Term Transfer	Far Term Transfer
INTERPERSONAL *dealing with others (social habits and skills)	Learning cooperative play; Learning to work in teams; Socialization skills	Conditioned social responses (e.g., socialized behaviors)	Interpersonal control skills (leadership, persuasion, prosocial skills, e.g., management skills)	Applying management skills from one domain to another (e.g., civilian to military life or vice versa)

In the Far Term Transfer Process of the Interpersonal domain our concentration is on learning ways to:

- **Re-examine,**
- **Negotiate,**
- **And manage relationships,**
- **And transfer these from one area of life to another, one culture to another,**

By using the techniques of:

- **Observing and modeling experts and**
- **Finding new ways to work in teams.**

An illustration of far term transfer can be found in the following. We have often been proponents of the draft or some enforced public service following high school graduation for all students. The value of this psychologically is that the learner is put into a situation, which 1) is free of the emotional and social baggage of the home; 2) provides a consistent structure; and 3) provides for consequences (rewards and discipline) based upon behavior of the learner. What can be developed is a set of skills that can be applied across domains. The skills are: management of one's time, respect for authority, and responsibility for one's actions. Such skills, while formed in the military or a related structured environment, can readily be transferred by the learner to college, the business world, personal, and family life. In fact, a survey of over 2,000 presidents and CEO's of American businesses (Schroyer et al., 1990) revealed that Army veterans were rated higher than the general population of applicants in: dependability, showing respect, punctuality, working as members of teams, cooperation, and many other interpersonal skills picked up as part of their military experience.

Far term transfer enables the learner to use the social skills, developed previously, in new situations that can promote furthering one's education or training. A recently proposed, novel example of this has been the suggestion that college students be given the choice to participate in "cooperative college examinations" (Zimbardo, Butler, & Wolfe, 2003). The procedure is roughly as follows: When taking exams, the students are allowed to choose a partner and the resulting grade is shared. These tests allow the student to use their acquired social skills to work with another student in the taking of a test. Students also obtain increased exposure to working with others, in which lessons in social learning are learned: "knowledge can be, or should be, shared with fellow students; differences in opinion can be rationally negotiated even under conditions of test pressures; and cooperative learning procedures can be enjoyable and productive" (Zimbardo et al., 2003, p. 120). It is proposed by the researchers that this technique produces significant improvements in academic performance, reduces test anxiety during studying and testing, encourages sharing knowledge, gives practice in negotiating differences, elevates confidence, decreases cheating, and increases the enjoyment of the course and subject matter.[1] Cooperation and teamwork have become almost a staple in the modern business community as well. "Competition is more likely among different teams and companies rather than within the home team or parent company. Yet there is little in the standard academic curriculum that prepares students to work harmoniously and productively in teams of peers with shared goals" (Zimbardo et al., 2003, p. 102). Cooperative college examinations teach individuals how to do this.

Specifics on how to implement cooperative examinations include:

o   Introduce the concept of cooperative examinations and stress the social and intellectual values; however, give the student the option of taking the test alone or with a fellow classmate;

o   Allow the student to take the examination with the classmate of his/her choice;

o   Encourage discussion of questions during the test;

o   Suggest for the students to use an agreed upon test-taking strategy other than relying on their notes or the texts;

o   Encourage the students not to divide the work in half because when one partner cannot recall the answer to a question from his or her half of the material, she or he cannot rely on the other team member for an educated answer;

o   Encourage the students to fully discuss their differences before agreeing on the best answer.

In addition to the direct benefits to the learner in college, as implied above, this technique is suggested for other reasons. Today most sports, companies, and business settings require cooperative teamwork. The following discussion on coaching amplifies this perspective.

Adult Interpersonal Skill Development
Considering adult interpersonal skill development, it's not so much that there has not been any previous learning. Rather, these earlier skills about how to deal with relationships need to be modified or replaced in order to cope with new, adult realities. This is not easy to do because what has enabled the individual to achieve as much as she or he has so far has been these earlier developments. These can be called "survivor skills;" these templates or schemas have helped us to survive horrible parenting, relationship problems in school, and other emotional potholes as we were growing up.

Unfortunately, there are many areas in our adult life where we have to either learn anew or adapt social skills developed during our childhood. Some of the more obvious are: entering into the military environment and having to learn the protocols of interacting in a hierarchically organized world, which has its own unique structure; being promoted in the corporate world beyond the individual skill level, such as becoming a foreman or supervisor or an executive; cross-cultural training for work in the State Department, where new protocols are necessary to learn based upon the country of assignment. It is not sufficient to simply learn the language of the nation we are visiting as tourists, we also need to learn the unique cultural patterns in order to adapt to the required interpersonal relational issues and accepted ways of interacting. These ways overlap with all manner of social skills, including gender interaction, eating habits and protocols, conversations between peers and those considered in different social strata, etc. Within the military there are courses in leadership development, mission planning, etc. In the corporate world there are courses in coaching. In many instances they represent the counterpart in the civilian world for military leadership development. In clinical practice, changing the ways to relate with others is a central focus to adjustment for clients. Reframing relationships, for example, could involve role-playing with an empty chair, or guided imagery to deal with an inner child, etc.

All of these require Far Term Transfer expertise, which means schema development at a meta-domain level. As an example, the instances where we can get in trouble easily on a diplomatic scale are when we assume that other nations do things the same way that we do. When we travel to England for example, we assume that because we seem to speak the same language (although the British would deny this and with some justification) that the only difference is that they have this peculiar habit of driving on the left side of the road. We have no appreciation unless we are forced to think about the fact that their historical traditions, which we in the United States have purposely grown away from, have yielded and maintained a culture, which is still much different from our own. These cultural issues are magnified of course manifold when we visit countries having different languages and religions from our own.

In this discussion, we illustrate available strategies using the military and corporate worlds. We start with details on corporate coaching. There are many different approaches to coaching; but they all have in common the concept of mentoring in order to accomplish change individually and/or organizationally. The focus is on interpersonal skill development. Basically, ask the questions: Do we have a shared vision for our organization? Are our roles clear within this vision? Are we being as productive as possible to reach the goals we set in our competitive world? If the answers are, "No," what changes need to be made?

Masterful coaching
According to Hargrove (2000), who is the architect of what is called "masterful coaching," coaching belongs at the center of all management. It is the basis for producing "*extraordinary* results in your business with colleagues amid change, complexity, and competition" (Hargrove, 2000, p. 8). Moreover, it encompasses everything that you as a leader do in running your business. Masterful coaching is not to accomplish the ordinary. Hargrove's goal for coaching is to help make leaders turn the impossible into the possible. "If you ask people what they are interested in doing and then give them the tools and encouragement to try it, they will come back with something extraordinary" (Hargrove, 1995, p.282).

An example of the application of Hargrove's ideas (1995) is contained in the "pull" approach for leadership development. The sequence of events has:

o   People declaring for the future (e.g., using personal and collective aspirations);
o   Identifying their own gaps (e.g., where they need learning); and
o   The coach providing the stimulus to ignite the learning process (e.g., teaching key attitudes and skills and having daily coaching conversations).

A number of practical exercises are provided in the Masterful Coaching Field book in order to accomplish these goals at various levels of the organization. Hargrove lists 10 rules for business consulting in the new economy. These are designed to help the coach and the organizational leadership stay focused on transformation to enable the organization to succeed (Hargrove, 2000, pp. 60-71).

1. "Keep the coaching conversational" (Managers need to rid themselves of hierarchical attitudes and keep the conversation two-way.).
2. "Use face to face, phone, and e-mail communication" (Use multiple means to sustain communication; don't be limited by face-to-face.).
3. "Focus on mind-set first, techniques second" (Shift thinking from efficiency to the creation of relationships. Behavior change will follow.).
4. "Shift knowledge workers to higher level thinking tasks and work products" (do not require talented knowledge workers to continue performing routine, repetitive tasks.).
5. "Create virtual mastermind groups and coach people on how to think and interact" (Juxtapose multiple perspectives, talents to increase creative possibilities.).
6. "Employ a breakthrough strategy, not just improvement technique" (See above "pull" sequence.).
7. "Create robust feedback loops" (Brainstorm with the group to create different kinds of quality feedback loops.).
8. "Expect something new from everyone."
9. "Coach customers to solve problems for themselves."
10. "Make sure that all processes are capable of just-in-time delivery" (Give people a view of the entire process, and simplify to reduce handoffs, eliminate waste, and ensure that products can be delivered to customers on a just in time basis.).

Other coaching approaches seem to focus more on the individual, who may be either a fast rising star in need of developing interpersonal skills for new managerial levels, or the person who needs remediational coaching almost as a last resort in order to retain her or his job.

One quality example is the Leadership Development Program at the University of Maryland's National Leadership Institute (NLI). NLI is a satellite organization of the nationally recognized Center for Creative Leadership in Research Triangle, North Carolina. Coaches complete training themselves; and evaluations are an integral part of the process of quality control over all the NLI activities.

Coaching Sequence at The National Leadership Institute

1. Assessment (completion of the number of testing instruments and extensive biographical inventory).
2. Training (participation in a structured, week's activities at the University) to include:

- Review of test results,
- Team building exercises,
- Synthesis/feedback coaching,
- Individual Development Plan (short term realistic goals and means to attain and measure progress in a two week period).
3.   Opportunity for follow-up coaching.

Military Leadership Development
Interpersonal skill learning is an integral part of the U.S. Army's leadership development program. For one example, the Non-commissioned Officers Educational System with the guidance of Field Manual 6-22, "Army Leadership," follows a program covering the development of interpersonal skills, including mentoring, coaching, and counseling. Recommendations have been made by the Army Training and Leader Development Panel (ATLDP Report (NCO), Final Report April 2, 2002), to improve it further for the transformed Army of the 21st century. Similar portions of officers' leadership development courses exist and their further development has also been recommended by the ATLDP in a companion Report (2001).

SECTION II:

SUPPORTING RESEARCH

As noted earlier in the Introduction to his chapter, the social cognitive theory proposed by Albert Bandura (1986, 2001) is supportive of our ideas on the process requirements of the interpersonal domain. A triadic model was proposed by Bandura (1986, 2001) to explain the interaction between the three domains in the development of the social self: Personal, Behavioral, and Environmental.

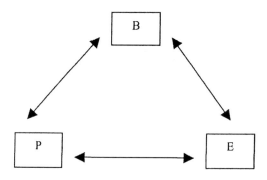

Figure 5.1. Bandura's Triadic Model

This model of *reciprocal determinism* involves "personal factors in the form of cognitive, affective, and biological events, behavioral patterns, and environmental events that all operate as interacting determinants that influence each other bidirectionally" (Bandura, 2001, p. 266). Bandura (2001) uses the term "reciprocal" to represent the mutual action between potentially causal factors. "Determinism" is used to signify the production of effects by certain factors. The complexities that may arise in his proposed reciprocity are indicated by his assertion that the strength of any causal relation will depend on the particular activities and circumstances. He cites the interdependence using the example of television watching. Personal choice determines the specific televised environment and separates it from the potentially identical one for all. Those of us, who surf the channels end up at different spots if we prefer football, drama, or the news. Secondly, within each of the factors, Behavioral, Personal, or Environmental, the reciprocal nature of influences also applies. Thus frightening thoughts can in turn produce internal stimuli, which can in turn, produce even more frightening thoughts (Bandura, 1986). All of these factors are needed to create an effect.

Similarly, Vygotsky (1978, 1997) proposed that patterns of thinking are not primarily innate, rather are products learned and practiced in social institutions of culture. The genesis and structure of mental processes are culturally and historically developed. Vgotsky believed that a child acquires knowledge and skills on a social level and on an individual level. They must first acquire the knowledge from a teacher, parent, or peer; then, they apply that knowledge as their own. Children transform their "spontaneous concepts," or intuitive ideas, to logically defined and highly structured "scientific concepts" through social interaction with others. Through the modeling and feedback of adults and peers, children learn more advanced, higher-order thinking.

Therefore, as discussed, pro-social skills are acquired through the process of social learning. However, inappropriate social skills, such as aggression, can also be learned through the process of social learning. Violence is a problem that we deal with at all ages, with both genders, and with all racial groups. The accessibility of guns, violence against children in schools and homes, and the widespread exposure to violent entertainment media contribute to the high level of violence and aggression in our society. There are many theories out there to describe the processes involved in the acquisition of aggression, including the social learning theory, as well as, cognitive neo-association, script, excitation transfer, and social interactionist theories.

Berkowitz (1989) proposed that aversive events produce negative effect. This negative affect stimulates various thoughts, memories, and physiological responses associated with fight and flight tendencies. This, in turn, gives rise to feelings of anger or fear. The cognitive neo-association theory suggests that these aggressive thoughts, emotions, and behavioral tendencies are linked together in memory. In another theory, it is suggested that scripts are learned then formed in one's mind to define a situation. When exposed to similar situations at later times, the script theory proposes that the individual behaves according to the pre-formed scripts. Aggressive scripts are acquired from observation of violence in the mass media and aggressive behavior stimulates the observation of media violence (Huesmann, 1986). Huesmann suggests that certain cues in the media may trigger the activation of aggressive scripts and thus stimulate aggressive behavior. The excitation transfer theory (Zillmann, 1983), as discussed in Chapter 4, suggests that physiological arousals are misattributed to a second event when two events are separated by a short period of time. When the event is related to anger, the additional arousal will make the individual angrier. This theory also suggests that angered feelings continue over longer periods of time if the individual attributes the heightened arousal to anger. After the arousal ends, the individual remains aggressive as long as the anger persists. The social interactionist theory (Tedeschi & Felson, 1994) suggests that the individual makes the choice to be aggressive in order to gain expected rewards or to obtain a different outcome. Social interaction and situational factors are a major concern in this theory. The aggressive acts are motivated by a goal. For example, the act of punishment is intended to produce the proximate outcome of harm, which is a result of the motive, which could be justice, status, or deterrence.

Anderson and Bushman (2002) have suggested a sensible approach to unify the theories proposed above. Using the general aggression model, Anderson and Bushman suggest that cognition, affect, and arousal mediate the effects of situational and personal variables on aggression. We would propose that personal variables operate maximally during the Acquisition phase. Personal variables include the things that the individual brings to the situation that also have been influenced by the environment and the individuals to whom they are exposed. These include traits, gender, beliefs, attitudes, values, long-term goals, and scripts. Situational variables include aggressive cues, provocation, frustration, pain and discomfort, drugs, and incentives. Key features of this theory "include the ideas that knowledge structures: develop out of experience; influence perception at multiple levels, from basic visual patterns to complex behavioral sequences; can become automatized with use; can contain affective states, behavioral programs, and beliefs; and are used to guide people's interpretations and behavioral responses to their social environment" (Anderson & Bushman, 2002, p. 33). This most nearly approximates the Automaticity phase of our proposed learning processes. Repeated exposure to certain factors can produce certain behaviors, such as aggression, and these long-term effects result from the knowledge structures that have been produced, and transfer to other similar and even novel situations.

Crick and Dodge (1994) propose a social processing model of human performance and social exchange. Their model is consistent with our view on the "development of templates" as we grow up. As we develop, we are influenced in our information processing by the ways in which we see our adult figures relating to the environment. This process helps us formulate, consciously and unconsciously, sets of rules, schemas, images, heuristics, etc. through which we filter and act upon new information. The information-processing model is neutral with respect to the types and intensities of reactions, which result from the filtering process. These are based upon our experiences up to the point of receiving new information. In agreement with the Freudians, and the "early experience" theorists, a lot of it takes place and gets set through the first five years. Modifications are made at various critical points in our developmental history; typically puberty, new schools, leaving high school, going away from home, trying to make it on your own, etc.

Acquisition Process

Interpersonal development can be traced to infancy, with the influences of mother and father including holding, fondling, talking, and emoting to and with the infant. With this, we have the beginning of interactions and interdependence among cognitive, motor, psychomotor, and affective domains. Bowlby (1969/1982) proposed the attachment theory, which stated that all infants form enduring emotional bonds (attachments) with their caregivers. Basically, this is how the initial social elements are acquired and initial habits formed, the Acquisition phase. These attachments form mental representations that become the basis for all future relationships and social interactions. Ainsworth et al. (1978) proposed two categories of attachment: secure attachment and insecure/anxious attachment (anxious-avoidant and anxious ambivalent). In secure attachment, the infant is comfortable in the mother's presence and explores their environment. The infant becomes distressed by the mother's absence but is comforted by her return. This attachment produces self-confident, self-soothing individuals who believe in relationships. Anxious-avoidant attachment involves an infant who is indifferent to the mother's presence and may or may not respond to the mothers' absence. Infants in this category are as easily comforted by a stranger than they are by their mother. Long-term patterns of relationships include avoidance of intimacy, fear of dependence, lack of trust in others, and low faith in relationships. An anxious-ambivalent infant is anxious in the mother's presence and has difficulty engaging in play or exploration. They become quite distressed in the mother's absence and are not comforted by the mother upon her return. Long term patterns include the desire and fear of intimacy, overly close but overly far reactions, extreme dependence or independence, lack of trust in others, and low faith in relationships. These attachments and behaviors are a result of the caretakers' behaviors and emotions toward their children.

The theories of Bowlby and Ainsworth have contributed to the understanding of the development of social behaviors and have sparked further research in this area of attachment organization. Their theories are consistent with our own template notions mentioned above, in that the early authority figures (usually Mom and Dad) provide the bases for future relationships by their approaches to bonding, providing intimacy experiences, etc. Piaget (1937) proposed that intelligence is a form of adaptation, wherein knowledge is constructed by each individual through the two complimentary processes of assimilation and accommodation. He theorized that as children interact with their physical and social environments, they organize information into groups of interrelated ideas called "schemes." When children encounter something new, they must either assimilate it into an existing scheme or create an entirely new scheme to deal with it (Wadsworth, 1996). This theoretical approach would seem to apply equally well to interpersonal scheme development as to cognitive learning; and the interpersonal schemes are aided by the modeling and mimicking process described above by social learning theory. "Schemes" and "schemas" would seem to be interchangeable without loss of meaning.

Similarly, Sternberg's notion of socialization is consistent with this view. Sternberg (1988) defines socialization as "the interaction between the social environment and the way an individual develops as a person" (p. 250). His approach highlights that socialization processes affect intelligence and its development. The purpose of this chapter is to describe how one learns to socialize (or to develop this social intelligence) and how this affects the educational process. Sternberg (1988) draws on evidence across cultures to support the notion that intelligence is a product of socialization. Parents "raise their children to be intelligent in accordance with their conception of what it means for a child to be intelligent" (p. 251). However, each community seeks to develop the intelligence of their children differently. The motivations, values, experiences, strategies, and resources may differ cross-culturally.

Child-care experiences are examples of community development of these social skills, and have a lasting effect on children's social competence and social intelligence. There have been various claims on the effects of daycare environments based on research with limited variables of time, age, or quality being considered. For example, some findings show that there is a negative correlation with pro-social behavior and being in daycare (DiLalla, 1998); others have shown that daycare has a positive effect on the child's social skills (Field, 1991); and some show that there is no effect, suggesting that in-home and out-of-home care produces similar social skills (Howes, Matheson, & Hamilton, 1994). DiLalla (1998) found that "children who experienced little or no daycare were more likely to behave pro-socially, suggesting that daycare may actually inhibit socialization for some children" (p. 223). However, the results may be inaccurate because in DiLalla's study, there was no control for the quality of daycare.

Field (1991), however, in a more comprehensive study, examined both the amount of time children are placed in daycare and the quality of the daycare that they attend. She found that the amount of time spent in full-time daycare was positively correlated with the number of friends and extracurricular activities. The time spent in daycare was positively correlated to the parents' ratings of the children's emotional well-being, leadership, popularity, attractiveness, and assertiveness and negatively correlated with aggression. Field (1991) also found that the children who spent "more time in high-quality daycare showed more physical affection during peer interactions, were more often assigned to the gifted programs, and received higher math grades" (p. 863). Howes et al. (1994) attempted to look at the relation of the maternal attachment (based on Bowlby's attachment theory, 1969) to social competence in peers and instead, found that children new to child-care at 4 years of age did not appear different in peer behaviors and maternal attachment quality than children with more child-care experience.

A recent report concerned secondary data analysis from 3 large-scale studies concerning child-care quality (Burchinal et al., 2000). It provides some insight into the questions about the timing of intervention, quality related to poverty level or minority ethnic background, and how well all of these variables predicted child development in terms of cognitive and social outcomes. First, they report that two of the most successful programs that provided full-time child-care were started during infancy. The studies in the subject of their report included children who were one to two years prior to entering kindergarten. Moreover, "... the highest quality care, the public preschool care, was provided to eligible children for less than one year and the next highest quality care, Headstart, was part-time care provided nine months per year..." (Burchinal et al., 2000, p. 163). Despite these limitations, the results of this analysis revealed that childcare quality was related to the incidence of behavior problems; i.e. better quality care resulted in fewer behavior problems, confirming the 1991 Field study results. Overall, the results supported the view that, "...good quality care is important for all children and may be especially important for children of ethnic minority groups" (Burchinal et al., 2000, p. 163). Secondly, even though the programs contained in this report were part-time or one year programs and did not show the large effects observed in the early intervention programs (the Abecedarian Project, or the Infant Health and Development Program), "...good-quality child-care programs do appear to enhance developmental outcomes for the enrolled to children whereas poor quality care may be detrimental to their development" (Burchinal et al., 2000, p. 163).

Campbell, Lamb, and Hwang (2000) performed an even more comprehensive study and found that it is the age the child enters, the amount of time in, and the quality of the daycare that shapes the child's social skills. Their results confirmed those of Field (1991) and support the position that daycare can be beneficial to the child's social development. The results suggest "that social competence with peers, as observed in out-of-home care settings, begins to stabilize at around 3 ½ years of age. Prior to this age, the amount of time spent in out-of-home care and the quality of early home and out-of-home care may play an important role in shaping the children's social skills" (Campbell et al., 2000, p. 174).

In conclusion, experiences in daycare early in life do influence social competence. In the interaction with different children of all ages, genders, and racial and cultural backgrounds and the supervision of caretakers, a child can learn a variety of social skills. These experiences may foster individual differences that remain stable through childhood and adolescence. This experience reflects again the point made earlier that children's attachments develop, from parents to daycare, as enduring emotional bonds with caregivers.

Automaticity Process

As the child moves to the Automaticity phase, these attachments become the basis for initial, conditioned social behaviors. These primary attachments, (we would say associations) whether secure or insecure, lay the foundation for adolescent developments and refinements. For example, Allen et al. (2000) found that security in attachment predicted relative increases in social skills and insecure-preoccupied attachment organization predicted increasing delinquency during ages 16 through

18 years. Allen, Marsh, McFarland, McElhaney, Land, Jodl, and Peck (2002) examined adolescent attachment organization as a predictor of the development of social skills and delinquent behavior during mid-adolescence. We began this discussion on attachment in the Acquisition section. Insecure adolescents, who dismiss attachment relationships, are often more likely to display conduct disorders. Insecure avoidance teens have been found to have conduct problems in infancy and childhood. Preoccupied teens interacting with highly autonomous mothers showed greater relative decreases in skill levels and increases in delinquent activity.

Attachment organization also appears to moderate the influence of other primary development processes on social functioning. An example is the increase in autonomy in adolescent-parent interactions. This is susceptible to disruption by attachment insecurity. "Increasing autonomy of adolescence may threaten preoccupied adolescents, lead them to dysfunctional anger, and then release controls on their behavior" (Allen et al., 2000, p. 58). Adolescents' levels of social problem-solving skills are negatively correlated with delinquency. Relevant at this point is the previously mentioned importance (see page 6 of this chapter) of the relational self noted by Andersen and Chen (2002). The relational self has inherent in it the notion of social identity and group commitment based upon the interactions and their salience as the individual grows. This would be in agreement with the position taken in the review by Ellemers, Spears, and Doosje (2002): "The impact of social groups on the way people see themselves and others around them cannot be understood without taking into consideration the broader social context in which they function" (p. 164-165).

Near Term Transfer Process

As discussed earlier, pro-social skills can be acquired through the process of social learning and early pro-social behavior contributes to children's development in academic and social domains. Pro-socialness (cooperating, helping, sharing, and consoling) had a strong positive impact on later academic achievement and social preferences in a study done by Caprara, Barbaranelli, Pastorelli, Bandura, and Zimbardo (2000). They found that pro-social behaviors measured in early childhood were good predictors of academic achievement and peer relations in adolescence five years later. Others (Hinshaw, 1992) have found that engagement in aggressive behaviors, including proneness to verbal and physical aggression, detracted from developing academically by undermining intellectual pursuits and creating socially-isolating situations.

Dalton, Sundblad, and Hylbert (1973) investigated the effects of social learning on the acquisition and transfer of accurate and empathic understanding. Those who were involved in a modeled-learning experience, which consisted of an advance organizer, modeled interviewing session, and covert practice session, displayed a significantly higher level of functioning in the communication of empathy and these differences were maintained overtime. The two other groups, who either received no instruction, or were given reading material about counseling behaviors, did not display high levels of understanding of empathy. The results of this study further support the view that our observations of others and their behaviors can provide a model for better understanding, learning, and transfer of social skills.

Ashwin (2003) investigated the approaches to studying and academic outcomes of students who participated in study group of peers, "Peer Support," when controlling for prior levels of academic achievement. He found that attendance at "Peer Support" sessions was positively and significantly correlated to academic performance. The idea of peer learning refers to "situations where students support each other in educational settings" (Ashwin, 2003, p. 159). Ashwin based his approach of "Peer Support" on Supplemental Instruction (SI), which was first developed at the University of Missouri, Kansas City in 1973 (Blanc et al., 1983). This also took place outside the mainstream curriculum and was voluntary. It consisted of a peer facilitator to structure the discussion and those students involved who took an active part in providing material for the discussion. The research suggested that SI users received higher grades than those who did not participate even when previous academic achievement, ethnicity, and double-exposure to course material was controlled for (Congos & Schoeps, 1993).

Ashwin (2003) extended the research on peer learning to first year students in an inner-city college over a school year in Chemistry and Pure Mathematics and Statistics classes. Once again, the groups were voluntary and took place during the free time of the students. Ashwin examined the relationship between students' previous academic performance and their levels of attendance at Peer Support, the students' approaches to studying before and after Peer Support, and the interaction between the students and Peer Supporters (leaders of the group). During the groups, the students concentrated on discussing how to answer past examination questions. He found that academic performance significantly increased and there was not a significant correlation between students' prior academic performance and attendance at Peer Support. Students adopted less meaning oriented approaches to studying; however, Ashwin suggested that this change in approach was not an indicator that quality fell, but a response to an increased awareness of the demands of the course and a more strategic approach to learning. The interaction between the students developed over time and improved as the students became more comfortable with the setting and situation. Those students reluctant to talk in the beginning became more willing to discuss, and those that were more forthcoming became tolerant with those who were slower to catch on. A sense of how to work with other individuals was developed. Ashwin's (2003) study showed that "at all levels of ability, the more Peer Support sessions attended, the better they performed in their end of year examination" (p. 167).

In the training field, these effects were demonstrated by Army trainees in learning to repair electronics where the faster students were required as part of the criterion of learning to train a slower student (Weingarten et al., 1972). Secondly, in learning the tasks of a supply clerk, Hagman (1986) found that, requiring students to practice in study groups of 2 or 4, where none of the group could advance to the next part of the course until all members of the group passed the interim tests resulted in superior course performance than having students work alone. The students also expressed a liking for this approach. The research suggests therefore that working with peers in a study group improves learning, may prevent negative attitudes to studying, and helps students better organize their study methods.

Considering social learning in a broader sense, Vaughan and Rogers' research (2000) demonstrates the value of entertainment-education as a communication medium, which can influence cultural change by starting with the individual's attitude shift, and broadening to interpersonal, pro-social skill developments. Vaughan and Rogers proposed a staged model to explain how communication messages have effects on individual behavior. They first observed the effects of an entertainment-education radio soap opera in Tanzania. Then they synthesized the ideas of the hierarchy-of-effects (HOE) model proposed by McGuire (1989), the stages-of-change (SOC) model proposed by Prochaska and others (1992), Bandura's social learning theory (1977, 1997), and the diffusion of innovations (DOI) by Rogers (1995). Their synthesis resulted in a six-staged model of communication effects that provides a useful framework for understanding the effects of an entertainment-education program and promotes progress in family planning methods.

Before discussing Vaughan and Roger's model, we give a brief description of the models that it was based on. The HOE model assumes "that a linear sequence of events begins with exposure to a mass communication campaign's messages, leading to knowledge of the message, which in turn leads to attitude change concerning the message content, which influences the individual's intention to change behavior, and ultimately to a change in overt behavior" (Vaughan & Rogers, 2000, p. 204). The problem with this model is that the impact for change is higher at the top of this hierarchy and as one steps down the hierarchy, the overt behavior change is minimal. SOC is a five-step model of change that was initially developed for individual behavior changes in addictive behaviors. Step 1 is "precontemplation," in which the individual is unaware of the need to change; Step 2 is "contemplation," in which the individual becomes aware of the problem and weighs the pros and cons of changing the behavior; Step 3 is "preparation," in which the decides to make a change; Step 4 is "action" in which the individual actively engages in the change; and Step 5 is "maintenance," the adoption of the behavior change. The individual can cycle through the SOC several times before successful completion of a behavior change. The social learning theory suggests that individuals can learn new behaviors by observing others' behaviors. The social learning theory process in positively reinforced by observing the benefits of the model's behavior and negatively reinforcing when observing behavior that results in a disadvantage. "Observation of the model by an individual thus serves as a vicarious trial-and-error of the new behavior for the observer" (Vaughan & Rogers, 2000, p. 206). Lastly, the DOI suggests that the adoption of a new idea is developed through "social networks of interpersonal communication" in a five-stage "innovation-decision process."

After considering the theories discussed above, Vaughan and Rogers (2000) suggested six stages of behavior change: precontemplation, contemplation, preparation, validation, action and maintenance. Their model "includes both cognitive and affective processes in the internal state of the individual, and interpersonal communication processes in the external environment of the individual" (Vaughan & Rogers, 2000, p. 208-09). The exposure to entertainment-education radio soap opera is the prerequisite for change. During Stage 1, precontemplation, the individual is unaware of the family planning methods or finds it irrelevant. At this point, he or she is exposed to the radio soap opera, which leads to recognizing and understanding the educational content as well as identifying with the characters. The outcome of the second stage, contemplation, "is a change in attitude as the individual forms a positive attitude toward the innovation of family planning and believes that the message is beneficial to people like themselves" (Vaughan & Rogers, 2000, p. 210). This is achieved by weighing the pros and cons of the innovation, by observing the benefits of pro-social behaviors of the characters and punishments for antisocial behaviors of characters, by identifying with or empathizing with a character on the program. During Stage 3, preparation, the individual starts to believe in the positive aspects of family planning and their ability to do so. He or she decides to adopt the innovation. Stage 4, validation, involves the interpersonal communication of family planning with their partner and the discussion each others' opinions. At Stage 5, action, the individual seeks outside help in their behavior change. This could involve communicating with a service provider to obtain contraceptives and literature. These behaviors are modeled on the show. The final stage, maintenance, "is achieved when an individual (1) consistently uses the new idea advocated by communication messages, and (2) recognizes the benefits of the innovation in his or her life" (Vaughan & Rogers, 2000, p. 211) through their experiences with family planning methods.

Far Term Transfer Process

So as noted above, learning to interact with others using social rules or schemata could influence how you see yourself as a person, emotionally, and cognitively as well. Successes or failures when acting according to your digested rules for interacting, like dating, or working in class, could have such an effect. Without repeating our earlier discussion in any depth of the value and effect of the application of Bandura's social learning principles in the media, we do wish to note that his research has shown cross-cultural benefits. In addition, the work of Andersen and Chen (2002) described briefly in Section I, both supports and extends the implications of Bandura and others regarding the development of self based on observation and modeling. Their research suggests that the templates we develop as children, the self in relation to significant others, form the basis for future interactions. New persons are seen as representations of previous ones through the process of "transference." In one paradigm, for example, participants were first asked to provide descriptors of significant others (SO). Next, they were asked to list adjectives that were irrelevant to those significant others (SO). They were then given sentences about a new person which were derived from the descriptive sentences for the significant others along with some filler sentences (the resemblance condition). These were compared with other participants where the sentences were derived from other people's sentences and therefore bore no relationship to their own SO. The research based on this paradigm "...has shown that participants in the resemblance condition report higher recognition-memory confidence about having been exposed to descriptors that had not actually been presented, but that do characterize their significant other, as compared with participants in the non-resemblance condition" (Andersen & Chen, 2002, p. 629). The authors report that numerous studies have yielded such inference-memory phenomena, including whether the SO had positive or negative characterizations, and could not be reduced to stereotype interpretations. The data show clearly that a new person will be evaluated, liked or disliked, based upon, similarities to a positively regarded SO or to a negatively regarded SO. Other studies, presenting stimuli subliminally, reveal that the transference occurs unconsciously. Still others show that facial expressions, when participants are reading descriptors of SO, positive or negatively regarded, reveal their emotional reactions in facial expressions. In their review of studies concerned with the development of automaticity and the role that it plays in our navigating efficiently through life, Bargh and Chartrand (1999) reveal how stereotyping can develop when individuals receive a blow to their self-esteem in the form of negative feedback. In the studies, the results supported the inference that, "...the threat to self-esteem put into motion a goal to denigrate others that was so automatic and efficient and its working better produce stereotyping of a minority group under attention-overload conditions, in which manifestations of stereotyping are normally not obtained" (p. 470). So the failure experience or negative feedback to one's self-esteem can automatically set off "...a well rehearsed goal and plan to restore the sense of self-worth. Unfortunately it comes at the expense of others" (p. 470). While we do not intend to treat the topic of stereotypes in this chapter (racial, ethnic, or otherwise), we simply note that these also follow the same developmental learning phases through automaticity and can also be influenced by instructional techniques.

Meyer (1996) has developed an Implicit Rules Model to explain "...how individuals acquire and store knowledge that allows them to adapt a request to communication-relevant situational features" (p. 582). Her model concerns the development of social schemas in situations where an individual makes a request to have another individual change his or her behavior. Her research takes into account four variables: the personality of the individual being communicated to (cooperative or disagreeable), the nature of the request, the rights of the communicator (either I have no right to ask this or I am entitled to ask this), the perceived resistance to change (high or low), and benefits to the listener for changing (high or low). The results demonstrate that social schemas do in fact develop, both with near term transfer implications (situational dependence) as well as far term transfer relevance (situational independence).

Adult Interpersonal Skill Development
The U.S. Army Research Institute (ARI) has been conducting research for many years to help the Army identify characteristics of effective leaders and thereby to make suggestions and recommendations for improving leadership development. (e.g., Fiedler, 1995; Jaques et al., 1986). At the 3 and 4-star General Officer levels,

the requirement for an international perspective with the accompanying understanding of cultural differences was found. Coaching and mentoring were recognized as essential elements of long-term development of leaders.

More recently, ARI has embarked upon research to study military leadership with a focus "on experience based, practically relevant knowledge...tacit knowledge" (Hedlund, Sternberg, & Psotka, 2000, p. 1). The work has been an attempt to extend the research of Sternberg and his associates (e.g., Sternberg, et al, 2000) from the civilian domain of real-world performance to that of the military. Scenarios have been designed to illustrate practical, difficult problems faced by battalion commanders, company commanders, and platoon leaders, and then to use these in a collaborative learning environment as teaching tools in order to enhance leadership skill development. Preliminary results (Lochbaum, Streeter, & Psotka, 2002) indicated that this approach has been valuable as a means of improving perceptions of better ways to deal with leadership situations; and by creating virtual groups through the use of on-line discussion, results can be much more representative for all individuals' participation, as opposed to face to face group meetings where one or two persons might dominate.

Conclusion

Interpersonal learning is a powerful and pervasive process that starts from birth, or perhaps in utero. Formal education needs to be aware of and capitalize on this process if students are to achieve. Bandura's efforts and those of others, such as Andersen and Chen and associates, have shown clearly that observation, modeling, and relating to significant others are the building blocks of templates that shape our development.

As Andersen and Chen (2002) note, "...transference occurs by means of the activation of mental representations of significant others, which accordingly evokes the associated self-with-significant other—or the relational self...It suggests that significant others are crucial to self-definition and its vicissitudes as well as to affective and motivational experience, self-regulation, and interpersonal behavior" (p. 638). The challenging task for education and training is to capitalize on this knowledge by building curricula that take advantage of the positive templates or schemas and sidestep the negative ones in order to aid the learner to maximize her/his achievement.

ENDNOTES

[1] The reader is cautioned that the research as reported to date is very preliminary and needs to be further developed. For example, it is unclear whether the improvement is confined to performance on the specific exam, or generalizes to greater understanding of the subject matter domain to be learned. We provide the information because it has received such widespread publicity; therefore, we feel obligated to inform the reader.

REFERENCES

Adams, D. M. & Hamm, M. E. (1990). *Cooperative learning: Critical thinking and collaboration across the curriculum.* Springfield, IL: Charles C. Thomas Publisher.

Ainsworth, M., Blehar, M. C., Waters, E., & Wall, S. (1978). *Patterns of attachment: A psychological study of the strange situation.* Oxford, England: Lawrence Erlbaum.

Allen, J. P, Marsh, P., McFarland, C., McElhaney, K. B., Land, D. J., Jodl, K. M., & Peck, S. (2002). Attachment and autonomy as predictors of the development of social skills and delinquency during midadolescence. *Journal of Consulting and Clinical Psychology, 70*(1), 56-66.

Anderson, C. A. & Bushman, B. J. (2002). Human aggression. *Annual Review of Psychology, 53,* 27-51.

Anderson, S. M. & Chen, S. (2002). The relational self: An interpersonal social-cognitive theory. *Psychological Review, 109*(4), 619-645.

Army Training and Leader Development Panel Reports on the Noncommissioned Officer (NCO) Study. Retrieved July 31, 2003, from http://www.army.mil/features/ATLDPNCO/default.htm.

Ashwin, P. (2003). Peer support: Relations between the context, process and outcomes for the students who are supported. *Instructional Science: An International Journal of Learning and Cognition, 31*(3), 159-173.

Bandura, A. (1977). *Social learning theory.* Englewood Cliffs, NJ: Prentice Hall.

Bandura, A. (1986). *Social foundations of thought and action: A social cognitive theory.* Englewood Cliffs, NJ: Prentice-Hall, Inc.

Bandura, A. (1997). *Self-efficacy: The exercise of control.* New York: Freeman.

Bandura, A. (2001). Social cognitive theory of mass communication. *Media Psychology, 3,* 265-299.

Bargh, J. A. & Chartrand, T. L. (1999), The unbearable automaticity of being. *American Psychologist, 54*(7), 462-479.

Berkowitz, L. (1989). Frustration-aggression hypothesis: Examination and reformulation. *Psychological Bulletin, 106,* 59-73.

Blanc, R. A., DeBuhr, L. E. & Martin, D.C. (1983). Breaking the attrition cycle: The effects of supplemental instruction on undergraduate performance and attrition. *Journal of Higher Education, 54,* 80-90.

Bowlby, J. (1982). *Attachment and loss: Volume 1.* New York: Basic Books. (Original work published in 1969).

Borba, M. (2003). *No more misbehavin': 38 difficult behaviors and how to stop them.* New York: Jossey-Bass Inc., Publishers.

Bradley, R. H., Corwyn, R. F., Burchinal, M., McAdoo, H. P., & Coll, C. G. (2001). The home environments of children in the United States, Part II: Relations with behavioral development through age thirteen. *Child Development, 72*(6), 1868-1886.

Burchinal, M. R., Peisner-Feinberg, E., Bryant, D. M., & Clifford, R. (2000). Children's social and cognitive development and child-care quality: Testing for differential associations related to poverty, gender, or ethnicity. *Applied Developmental Science, 4*(3), 149-165.

Campbell, J. J., Lamb, M. E., & Hwang, C. P. (2000). Early child-care experiences and children's social competence between 1 ½ and 15 years of age. *Applied Developmental Science, 4*(3), 166-175.

Caprara, G. V., Barbaranelli, C., Pastorelli, C., Bandura, A., & Zimbardo, P. G. (2000). Prosocial foundations of children's academic achievement. *Psychological Science*, 11(4), 302-306.

Congos, D. H. & Schoeps, N. (1993). Does Supplemental Instruction really work and what is it anyway? *Studies in Higher Education, 18,* 165-176.

Crary, E. (1996a). *I can't wait.* Seattle, WA: Parenting Press, Inc.

Crary, E. (1996b). *I want to play.* Seattle, WA: Parenting Press, Inc.

Crary, E. (1996c). *I want it.* Seattle, WA: Parenting Press, Inc.

Crary, E. (1996d). *Mommy don't go.* Seattle, WA: Parenting Press, Inc.

Crick, N. R. & Dodge, K. A. (1994). A review of reformulation of social information-processing mechanisms in children's social adjustment. *Psychological Bulletin, 115*(1), 74-101.

Coleman, W. L. & Lindsay, R. L. (1992). Interpersonal disabilities. Social skills in older children and adolescents: Their description, assessment, and management. *The Pediatric Clinics of North America, 39*(3), 551-567.

Dalton, R. F., Sundblad, L. M., & Hylbert, K. W. (1973). An application of principles of social learning to training in communication of empathy. *Journal of Counseling Psychology, 20*(4), 378-383.

De Vito, D., Shamberg, M., Sher, S. & Dahl, L. (Producers), & De Vito, D. (Director). (1996). *Matilda* [Motion picture]. (Available from Tristar Films. 10202 West Washington Boulevard, Culver City, CA 90232).

DiLalla, L. F. (1998). Daycare, child, and family influences on preschoolers' social behaviors in a peer play setting. *Child Study Journal, 28*, 223-244.

Ellemers, N., Spears, R., & Doosje, B. (2002). Self and social identity. *Annual Review of Psychology, 53*, 161-186.

Field, T. (1991). Quality infant day-care and grade school behavior and performance. *Child Development, 62*, 863-870.

Fiedler, F. E. (1995). Cognitive resources and leadership performance. *Applied psychology: An international review, 44*, 5-28.

Frankel, F. (1996). *Good friends are hard to find: Help your child find, make and keep friends.* Pasadena, CA: Perspective Publishing, Inc.

Gardner, H. (1983). *Frames of mind: The theory of multiple intelligences.* New York: Basic Books.

Gardner, H. (1993). *Multiple Intelligences: The theory in practice.* New York: Basic Books.

Gilmore, W. S. & de la Torre, D. (Producers), & Evans, D. (Director). (1993). *The Sand Lot* [Motion Picture]. (Available from 20th Century Fox, P.O. Box 900, Beverly Hills, CA 90213).

Glazer, B. (Producer) & Zieff, H. (Director). (1991). *My Girl* [Motion Picture]. (Available from Columbia Tristar Home Video, 3500 West Olive Ave., Burbank, CA 91521).

Gut, D. M. & Safran, S. P. (2002). Cooperative learning and social stories: Effective social skills strategies for reading teachers. *Reading & Writing Quarterly, 18*, 87-91.

Guthrie, J. T. & Cox, K. E. (2001). Classroom conditions for motivation and engagement in reading. *Educational Psychology Review, 13*(3), 283-302.

Hagman, J. D. & Hayes, J. F. (1986). *Cooperative learning: Effects of task, reward, and group size on individual achievement* (Technical Rep. 704, January, 1986). Alexandria, VA: US Army Research Institute.

Hargrove, R. (1995). *Masterful coaching.* San Francisco: Jossey-Bass/ Pfeiffer.

Hargrove, R. (2000). *Masterful coaching field book.* San Francisco, CA: Jossey-Bass/Pfeiffer.

Hebert, T. P. & Speirs Neumeister, K. L. (2002). Fostering the social and emotional development of gifted children through guided viewing of film. *Roeper Review, 25*(1), 17-21.

Hedlund, J., Sternberg R., & Psotka, J. (2000). *Tacit knowledge for military leadership: Seeking insight into the acquisition and use of practical knowledge.* U.S. Army research Institute: Technical Report 1105.

Hinshaw, S. P. (1992). Externalizing behavior problems and academic underachievement in childhood and adolescence: Causal relationships and underlying mechanisms. *Psychological Bulletin, 111*(1), 127-155.

Honig, W. K. (Ed.). (1966). *Operant behavior: Areas of research and application.* New York: Meredith Publishing Company.

Howes, C., Matheson, C. C., & Hamilton, C. E. (1994). Maternal, teacher, and child care history correlates of children's relationships with peers. *Child Development, 65*, 264-273.

Huesmann, L. R. (1986). Psychological processes promoting the relation between exposure to media violence and aggressive behavior by the viewer. *Journal of Social Issues, 42*, 125-140.

Jaques, E., Clement, S., Rigby, C., & Jacobs, T. O. (1986, January). Senior leadership performance requirements at the executive level. Research Report for the U. S. Army Research Institute for the Behavioral and Social Sciences, 1420.

Krischanitz, R. (1999). *Nobody likes me.* New York: North-South Books.

Lachner, D. (2000). *Danny, the angry lion.* New York: North-South Books.

Lochbaum, K., Streeter, L., & Psotka, J. (2002). Exploiting technology to harness the power of peers. Presentation at Interservice/Industry Training, Simulation and Education Conference, Orlando, FL, December 2-5, 2002.

Lovell, P. (2001). *Stand tall, Molly Lou Melon.* New York: Penguin Putnam, Inc.

Mastrilli, J. (2003, Spring). Play for balanced living. *Healing Magazine, 8*(1), 12-13.

McClary, A. J. (Producer & Director). (1995). *Annie O.* [Motion Picture]. (Available from Hallmark, 116 N. Robertson, #506, Los Angeles, CA 90048).

McGinnis, E. & Goldstein, A. P. (1997a). *Skillstreaming the elementary school child: New strategies and perspectives for teaching prosocial skills.* Ottawa, ON: Research Press.

McGinnis, E. & Goldstein, A. P. (1997b). *Skillstreaming the adolescent: New strategies and perspectives for teaching prosocial skills.* Ottawa, ON: Research Press.

McGuire, W. J. (1989). Theoretical foundations of campaigns. In R. E. Rice & C. K. Atkin (Eds.), *Public communication campaigns.* Newbury Park, CA: Sage.

Meyer, J. R. (1996). Retrieving knowledge in social situations: A test of the implicit rules model. *Communications Research, 23*(5), 581-611.

Moser, A. (2002). *Don't be a menace on Sundays: The children's antiviolence book.* Kansas City, Missouri: Landmark Publishers.

Munson, D. (2000). *Enemy pie.* San Francisco: Chronicle Books, LLC.

Piaget, J. (1937). *The construction of reality in the child.* New York: Basic Books.

Pincus-Ward, D. (1996). *Manners matter: Activities to teach young people social skills.* Columbus, OH: McGraw-Hill Publishing.

Prochaska, J. O., DiClemente, C. C., & Norcross, J. C. (1992). In search of how people change: Applications of addictive behaviors. *American Psychologist, 47*(9), 1102-1114.

Project ACHIEVE: Project overview and focus on creating a building-based social skills, discipline/behavior management, and school safety system. (1999). Retrieved August 18, 2003, from http://cecp.air.org/teams/greenhouses/projach.pdf.

Rogers, E. M. (1995). *Diffusion of innovations* (4th ed.). New York: Free Press.

Romain, T. (1998). *Cliques, phonies, and other baloney.* Minneapolis, MN: Free Spirit Publishing, Inc.

Rudin, S., Wisnievitz, D., & Hohrberg, W. (Producers), & Zaillian, S. (Director). (1993). *Searching for Bobby Fischer* [Motion Picture]. (Available from Paramount Pictures, Melrose Avenue, Hollywood, CA 90038).

Schroyer, C. J., Hansen, L. A., Pasquale, A. L., & Benedict, M. E. (1990). *Analysis of the 1990 ARI Survey of Employers,* U.S. Army Research Institute Research Report 1573.

Smith, D. (2002). The theory heard 'round the world. *Monitor on Psychology, 33*(9), 30-32.

Sternberg, R. J. (1988) *The triarchic mind: A new theory of human intelligence.* New York: Penguin Books.

Sternberg, R. J., Forsythe, G. B., Hedlund, J., Horvath, J. A., Wagner, R. K., Williams, W. M., Snook, S., & Grigorenko, E. L. (2000). *Practical intelligence in everyday life.* New York: Cambridge University Press.

Substance Abuse & Mental Health Services Administration: An agency of the U.S. Department of Health and Human Services. (2003). Retrieved August 19, 2003, from http://www.samhsa.gov.

Tedeschi, J. T. & Felson, R. B. (1994). *Violence, aggression, and coercive actions.* Washington DC: American Psychological Association.

Vaughan, P. W. & Rogers, E. M. (2000). A staged model of communication effects: Evidence from an entertainment-education radio soap opera in Tanzania. *Journal of Health Communication, 5,* 203-227.

Vygotsky, L. S. (1978). *Mind in society: The development of higher psychological processes* (M. Cole, V. John-Steiner, S. Scribner, & E. Souberman, Eds.). Cambridge, MA: Harvard University Press.

Vygotsky, L. S. (1997). *Educational psychology* (R. Silverman, Trans.). Boca Raton, FL: St. Lucie Press.

Wadsworth, B. J. (1996). *Piaget's theory of cognitive and affective development.* White Plains, NY: Longman.

Ward, K. (2000). *The shy child: Helping children triumph over shyness.* New York: Warner Books.

Weingarten, K., Hungerland, J., & Brennan, M. (1972). *Development and implementation of a quality-assured, peer-instructional model* (Technical Rep. 72-35, November, 1972). Alexandria, VA: HumRRO.

The Western Psychological Services Creative Therapy Store (2003). Retrieved May 19, 2003, from http://www.creativetherapystore.com.

White, E. B. (1974). Charlotte's Web. New York: HarperCollins Publishers.

Woods, C. & Konrad, C. (Producers) & Shyamalan, M. N. (Director). (1997). *Wide Awake* [Motion Picture]. (Available from Buena Visat Home Entertainment, Dept. C. S., Burbank, CA 91521).

Zillmann, D. (1983). Arousal and aggression. In R. G. Geen & E. Donnerstein (Eds.), *Aggression: Theoretical and empirical reviews, Volume 1,* (pp. 75-102). New York: Academic.

Zimbardo, P. G., Butler, L. D., & Wolfe, V. A. (2003). Cooperative college examinations: More gain, less pain when students share information and grades. *The Journal of Experimental Education, 71*(2), 101-125.

CHAPTER 6

SUGGESTIONS FOR THE INTEGRATION OF TECHNOLOGY

Heuristics highlighted in this chapter on the Integration of Technology:

- *Be explicit about the purpose for which the technology is being used.*
- *Conduct appropriate evaluations: matching the purposes for using the technology with the appropriate methods and measurements.*
- *Manage the implementation process by incorporating empirically tested principles for successful integration of technology.*
- *Distinguish between developing instruction with technology and delivering instruction with technology.*
- *In developing instruction, choose the appropriate authoring system or language with systematic examination of the development requirements and the functions of the authoring system.*
- *For delivering instruction, apply the technology appropriate to the learning phase.*

This next chapter covers a topic that may appear at first glance not to fit with the rest of the book. However, using information and communication (i.e., computer and internet) technology in learning provides an excellent example of how all four domains can interrelate and overlap during the various learning phases. The learner must first learn how to navigate the computer system prior to learning the domain contents in the technology-based system. One must cognitively understand the content of what appears on the computer screen. One would use interpersonal skills when communicating with others through the Internet and affectively understand their own and others' thoughts and feelings just as if they were together in the same classroom. Motivation to self-direct one's learning through technology is similarly developed (Keller, 1999); therefore, as the reader can see, using the computer/Internet involves all domains of learning. Similarly, the technology may be used to aid learning during any and all of the four phases: Acquisition, Automaticity, Near and Far Term Transfer.

As simple illustrations, it would not at all be unusual to use a tutorial approach with the computer during a concept acquisition phase of learning. Next, the drill and practice technique has been used almost since the beginning of the introduction of the computer in learning as a means of aiding the automaticity of math and language arts schemas or rules. Further, one of the most creative uses of the computer has been for the learner to use the computer in simulation or gaming environments as an assistant to help in learning how to solve problems, whether in math, science, or the creation of artistic products. While simulations could be useful in drill work, they are particularly helpful during integration of lower order skills. This could take place during Automaticity; but simulations are particularly helpful during transfer. Here, the learner is involved in developing schemas both for transfer across examples within a domain and, with the proper instruction, can learn schemas for transfer across domains as well (e.g., see Atkinson & Wilson, 1969 for discussion of the various types of early computer usage in instruction). With the developments in artificial intelligence, recent uses of the computer such as an adviser or collaborator in problem solving have become more feasible (e.g., Cognition & Technology Group at Vanderbilt, 2003; White, 2003). Some of these are noted below.

All of the strategies that we have discussed earlier can be implemented with more or less greater efficiency or effectiveness with computing technology. However, a few caveats are in order before the developer can consider these.

It is extremely important that the reader keeps in mind the distinction between computing technology and instructional technology. As we have noted in the introduction, instructional technology is the application of principles and research findings in learning psychology and teaching for the design, development and implementation of instructional materials and programs; computing technology (hardware and software) is the application of engineering and scientific knowledge for the improvement of system functions and capacity. With the use of multimedia or computing technologies, the instructional developer is given incredible capabilities for expanding the repertoire of both the process and the product of his or her instructional creations.

The two kinds of technologies, instructional versus computing, should not be confused. Analogies can be convenient and might go as follows. We must keep in mind the distinction between the recipe and the ingredients and the decision-making, which goes into the creation of a cake for example, as opposed to the oven, the microwave, or the refrigerator, which can house the ingredients and the product. Similarly, we must distinguish between the vehicle that carries the vegetables from the vegetables themselves. And finally, in this day and age the analogy could be made that we must certainly keep in mind the distinction between the pipes and the pumps, which can deliver the oil from the oil itself. The analogy applies for the distinction between the Internet and the information being delivered on the Internet. So too, must we as instructional developers distinguish between the course material, curriculum organization, and our systematic, instructional decision-making from the hardware and software which can provide tremendous capacities for developing and delivering this material to the learner. Any expert system, for example, must have a knowledgebase, but that knowledgebase must be parsed appropriately in order to facilitate learning. Therefore an appropriate instructional model must be part of the intelligence of the system (see for example: Park, Perez, & Seidel, 1987).

We have also discussed the fact that multimedia can be used most effectively to enhance learning when the features and functions of multimedia are appropriately used for the learning requirements of the given tasks for the given students. Once again we must emphasize that the media must be complementary to one another and not acting as distractors if the learning is to be enhanced and not hindered. Thus, sound images and visual images can be used effectively to help the learner use their multi dimensional sensory modalities in optimal ways to facilitate the understanding of the alphabet, to encode for example the ABC's. On the other hand, if the visual or auditory images are presented to give the learner an interesting context for engaging the learner rather than teaching the ABC's itself, those visual images must not be too interesting because if they are too colorful, dynamic, and attractive in their own right, they will distract the student's attention from the target learning task and consequently detract from the ability of the student to encode ABC, etc.

We must also acknowledge the incredible advances that computing technology has made in the past 40 years. Increases in power and speed have been accompanied by comparable reductions in price and size. Miniaturization has led recently to handhelds that are equivalent in capabilities to previous, large computers, which used to occupy a small room. Of course, the other advantage of the palm size computers is that they are faster! Nevertheless, as the following quote cautions us, we need to be wary of technological seduction, especially when to exploit the use of this technology, we are required to re-think, the how, and the what we wish to accomplish in society.

> If people's immediate worlds are responsive to them, then they believe they are living the good life. We have become ensconced in technological cocoons, with remote controls for our television sets, our compact disc players, our videotape players. We have cordless telephones, fax machines, and personal computers connected through modems to sources of information around the world. We are not questioning these technological advances. We are suggesting that such devices are seductive, that they promise more than they actually deliver. Rather than allowing us to get to the substance of life in a more efficient way, they have become the substance itself, crowding other matters -- murkier and less responsive to be sure -- out of the scene (Peterson, Maier, & Seligman, 1993, p. 310).

Nowhere is this more evident than in education and training, where traditionally instructing has proceeded with the teacher in front of a classroom full of students. With the power of the computer and the fingertip availability of resources from the Internet, how do we make the transition from an instructor-centered system to a learner/student centered system? The instructor must become the guide for the active, inquisitive learner to enable her or him to maximize the use of these technological resources. In the following discussions, we separately review the advances in technology and the remaining issues to implement these advances meaningfully in the cultures of education and training. Along the way, we follow a similar format to the previous chapters by providing an Instructional Guidance Section and a Research Section.

TECHNOLOGICAL ACCOMPLISHMENTS

From the early days of programmed instruction, through the use of computer-based instruction and on to distance learning and the use of virtual reality, technology has provided the opportunities for, both individualized education and training, as well as for real and virtual, collaborative learning. At the very least, programmed texts and computer-based drill and practice have provided more time on task for the learner. The development of simulations, simulators, and telecommunications have further held the promise for the learners to go far beyond what was previously possible in non-technological instructional environment. Many analyses, meta-analyses and reviews have been conducted (e.g. Kulik, 1994; Fletcher, 2003; Moore & Kearsley, 1996; Seidel & Chatelier, 1993, 1995; Seidel & Perez, 1994). All studies attest to the fact that technology in the proper circumstances can both improve the way in which traditional instruction has been delivered for the learner as well as promising to allow learning in ways that could never have been accomplished prior to the development of the computer (Adelsberger et al., 2002; Becker, 1991, 2000; Seidel & Chatelier, 1997). Bellman (1997) described cases where students collaborated in virtual, multi-dimensional user environments (or MUDS) to exchange information, create cultures, etc. Jones (1997) illustrated the beginning of the ability to perform surgery at a distance. In a recent example, White (2003) has shown how, students in a school environment can engage in collaborative work with artificially intelligent technological "advisers", and interact with learning simulations as an integral part of the learning process.

In sum, the integration of technology and instructional delivery can be seen from the perspective of: using technology to aid traditional instruction, using technology with instruction to accomplish instructional reform, and lastly, to accomplish instructional transformation with a fusion of technology and instruction, re-making our instructional system into a learner-centered environment. Collis (2002) describes this integration process as one of "convergence" on three different levels (involving changing roles of institutions, teachers, and learners, and utilization of resources). However, we must be careful when building theory into practice in learning and instruction. There have been attempts to connect descriptive learning theories with prescriptive instructional design principles and Spector (2000) feels that this theory-into-practice principle is "rarely followed with much rigor or success" (p. 79). He suggests that we "adopt more appropriate attitudes with regard to theory and praxis" (p. 88). In other words, the developer should "acknowledge that positions within an inquiry or an advocacy context should be held with an appropriate degree of uncertainty. Likewise, positions with regard to practical outcomes and what works best should be held with similar degrees of uncertainty" (p. 89). This position emphasizes the significant point that the successful practice of instruction requires not only knowledge (i.e., theories), but also expertise that is an integration of knowledge, experience, insight, and other intangible, artistic skills. As we have written elsewhere (Seidel & Cox, 2003; and Seidel & Perez, 1994), successful implementation of innovations of instructional technology in educational/training systems and minimizing uncertainty requires partnerships among all stakeholders; and building and maintaining such a partnership demands such integration expertise in the leadership of the implementation team. Indeed, we cite a couple of these in education where the National Education Association has been the catalyst, and one in Army training where the Army Research Institute has been the initiating member of such a partnership. In both cases, the policy makers, the education/training practitioners, the surrounding respective communities, and the researchers participated as full partners. When one speaks of "informing" research or "informing" practice, too often this mind set is associated with a distinct separation of what should be equal partners going forward through process and product together. The partner-relationship should result in a jointly accepted, cybernetic process where successive iterations are planned for, funded for, and carried out with all functional partners involved. In this way, it could be said that one part of the process informs another. Indeed from the examples discussed by Spector (2000), he seems to share this viewpoint. We briefly elaborate on these points later.

In this chapter, therefore, the authors attempt to connect education through technology with the principles described in the book; however, we are cautious in drawing any firm conclusions regarding use of particular technologies for specific learning phases. Although we make some suggestions, we acknowledge the limitations.

SECTION I:

INSTRUCTIONAL GUIDANCE

Acquisition Process

In the Acquisition phase, use a tutorial approach (traditional Computer Assisted Instruction, CAI) with the computer when the learner is attempting to learn the elements of a new domain. For example, as noted in Chapter 2, when the young or naïve learner is trying to learn the alphabet, a CAI tutorial with sound as well as visual symbols could be used to supplement the work of the classroom teacher. Some of the earliest successful CAI programs in reading were accomplished by Atkinson and his associates at Stanford (see Atkinson, 1969; Wilson & Atkinson, 1967 for a summary of the research and illustrative procedures for both tutorial and drill and practice techniques). Examples from the area of reading are as follows.

- **+Fast ForWord Language** is a CD Rom program that provides training in oral language comprehension for learning disabled and beginning readers. It is based on the hypothesis that students who have difficulty distinguishing phonemes at normal speeds of fluent speech may be successful when the speech is acoustically modified and slowed down. Thus, students using this program learn to recognize word sounds first in isolation, then in groups of sounds, then as words, and finally as sentences. The exercises are presented with altered speech sounds that have been slowed down and amplified or digitally enhanced to facilitate understanding. The speech sounds gradually change toward natural speech sounds as the student progresses through the exercises and the software increases or decreases in difficulty based on the student's progress. The effects of training are most consistently found for basic language processing skills and effects on phonemic awareness (Hook, et al, 2001; Torgesen, et al, 2001; see www.scientificlearning.com for more program details).

• **Kid Pix** *slide show making program:* Kid Pix, an educational software program, contains a slide show making program, which can aide phonics instruction. Students make slides composed of a combination of picture and text. Students then make their own word banks, which represent new words pulled from a book or piece of writing. Practicing these new sight words will foster development of automatic word recognition, one of the goals of exemplary phonics instruction. Students can also use Kid Pix to make slide shows of words in particular word families. For example, students can make slides of a *cat*, a *hat,* a *mat*, a *bat*, and a *rat* in order to help them note orthographic patterns and relationships between these patterns and isolated sounds (see http://www.kidpix.com for more program details).

Suffice it to say, any of the strategies or guidance proposed in Chapter 2 could be implemented using the capabilities of the computer. For example, we discussed the procedures for using storybook reading, decoding skills, or the teaching of word-recognition and sight-reading skills. Any of these can be implemented with the computer. By tutorial, generically, we therefore refer to using the computer to present new data elements within the targeted domain content (such as teaching the reader to encode and decode letters, etc.) and then having the learner practice associating and memorizing these data elements.

Automaticity Process

In Chapter 2's Automaticity phase, we highlighted the instructional guidance below.

• Teach word recognition and vocabulary;
• Use oral and expressive reading to develop fluency;
• Practice with appropriate levels of familiar texts;
• Maximize time spent reading.

The drill and practice technique can be used to practice with these newly acquired symbols as a means of aiding the automaticity of the reading (or, math and language arts) rules. As noted in the description of the Stanford Reading program, a typical sequence for learning new words could be "characterized as applied psycholinguistics..." with rules about learning to read "formulated on the basis of linguistic information, observations of language use, and an analysis of the function of the written code" (Atkinson, 1969, p. 147). A more recent specific program from the Reading area is Wiggleworks (www.scholastic.com/wiggleworks):

- **Wiggleworks: *Scholastic beginning literacy system.*** This program consists of a series of compact discs that contain electronic versions of trade books. The books are categorized into three levels of difficulty, based on sentence length, repetition of text, and complexity of syntax and vocabulary. Students can choose books at their own instructional level. Readers can change the size of the print, and they can request the computer to read text slowly (word by word) or quickly (with fluency). They can program the computer to read the whole page, the whole sentence, the whole line, or the whole word. Students can change the color of the text, and they can change the background color, so children with particular visual difficulties can modify the screen to better suit their needs. Furthermore, students log in when they begin, and so any modifications they have made will be saved so that the program is adapted to provide just the right amount of scaffolding.

  Students can also use *Wiggleworks* to work on their writing. The original text can be erased from each page so that students can rewrite the book using their own words. The program will then read their own story to them, giving direct, clear feedback about the pronunciation of their invented spellings. *Wiggleworks* also has a built-in tape recorder, which allows children to record their own version of the story. If the results of the taping are not satisfactory to the child, she can record again until she is happy. Thus the readers are developing fluency of reading and automatic word recognition. *Wiggleworks* has one more feature, which contributes to the phonics curriculum. Each program contains a notebook on which the student can copy words from the text (for students who cannot yet type, simply clicking the mouse on the word in the text will copy it onto the notebook). This notebook can be used in a variety of ways. Students can copy sight words, unknown words, or words from particular word families. These words can then be the content of directed phonics lessons. (See Schultz, 1995 for details on validation and www.scholastic.com/wiggleworks for more details about the specifics of the program.)

Numerous technology-based programs have also been developed for aiding in remediational teaching of at-risk (below average or disabled) readers.

- **Daisy's Castle and DaisyQuest II** are two that successfully teach a variety of skills, including rhyming, identifying words with the same beginning, middle or ending sounds, recognizing onsets and rimes, and counting phonemes (Fox & Mitchell, 2001; Torgesen & Barker, 1995). See http://www.smartkidssoftware.com/mdgws1.htm for more details.

In Chapter 3, in the Automaticity phase of the Psychomotor Domain, we gave the following suggested strategies:

- The use of numerous and varied examples and opportunities for practice;
- Maintaining short time intervals between practicing the numerous and varied examples and application to the transfer task;
- Making the practice as interesting as possible to maintain motivation with advanced learners;
- Involving the learner in the modeling process to facilitate understanding of how the skill is to be performed.

All of these can be implemented readily with simulations and simulators. For example, there are numerous golf programs available either for fun at a sports bar (see www.deadsolidgolf.com), or for detailed analysis and suggested techniques for practice of part-skills and integration (see www.holidaygolf.biz). Without endorsing the quality of either of these commercial efforts, we simply note with these examples that the technology exists to implement the acquisition and automaticity strategies we have proposed.

Near and Far Term Transfer Processes

Following through with the reading example, the computer could be used to aid in the development of comprehension strategies. It could be used with an interactive game-like format to better engage the learner. As will be noted in the Research Section, one of the most creative uses of the computer has been for the learner to use the computer as an assistant to help in learning how to solve problems, whether in reading, math, science, or the creation of artistic products. Here, the learner is involved in developing schemas both to transfer over examples within a domain and with the proper instruction, schemas to transfer across domains as well. As Spiro and his associates note (1995), and we discussed earlier, in ill-structured domains, the learner benefits by having many potential combinations available so that she or he can develop "...a rich palette to paint a knowledge structure well fit to helping understand and act on a particular case at hand" (Spiro, et al., 1995, p. 100). The value of a hypertext computer environment is that it readily provides the variations to the learner to create such a palette (see Spiro & Jehng, 1990; Romiszowski, 1990). Indeed, reading is such an ill-structured domain, which can benefit from this technology. As we have asserted earlier in Chapter 1, our choice of reading as the Cognitive Domain example is because its schemas are easily transferable or applicable for near term or far term transfer.

Some successful programs that support reading comprehension include programs that scaffold reading strategy use, such as *Kidspiration* and *Inspiration* for graphic organizing and concept mapping (see the following website for more details: http://www.inspiration.com/productinfo/index.cfm).

- *Kidspiration* **and** *Inspiration*: Students build graphic organizers by combining pictures, text and spoken words to represent thoughts and information. Inspiration, designed for students in grade six to adult, can be used across the curriculum for brainstorming, webbing, diagramming, planning, concept mapping, organizing, and outlining. *Kidspiration*, for students in kindergarten through grade five, helps students brainstorm ideas with pictures and words, organize and categorize information visually, and create stories and descriptions. Students create the hierarchical structure of knowledge, including main ideas and supporting details and the program offers a useful tool for organization (e.g., in reading, students can represent the macro and micro structure of the text in a computer concept map). Both offer the integrated graphic organizer tool and outline tool that work together to help students comprehend concepts and information. This program provides a very strong example of how technology can aid not just near term transfer in this case targeted toward reading. But concept mapping is clearly of benefit at a meta-domain level (e.g., for organizing science, social studies, etc.), thus aiding far term transfer as well.

Another program, which deals with measuring conceptual development and could be complementary to the above, *Pathfinder,* assesses the degree of a learner's knowledge structure. It has been successfully used in a few studies with elementary students.

- **Pathfinder:** Students perform a task on the computer in which they rate the relatedness of pairs of words drawn from the computer-based learning passages. The computer program generates a hierarchical structure of students' knowledge based on the pairs and computes a correlation (Pearson- r) between a student's ratings and an expert's ratings of all pairs of words. These correlation coefficients range from -1 to $+1$, and represent a measure of the extent that the student's knowledge structure approximates that of an expert. Pathfinder also generates graphic network representations for quantitative or qualitative analysis (Johnson, Goldsmith, & Teague, 1994).

Lastly, we cite a software tool that has the sophisticated reader acting as an author. For us, it is a prime example of how technology can benefit development of far term transfer, and also provides further support for our selection of reading as the cognitive domain example in this book.

- **HyperCard and hypermedia:** Students can be placed in an authoring role through creating multi-media book review databases by using tools for drawing, copying, and pasting graphics, creating buttons and text fields, and linking cards. These multimedia book reviews can be used as an alternative to conventional book reports. The reports can be entered into a database for use by other students, teachers, and parents (Blanchard & Rottenberg, 1990). Reinking and Watkins (1997) found that students were more engaged in learning and using the technology related to the multimedia book reviews than in other academic activities. See also Leu (2000) for further discussion of hypermedia and the emerging connections between literacy and technology in the information society.

In the Interpersonal Domain, simulations and use of game-like environments can readily be used to implement the strategies suggested earlier.

- Leadership and persuasion by
- Observation of positive role models through various media,
- Imitating behaviors, and
- Integrating these developments into everyday life.

For examples, we have already mentioned that students can learn how to solve problems with live collaborators in a distance learning, MUDS (multi-user domains) setting (Bellman, 1997) or with technological advisers to aid learning in a simulation environment (White, 2003).

An Example of Instructional Technology Across Phases and Domains

In order to further understand the interrelatedness of domains across the phases, the authors describe a strategy called "Structural Communication Methodology," originally designed by Hodgson (1972) and modified by Romizsowski (1990; Romiszowski & Chang, 1992). As stated by Romiszowski (2000), its purpose is "to better communicate understanding and simulate a dialogue between an author of instructional materials and the students." Romiszowski (2000) further modified the technique to operate in a Web-based learning environment. According to his discussion, implementation of it in a technology-based learning environment was highly motivating for both learners and instructors. The strategy is implemented as follows:

- *Intention:* "The opening statement, which defines what is to be studied, provides an overview" (Romiszowksi, 2000, p. 4) rationale, and context for the instructional material.
- *Presentation*: The focus of the unit to be studied; i.e. materials, exercise, etc. presenting the essential facts and concepts. It could involve a video or simulation or real-life experience depending upon the nature of the exercise. It could also include computer-based instruction and or simulations.

We would characterize these first two stages of the Structural Communication technique as relevant to the Acquisition and Automaticity phases of the learning process, where the learner is acquiring and becoming comfortable with the targeted data base.

- *Investigation*: A set of problems to be solved. Here the purpose is for the learner to interact with subject matter and to present the intellectual challenge essential for Structural Communication methodology. The problems are "interrelated and are open ended to allow multiple responses and viewpoints" (Romiszowksi, 2000, p. 4). According to Romiszowski's description one can infer that the learner has met the challenge if the student shows his or her ability to use knowledge appropriately in various contexts and to organize the knowledge with organizing principles that are specified for him. Originally designed, "to promote learning for social action" (p. 4) in a face-to-face environment, Romiszowski redesigned the methodology to be used in a virtual collaborative learning environment.

This section would seem relevant for near term transfer as do the remaining sections described below.

- *Response Matrix*: "A randomized array of items which summarize key parts, concepts or principles from the knowledge base that is being used and studied in the exercise. Often it resembles a 'key point summary' of the *Presentation*. The student composes a response (outlines an essay) by selecting any number of these items as a 'best' response to a given problem" (Romiszowksi, 2000, p. 4)
- *Discussion*: The discussion has two parts: a Discussion Guide and a set of Discussion Components. The Guide is a set of if-then rules, which test the student's response for omission or inclusion of certain significant items, or combination of items. The Comments are constructive statements that discuss in depth the rationale for including or excluding certain items.
- *Viewpoints*: "An outline of the author's, and other alternative viewpoints; this may review some aspects stated in the *Intention*, make explicit some biases or standpoints held dear by the author, draw attention to other views in the literature, etc. Ideally, the viewpoint section plays a final, interactive role between author and learner" (p. 4).

The modification by Romiszowski (2000) incorporates open ended discussion environments where students can "share, argue, persuade, and negotiate their perspectives on the expert's feedback comments as well as on their own opinions" (p. 5). (This type of Interpersonal learning is highlighted in Chapter 5.) In his virtual environment the software both supports and controls the nature of the collaborative activity such as creating discussion logs, accessing various expert feedback, constructing opinions, and justifying with their own words those opinions, or alternatively being able to select from a long list in order to present an opinion. The organization of the interaction process is along "simple-to-complex interaction structures." In sum, the Structural Communication methodology encourages first the acquisition of a database, and then follows with various kinds of open discussion, which would seem to promote near term transfer; and Romiszowski's technological application illustrates how the Web-based environment can facilitate this method.

Developer Guidance for Technology Integration

- Establish agreement among the stakeholders for the Purpose of incorporating Technology;
- Align the Purpose for incorporating the technology with appropriate measures.

Each of the following purposes, plus a cost-effectiveness purpose, as we have noted, required specific measures of effectiveness and ways to go about accomplishing that measurement. We briefly list these below; and the reader is referred to the referenced paper for a complete discussion (Seidel, 1980; Seidel, 1992). Looked at from a Bloom perspective, it has been called applying the principle of "congruence" (e.g., Chyung & Stepich, 2003). These authors note that the principle says "... in any situation, learning goals, instructional strategies, and assessment methods should be carefully matched or congruent" (p. 317). In our approach, the key is to satisfy the need for operational uniqueness in all of these factors. Taking the **value added** purposes first, we present the lists of measures to illustrate their requirements. Lastly, we present the list showing the measures required for cost-effectiveness.

Purpose: Computing Opportunity

Measures of Effectiveness:
- Access to Computing Facilities
- A Separate Budget for Instructional Computing
- Time Set-aside for Student and Instructor Use
- Convenient Locations of Terminals
- Documentation Available
- Consultation Available

Purpose: Computing Literacy

Measures of Effectiveness:
- o Courses in:
  - Understanding of Computers and Impact on Society or (Awareness)
  - Computer Applications in Own Discipline (Knowledge)
  - Computer Science and Programming (Skills)
- o Percent of Target Population Served:
  - Student
  - Faculty

- o Achievement in Courses
    - • Value Change Following Course

Purpose: Educational Reform

Measures of Effectiveness:
- • Individual Student Progression
- • Varieties of Learning Locations
- • Changes from Credentials to Competencies
- • New Approaches to Learning, the learner as explorer of a technological world of resources
- • New Values

Purpose: Curricular Enhancement

Measures of effectiveness:
- o Time
    - • Average Training Time in Course
    - • Average Testing Time in Course
    - • Average Course Time
- o Achievement (Final Criterion Test Results)
    - • Accuracy or Speed Scores
    - • Gain scores
    - • Number of objectives passed
    - • Percent Students Failed
- o Other Effectiveness Measures
    - • Student Attitudes
    - • Instructor Ratings
    - • Attrition Rates
    - • Absentee Rates

Purpose: Cost-effectiveness

Measures:
- • Student Efficiency (Achievement/Time, Money)
- • Cost Avoidance
- • Student Enrollment
- • Attendance
- • Attrition

Choose an authoring system that can be used precisely for the given situation and the unique learner needs with which you were concerned. Useful criteria for selecting an authoring system are exemplified in the following questions (Seidel & Park, 1993, pp. 12-17).

- Are there built-in instructional design aids (a framework for representing various kinds of courseware components in an organized structure)?
- Are there built-in development (programming) aids (provisions for the novice user to develop various types of courseware components-- presentation displays and student-computer interaction specifications)?
- Does the system possess the capability to be expanded?
- Is it user-friendly (ease of procedures for developing or revising materials, provision of development templates, ease of integrating materials, adaptation to author skill levels, help features, and an adequate manual)?
- What are the costs and affordability factors in using the system; i.e. what are hardware requirements, system price, contract terms, and training expenses?

Focusing on the learner, design motivational tactics into the technology integrated instruction. Keller's model has been applied successfully various types of learning environments, including computer-based instruction, distance learning, and multimedia environments (Keller, 1999).

Steps to implement the motivational tactics include:

- Identify salient characteristics of the learners' overall motivation to learn.
- Judge how appealing the learning task will be to the learners.
- Identify learners' expected positive or negative attitudes toward the medium of instruction and the instructional materials.
- Based on the above information, decide how much motivational support is required and what types of tactic to use.
- Include predetermined "checkpoints" throughout the program that involve a screen asking several questions about the student's motivational attitude.
- Based on her/his responses to these screens, supply motivational tactics to improve attention, relevance, or confidence such as including personal messages when the tutor deems appropriate (greeting cards, reminders, etc).

SECTION II:

SUPPORTING RESEARCH

Comparable to the advances to help the learner, computing technology has provided instructional designers with capabilities for more effective and efficient development of instructional materials. Computers have also had a long and varied history of providing this kind of support as well. Generically, this has fallen under the rubric of authoring languages and ultimately authoring systems. (see Hunter,

Kastner, Rubin, & Seidel, 1975 for discussion of the earlier authoring languages; and for a review of authoring systems, Seidel & Park, 1993). The goal of these computing aids has been to provide an efficient and effective means to help the training or educational instructional designer develop and manage materials. One of the advantages gained as a user of authoring systems was that you, the designer/creator of instruction, were forced to be explicit about what you were trying to have the student learn. Therefore, as a developer, your requirements for selecting an authoring system needed to be determined precisely for the given situation and the unique learner needs with which you were concerned. Useful criteria for selecting an authoring system are exemplified in the following questions (Seidel & Park, 1993, pp. 12-17).

- Are there built-in instructional design aids (a framework for representing various kinds of courseware components in an organized structure)?
- Are there built-in development (programming) aids (provisions for the novice user to develop various types of courseware components-- presentation displays and student-computer interaction specifications)?
- Does the system possess the capability to be expanded?
- Is it user-friendly (ease of procedures for developing or revising materials, provision of development templates, ease of integrating materials, adaptation to author skill levels, help features, and an adequate manual)?
- What are the costs and affordability factors in using the system; i.e. what are hardware requirements, system price, contract terms, and training expenses?

Over the years, these authoring systems have become increasingly more sophisticated. For example, Scandura (2003) has developed and is marketing an expert system-based authoring system including an intelligent tutor. Another of the more creative products has been developed by Gibbons (2003). His approach conceptualizes the instructional development process in the context of a layered design architecture. Gibbons takes into account the fact that there are development team members with different specialties, who must interact with the developing materials and must relate to one another. He characterizes seven layers of instructional design: content, strategy, control, message, representation, media-logic, and data management. The team members who must interact and deal with these various layers he describes as the designer, the subject matter expert, the writer, the artist, and the programmer. Each of these parties has typically their own language and their own goals for design at their layer. A design system, in order to enable communication amongst the layers and therefore the team members, thus must be coherent and must be able to articulate the multiple design languages required for solving problems unique to each of the layers. The goal of both of the systems proposed by Scandura and Gibbons is to automate as much as possible the design process. These are but two examples of many interesting approaches to authoring discussed at the 2003 American Educational Research Association meeting. (see for example Paquette, 2003; Shute, 2003; van Merrienboer & de Croock, 2003).

The technical advances in computing technology continue to show us how we can improve education and training. So, why has its use not been universal? The next section addresses this question in terms of organizational and user issues, which have not been as systematically addressed as have the technical developments.

HUMAN CONCERNS: CULTURE, ORGANIZATION, AND INDIVIDUAL

Learner Motivation

When using technology for instruction, such as in distance learning and computer-based instruction, motivation plays a big factor in the implementation, continued use/attrition, and successful completion of the task at hand. As Keller (1999) suggests, "there is no doubt that there are serious motivational challenges among distance learners." In order to use the ARCS method of instruction, motivation learned from prior domains must be transferred here. Keller's ARCS Motivational Process model (1987a, 1987b), discussed in Chapter 4, provides a systematic, seven-step approach (Keller, 1997) to designing motivational tactics into instruction. This model has been applied to various types of learning environments, including computer-based instruction, and multimedia (Keller, 1999). Keller (1999) reviewed implementation and research of his ARCS Motivational Process Model that provided successful examples of its easy and diverse use. He cited three specific unpublished studies that extended the ARCS motivational process model in different directions: refinement of systematic approaches to motivational design, varied contexts of application, and multicultural audiences.

The first study (Suzuki & Keller, 1996) developed a simplified approach to Keller's motivational design (see Guidance section). Suzuki and Keller (1996) developed an approach, which identified key motivational characteristics in the learners, in the content area to be taught, and in the hardware or software to be used. This information was evaluated and the authors then listed tactics based on identified motivational problems. In the evaluation of the effectiveness of this motivational design process verified that the teachers were able to implement the steps accurately and more than two-thirds felt that it helped them produce a more effective motivational design. This simplified model provided "an efficient and effective means of supporting educators in improving the motivational aspects of learning environments" (Keller, 1999, p. 46). Steps to implementation of the motivational program are described above in Section I.

The second study (Song, 1998) designed a motivationally adaptive computer-based instruction in genetics for junior high school students based off the ARCS model design (see Guidance section). He included "checkpoints" throughout the instructional program that were then evaluated to create specific tactics for the user based off the ARCS model design. After analyzing the students' motivation and performance levels, it was concluded that both adaptive and full-featured treatments were superior to minimalist treatment. More sophisticated programs that are designed to the individual student have stronger effects. However, these programs are lengthy and costly.

The final study (Visser, 1998) that Keller discussed was an extension of his design process in distance learning and provided an example of the multicultural nature of his work. Visser's (1998) extension of Keller's design process in distance learning used textual material supplemented by audio or videocassettes. Motivational challenges of distance learners, including feelings of isolation, lack of isolation, lack of feeling of making steady progress, and doubts about the ability to complete the course given the students' other responsibilities, were addressed. Visser used the simplified ARCS model to analyze the audience and conditions of a distance learning course offered by a university in the United Kingdom and offered potential solutions. She found that supplying generic and personalized motivational messages to students throughout the course improved retention rates of 70 to 80 percent. Visser's suggestions for implementing motivational messages to all students is described in Section I.

The final two studies (Song, 1998; Visser, 1998) illustrated "how systematic motivational design can be incorporated into formal instructional design and curriculum development projects, how it can serve as a basis for motivationally adaptive computer-based instruction, and how it can increase student motivation and performance by improving the student support system in distance learning" (Keller, 1999, p. 46). Finally, Keller discussed applications supporting the multicultural and multinational relevance of his design. He notes that the ARCS model is being used in different countries across the world, including countries in Asia and Europe (Keller, 1999).

Over the many years in working with computers, we at HumRRO and the Army Research Institute have conducted research with computers, conducted surveys about using computers in education and training, performed both project and program evaluations on attempts to incorporate technology as an integral part of instruction. From a technical standpoint, the findings, as noted above, are universal. The use of computer technology can and should be considered integral to the process of developing and delivering instruction. This is true whether in a training institution or an educational institution. Indeed, numerous predictions in the late '60's and '70s strongly suggested widespread use of computers in education and training by the late 1980's (For a review, see Hunter, Kastner, Rubin, & Seidel, 1975).

While the use of computers has been increasing at all levels and there is agreement about the potential value of computers in education "... the degree of change attributed to computer implementation is significantly lower than anticipated" (Seidel & Cox, 2003, pp. 323-24). We agree with Peterson et al. (1993) that the technology itself is seductive, and that the availability of computers has increased dramatically. According to a 1997 study, roughly 40 percent of the homes have computers (Seidel & Cox, 2003). Undoubtedly, with the lowering of prices for personal computers, this has continued to increase. Availability in schools has increased dramatically as well (Seidel & Perez, 1994; Becker, 2000). So the question arises: why has technology not become an integral part of instruction. Or conversely: why has instruction not become integral with technology? Clearly, the answer lies not in the technical aspects of computer usage or development; rather, the answer to that puzzle rests with the human and organizational dimensions as they relate to coping with the problems of change. Becker noted in his 2000 report that larger numbers of computers have become available, yet usage by teachers in U.S. schools is still quite limited. Computers in schools "...number over 10 million..." yet "the most common frequent uses are in computer and business classes" (Becker, 2000, p. 2).

Years ago the senior author was asked to write a paper dealing with just such a puzzle (Seidel, 1980). At that time confusion was rampant in the educational field concerning how to evaluate the potential value of computers as they might assist the instructional process. For example, in the early 1970s there was an excellent program developed by researchers at the Pennsylvania State University. The purpose of the development was to provide mobile computing capability around the state of Pennsylvania so that special education teachers could receive training which they otherwise would not be able to receive since they could not attend classes on campus. The program was closed down by the fiscal officers at Penn State because they said it was not cost-effective. By that, the administrators meant that the courses could be attained less expensively by campus attendance. Clearly, these two sets of decisions were based upon different purposes. These and similar misunderstandings led us to conclude that there were multiple purposes for which computers might be used, and that each purpose required both its own method of evaluation and its own set of measures of effectiveness of the instruction using the computer as part of its process. The first dichotomy we uncovered was the difference between value added, in the sense that things could be done with computers that previously could not be done (note the example above); and secondly, a cost-effectiveness approach or purpose which would involve comparing delivery of the same instruction with or without the use of the computer. Upon closer examination, we determined that there were at least four value added purposes for the use of the computer. First, schools could be interested in adding facilities, computing opportunities; secondly, they might want to focus on what the term computer means and how to use it, computer literacy; thirdly, they might be interested in attaining new objectives in the curriculum by using the computer, curriculum enhancement; and the fourth value added purpose, and by far the most ambitious, would be to reform the entire process of training or education; for example, by setting individualized curricula and graduation, or even obtaining a high school education at home.

Each of these purposes, plus a cost-effectiveness purpose, as we have noted, required specific measures of effectiveness and ways to go about accomplishing that measurement. These were given in a detailed listing as part of the Instructional Guidance Section.

As the reader will note, these approaches imply clearly different ways to examine the value of incorporating technology into the instructional process. Teachers and administrators need to be trained to understand the possible uses they can make of the technology. Added to this need to be clear on why you might wish to incorporate the computer into instruction, there are all manner of organizational issues, which can impede or facilitate widespread, instructional use. In fact, because conditions between using the computer and not using the computer were rarely comparable, it made more sense to use the phrase "tolerable costs" rather than cost-effectiveness. In other words, it was common for administrators to ask, "How much is a given gain with the computer usage worth to me since it's going to cost me so many dollars to have that gain?" or "How much dollar investment am I willing to tolerate to achieve x-amount of improvement in instruction by including the computer as an integral part of it?"

We have stated that the reason for the lack of both universal use of computers in education stems at least in large part from the fact that the human and the organization had not been taken into account by the technologists. Mayer (2003) has his own take on that, which is in one sense similar to ours in another sense dissimilar. He states: "One answer is that the focus was on giving people access to the latest technology rather than on promoting human cognition through the aid of technology" (Mayer, 2003, p.132). We agree and asserted this previously (Kopstein & Seidel, 1968) that the use of computers can easily be viewed and appropriately so as an amplification of intelligence or cognition. While Mayer confined his comments regarding why computers are not universal use in education to the shortcoming quoted above, we simply assert that this is one of the reasons and not the totality of the reasons. Nevertheless, it is the case that the reasons for nonproliferation of computer use relate to both the conception of the individual mind and how the teaching structure can change to a learner centered environment and how well the educational system is prepared to accept change in the roles that teachers, administrators, and support staff play in a learner centered world.

Without being too redundant, we also assert that the use of technology to help a learner will include drill and practice plus tutorials during the initial stages of the learning processes i.e., acquisition and automaticity. In building our curriculum with technology towards aiding the student to develop schemas or principles for transfer both within a domain (near term transfer) and across domains (far term transfer), simulations and problem-solving tools are of paramount importance. Therefore, it is our contention and literature agrees that technology has been shown to be important in all phases of the learning process (e.g., Atkinson & Wilson, 1969; Kulik, 1994; Mayer, 2003; Suppes, 1969; Suppes, Jerman, & Brian, 1968; Vinsonhaler & Bass, 1972)

Typical classroom instruction takes place in a very rich environment. The environmental variables contributing to that richness impinge upon classroom, school, school system, and the community surrounding the school system all have influence. They and their needs must be taken into account if sustained achievements using a computer innovation are to be accomplished. Any attempt to integrate computer usage with instruction must therefore take into account these levels of decision makers and their unique needs it the systematic inquiry of the intervention affects can be accomplished. We, therefore, proposed a process model of evaluation (Seidel & Perez, 1994), which takes into account several important dimensions, including the objectives of the innovative project, intended computer usage, and the maturity of the project itself. The model involves three major stages, which we call adoption, implementation, and institutionalization, as well as two principal processes, assimilation of the innovation and accommodation to the innovation. The third dimension for consideration in any evaluation consists of the multiple stakeholders, which we noted above: the community, school system, the classroom, and most importantly, the student. To adopt the innovation means to use it initially within an administrative unit; to implement the technological innovation is to go beyond a typical department or course and to use it in an entire school system within a local organizational structure. Finally, institutionalization can only take place following a successful usage in the first two stages.

By institutionalization, we refer to the incorporation of the technology as part of the overall school or training budget. It is our contention that successful institutionalization needs to proceed by first assimilating the innovative technology into the existing environment (applying computer use in much the same way pencils and papers were used previously, record keeping, simple use of drill and practice etc.). Attending to assimilation first provides the opportunity for the new user to get comfortable with the technology; following upon this, we can indeed plan for adapting our instruction to the innovation. Thus, we can introduce local area networks to increase collaborative work among students, include simulations as a principal part of the instruction, and flexibly adapt our education and training process to incorporate learning on demand, individual course completion, distance learning, and competency-based models of learning in a changed organizational structure.

Such lofty goals and expectations clearly require, as was noted above, the involvement of the entire community of decision makers in our multilevel model. This means that policymakers, politicians, various teachers unions and associations, PTAs, business leaders, and local groups of citizens need to be involved. In a training environment similar or analogous groups and levels exist within companies or the military; and all stakeholders need to be involved from the outset of the innovation in order for success to take place.

We have had an opportunity to incorporate all of these factors in conducting an actual program evaluation of innovative technological use in a consortium of school districts (Seidel & Wallace, 2001, 2002). We were called on to provide an evaluation of the management process during the implementation of technology in this joint effort of some 20 schools, and the surrounding communities. As part of this evaluation we designed, administered, and analyzed results from a questionnaire, individual interviews, and focus groups. All methods were intended to provide formative information in order to enable a consortium to continue to build a viable partnership during the process of implementing technology in the schools. Through a continual series of meetings with the various, principal participants involved in this partnership, the use of the focus groups, and the multidimensional structure questionnaire, all levels and types of decision-makers were included; and the process of implementation of technology was successfully managed.

With the advent of online or electronic learning, the potential for transforming education into a learner managed learning environment seems quite pronounced. Evolving technology has brought us to that point where learners may have easy access: to resources, human and material, synchronous or asynchronous dialogs, access to different levels and types of feedback as well as support, and to other media including simulations, and perhaps even choices of learning styles for the same materials. Pilot global programs are described in a volume edited by Stephenson (2001). What is required of course is continuing commitment towards evolving different kinds of educational institutions permitting increased variability and control of the learning process by the learner. Therefore, there will need to be a transformation of the current culture; perhaps it may be a generational transition similar to the computing literacy phenomenon, before the full realization may take place. Our children currently are growing up with all sorts of video and computing experiences, even by the time they hit grammar school.

Before closing, it is worth noting yet one more way that technology can have a perverse and unintended effect on education and its culture. One of the sports writers in the Washington Post newspaper penned a very insightful article on how technology has created technological athletic conferences in collegiate athletics at the expense of the primary goal of higher educational institutions---the academic enlightenment of students (Jenkins, May 17, 2003). Instead of athletics being of secondary value to education, and a way for geographically co-located schools to develop friendly competition, the process of the NCAA has subverted and inverted the goals, through the developments in television, satellite communications, computers, etc. Now, conferences are changing, strictly guided by the revenue which can be brought to the university by sports. Education of students has become secondary!

Once again to emphasize the importance of the consideration of organizational and people concerns when implementing technology, we draw upon a significant quotation from Peterson, Maier, and Seligman (1993):

> Our technological world provides a quick fix, the psychological equivalent of junk food.... Many of us have become addicted to technological gadgets because other sources of potential satisfaction are not nearly so responsive.... What we decry is the crowding out of other concerns. Our task as a society is to find better ways of dealing with control, so that we end up with fewer casualties.... To begin with, we should endeavor to make the social world as responsive as the world of technology.... We need to make the interdependence of people something that we value. Only when we start to take other people's welfare seriously will they start to do so for us. This seems to be a prerequisite for creating a world that is responsive, one that will encourage efficacy on the part of all. When we stop competing against one another in destructive ways, we all can be satisfied about our accomplishments (pp. 307-309).

The authors then go on to propose the establishment of optimism institutes.

> ...We envision the creation of Optimism Institutes, centers in which research on personal control is conducted and then applied, to schools, to work settings, to society itself...Involve citizens in the planning and evaluation...Let society judge whether these ideas are preferable to those that pervade our current age of personal control"(Peterson, Maier, & Seligman , 1993, p. 310).

We have attempted in this chapter to show how technology can play an important role in implementing instructional strategies and how the human considerations of organizational structure, culture, and individual stakeholders can make or break successful integration of technology with instruction. Negroponte (1995) wrote eloquently about the consequences of "being digital." As he noted, "Better and more efficient delivery of what already exists is what most executives think and talk about in the context of being digital. But like the Trojan horse, the consequence of this gift will be surprising. Wholly new content will emerge from being digital, as will new players, new economic models, and likely a cottage industry of information and entertainment providers" (p. 18). In the language we used above, the assimilation process of information innovation was taking place in society in 1995. It is still taking place within education today. The transition to accommodation of the technology, however, is sporadic. Again, as we have stated above, only with careful attention to the human side of technological innovation, will education and society as a whole be able to take full advantage of the potential which technology offers.

REFERENCES

Adelsberger, H. H., Collis, B., & Pawlowski, J. M. (2002). *Handbook on information technologies for education and training*. London: Springer.

Atkinson, R. C. (1969). Computerized instruction and the learning process. In R. C. Atkinson & H. A. Wilson, *Computer-assisted instruction* (pp. 143-165). New York: Academic Press.

Atkinson, R. C. & Wilson, H. A. (1969). *Computer-assisted instruction*. New York: Academic Press.

Becker, H. (1991). How computers are used in United States schools: Basic data from the I.E.A. computers in education survey. *Journal of Educational Computing Research, 7*(4), 385-406.

Becker, H. (2000, January). Findings from the teaching, learning, and computing survey: Is Larry Cuban right? Paper presented at the School Technology Leadership Conference of the Council of Chief State School Officers, Washington D.C.

Bellman, K. (1997). Playing in the mud: Turning virtual reality into real education and training. In R. J. Seidel & P. K. Chatelier (Eds.), *Virtual reality, training's future?: Perspectives on virtual reality and other related emerging technologies* (pp. 9-18). New York: Plenum Press.

Blanchard, J. S. & Rottenberg, C. J. (1990). Hypertext and hypermedia: Discovering and creating meaningful learning environments. *The Reading Teacher, 43,* 656-661.

Chyung, S. Y. & Stepich, D. (2003). Applying the "congruence" principle of Bloom's taxonomy to designing online instruction. *The Quarterly Review of Distance Education, 4*(3), 317- 330.

Cognition and Technology Group at Vanderbilt. (2003). Connecting learning theory and instructional practice: Leveraging some powerful affordances of technology. In H. S. O'Neill & R. S. Perez (Eds.), *Technology applications in education: A learning view* (pp.173-209). Mahwah, NJ: Lawrence Erlbaum Associates.

Collis, B. (2002). Information technologies for education and training. In H. H. Adelsberger, B. Collis, & J. M. Pawlowski (Eds.), *Handbook on information technologies for education and training* (pp. 1-20). London: Springer.

Dead Solid Golf.com (2003). Retrieved April 16, 2004, from http://www.deadsolidgolf.com.

Fletcher, J. D. (2003). Evidence for learning from technology-assisted instruction. In H. F. O'Neil & R. S. Perez (Eds.), *Technology applications in education: A learning view* (pp. 323-339). Mahwah, NJ: Lawrence Erlbaum Associates, Publishers.

Fox, B. & Mitchell, M. J. (2001). The effects of computer software for developing phonological awareness in low-progressing readers. *Reading Research and Instruction, 40,* 315-332.

Gibbons, A. S. (2003, April). The architecture of instructional design and its implications of the generation of online instruction. Power Point Presentation presented at the meeting of the American Education Research Association, Chicago, IL.

Hodgson, A. M. (1972). Structural learning in social settings: Some notes on work in progress. *Programmed Learning and Educational Technology, 9*(2), 79-86.

Holiday Golf: Golf for the 21st Century (2002). Retrieved April 16, 2004, from http://www.holidaygolf.biz.

Hook, P. E., Macaruso, P., & Jones, S. (2001). Efficacy of Fast ForWord training on facilitating acquisition of reading skills by children with reading difficulties: A longitudinal study. *Annals of Dyslexia, 51*, 75-96.

Hunter, B., Kastner, C., Rubin, M., & Seidel, R. J. (1975). *Learning alternatives in U.S. education: Where student and computer meet.* Anglewood Cliffs, NJ: Educational Technology Publications, Inc.

Jenkins, S. (2003, May 17). How to curb big-time schools? Hit them with big-time taxes. *The Washington Post*, pp. D1, D10.

Johnson, P. J., Goldsmith, T. E., & Teague, K. W. (1994). Locus of the predictive advantage in Pathfinder-based representations of classroom knowledge. *Journal of Educational Psychology, 86*(4), 617-626.

Jones, S. B. (1997). Surgery 2001. In R. J. Seidel & P. K. Chatelier (Eds.), *Virtual reality ‚training's future?: Perspectives on virtual reality and other related emerging technologies*, (pp. 65-67). New York, NY: Plenum Press.

Keller, J. M. (1987a). Strategies for stimulating the motivation to learn. *Performance and Instruction, 26*(8), 1-7.

Keller, J. M. (1987b). The systematic process of motivational design. *Performance and Instruction, 26*(9), 1-8.

Keller, J. M. (1997). Motivational design and multimedia: Beyond the novelty effect. *Strategic Human Resource Development Review, 1*(1), 188-203.

Keller, J. M. (1999). Using the ARCS motivational process in computer-based instruction and distance education. *New Directions for Teaching and Learning, 78*, 39-47.

Kid Pix. (2003). Retrieved April 16, 2004, from http://www.kidpix.com.

Kopstein, F. F. & Seidel, R. J. (1968). Computer-administered instruction versus traditionally administered instruction: Economics. *AV Communication Review, 16*(2).

Kulik, J. A. (1994). Meta-analytic studies of findings on computer-based instruction. In E. L. Baker & H. F. O'Neil, Jr. (Eds.), *Technology assessment in education and training.* Hillsdale, NJ: Lawrence Erlbaum Associates.

Leu, D. J. (2000). Literacy and technology: Deictic consequences for literacy education in an information age. In M. L. Kamil, P. B. Mosenthal, P. D. Pearson, & R. Barr (Eds.), *Handbook of reading research, Vol. III.* Mahwah, NJ: Erlbaum.

Mayer, R. E. (2003). Theories of learning and their application to technology. In H. F. O'Neill & R. S. Perez (Eds.), *Technology applications in education: A learning view* (pp. 127-157). Mahwah, NJ: Lawrence Erlbaum Associates, Publishers.

Moore, M. G. & Kearsley, G. (1996). *Distance education: A systems view.* Belmont, CA: Wadsworth Publishing Company.

Negroponte, N. (1995). *Being digital.* New York: Alfred A. Knopf, Inc.

Park, O. K., Perez, R. S., & Seidel, R. J. (1987). Intelligent CAI: Old wine in new bottles or a new vintage? In G. P. Kearsley (Ed.), *Artificial intelligence and instruction applications and methods.* Reading, MA: Addison-Wesley.

Paquette, G. (2003, April). Next generation distance learning: From mechanistic to knowledge-based authoring. Presentation at the meeting of the American Education Research Association, Chicago, IL.

Peterson, C., Maier, S. F., & Seligman, M. E. P. (1993). *Learned helplessness.* New York: Oxford University Press.

Reinking, D. & Watkins, J. (1997). A formative experiment investigating the use of multimedia book reviews to increase elementary students' independent reading (Reading Research Report No. 73). Athens: GA: Universities of GA and MD, National Reading Research Center.

Romiszowski, A. J. (1990). Computer-mediated communication and hypertext: The instructional use of two converging technologies. *Interactive Learning International, 6*, 5-29.

Romiszowski, A. J. (2000). A methodology for case-study in virtual groups. Presentation at the Annual International Conference of the Brazilian Association for Distance Education (ABED).

Romiszowski, A. J. & Chang, E. (1992). Hypertext's contribution to computer-mediated communication: In Search of an instructional model. In M. Giardina (Ed.), *Interactive multimedia environments* (pp. 111-130). Heidelberg: Spring-Verlag.

Scandura, J. M. (2003, April). Expert model authoring system and general purpose intelligent tutor for procedural, declarative, and model-based domain specific knowledge. Presentation at the meeting of the American Education Research Association, Chicago, IL.

Scholastic: WiggleWorks: Scholastic Beginning Literacy System. (2004). Retrieved April 16, 2004, from http://www.scholastic.com/wiggleworks.

Schultz, L. H. (1995). A validation study of Wiggleworks, the Scholastic Beginning Literacy System. (Available from Scholastic, Inc., 555 Broadway, New York, N.Y. 10012-3999).

Scientific Learning. (2004). Retrieved April 16, 2004, from http://www.scientificlearning.com.

Seidel, R. J. (1980). It's 1980: Do you know where your computer is? *Professional Paper, 1-80,* 1-18.

Seidel, R. J. (1992). 1992: Have you found your computer yet? *Technological Horizons in Education Journal.*

Seidel, R. J. & Chatelier, P. K. (1993). *Advanced technologies applied to training design.* New York: Plenum Press.

Seidel, R. J. & Chatelier, P. K. (1995). *Learning without boundaries.* New York: Kluwer Academic Publishers.

Seidel, R. J. & Chatelier, P. K. (Eds.). (1997). *Virtual reality, training's future?: Perspectives on virtual reality and other related emerging technologies.* New York, NY: Plenum Press.

Seidel R. J. & Cox, K. E. (2003). Management issues in implementing education and training technology. In H. F. O'Neil & R. S. Perez (Eds.), *Technology applications in education: A learning view* (pp. 323-339). Mahwah, NJ: Lawrence Erlbaum Associates, Publishers.

Seidel, R. J. & Park, O. (1993). Evaluation of CBT authoring systems. In R. J. Seidel. & P. R. Chatelier (Eds.). *Advanced technologies applied to training design* (pp.23-36). New York: Plenum Press.

Seidel, R. J. & Perez, R. S. (1994). An evaluation model for investigating the impact of innovative educational technology. In H. F. O'Neil & E. L. Baker (Eds.), *Technology Assessment* (pp. 177-212). Hillsdale, NJ: Lawrence Erlbaum Associates, Publishers.

Seidel, R. J. & Wallace, D. K. (2001, October). Brazos-Sabine Connection Evaluation Report: Survey of program management consultant report.

Seidel, R. J. & Wallace, D. K. (2002, October). Brazos-Sabine Connection Evaluation Report: Management of implementation consultant report.

Shute, V. (2003, April). Under the hood of adaptive e- learning: Diagnostic assessment, student modeling, and selection rules. Presentation at the meeting of the American Education Research Association, Chicago, IL.

Song, S. H. (1998). The effects of motivationally adaptive computer-assisted instruction developed through the ARCS model. Unpublished doctoral dissertation, College of Education, Florida State University, Tallahassee, FL.

Smart Kids Software: Children's Educational Software. (2004). Retrieved April 23, 2004, from http://www.smartkidssoftware.com/mdgws1.htm.

Spector, J. M. (2000). Building theory into practice in learning and instruction. In J. M. Spector & T. M. Anderson (Eds.), *Integrated and holistic perspectives on learning, instruction, and technology: Understanding complexity* (pp. 79-90). The Netherlands: Kluwer Academic Publishers.

Spiro, R. J., Feltovich, P. J., Jacobson M. J., & Coulson R. L. (1995). Cognitive flexibility, constructivism, and hypertext: Random-access instruction for advanced knowledge acquisition in ill-structured domains. In L. P. Steffe & J. E. Gale (Eds.), *Constructivism in education* (pp. 85-107). Hillsdale, NJ: Lawrence Erlbaum Asssociates.

Spiro, R. J. & Jehng, J. C. (1990). Cognitive flexibility and hypertext: Theory and technology for the nonlinear and multidimensional traversal of complex subject matter. In D. Nix & R. J. Spiro (Eds.), *Cognition, education, and multimedia: Exploring ideas in high technology* (pp. 163-205). Hillsdale, NJ, England: Lawrence Erlbaum Associates, Inc.

Stephenson, J. (Ed.). (2001). *Teaching and learning online: Pedagogies for new technologies.* London: Kogan Page Limited.

Suppes, P. (1969). Computer technology and the future of education. In R. C. Atkinson & H. A. Wilson (Eds.), *Computer-assisted instruction: A book of readings* (pp.41-47). New York: Academic Press.

Suppes, P, Jerman, M., & Brian, D. (1968). *Computer-assisted instruction at Stanford:The1965-66 arithmetic drill-and-practice program.* New York: Academic Press.

Suzuki, K. & Keller, J. M. (1996). Creation and cross-cultural validation of an ARCS motivational design matrix. Paper presented at the annual meeting of the Japanese Association for Educational Technology, Kanazawa, Japan.

Torgesen, J. K., Alexander, A. W., Wagner, R. K., Rashotte, C. A., Voeller, K., Conway, T. & Rose, E. (2001). Intensive remedial instruction for children with severe reading disabilities: Immediate and long-term outcomes from two instructional approaches. *Journal of Learning Disabilities, 34*, 33-58.

Torgesen, J. K. & Barker, T. A. (1995). Computers as aids in the prevention and remediation of reading disabilities. *Learning Disability Quarterly, 18*(2), 76-87.

van Merrienboer, J. & de Croock, M. (2003, April). Dynamic task selection in adaptive e-learning. Presentation at the meeting of the American Education Research Association, Chicago, IL.

Vinsonhaler, J. P. & Bass, R. K. (1972). A summary of ten major studies in CAI drill and practice. *Educational Technology, 11*(7), 29-32.

Visser, L. (1998). The development of motivational communication in distance education support. Unpublished doctoral dissertation, Education Technology Department, University of Twente, the Netherlands.

White, B. (2003, April). Engaging learners in meta-cognitive modeling and inquiry. Presentation at the meeting of the American Education Research Association, Chicago, IL.

Wilson, H. A. & Atkinson, R. C. (1967, August). Computer-based instruction in initial reading: A progress report on the Stanford project. Technical Report, No. 119. Institution for Mathematical Studies in the Social Sciences, Stanford University.

CHAPTER 7

SUMMARY

As stated in the Introduction, our purpose for this book is to provide strategies for instruction, or guidance, drawing upon empirically based principles or heuristics from the psychological literature describing how we learn. The premise is that there is a necessary triadic relationship between psychology, training, and education. The descriptive laws of psychology provide the basis for how cognitive development, learning, meta-cognition, and other psychological organizing principles intrinsically relate to one another; therefore, they can provide the basis for prescriptions of instructional strategies. Both training and education can inform new psychological research possibilities based upon evidence from their applications. Ideally, there should be an ongoing cybernetic relationship amongst all three disciplines.

Too often, one or the other of these disciplines has proceeded as if the others did not exist and could not provide any fruitful advice. For example, in recent years such terms as "situated learning" and "authentic learning," among others, have been held as new constructs for education. Yet both terms have roots earlier in the training literature and in the psychology of learning literature.

The hope is that the recommendations based on this broad empirical perspective will enable education and training developers to make comfortable decisions on how to build sound instructional materials. In order to make our case, the most formidable task for us was to develop a coherent taxonomy that would permit a consistent crosswalk from the learning heuristics to targeted instructional tasks. This we presented in Chapter 1. We identified four phases of the learning process, which govern the development of knowledge and skills: Acquisition, Automaticity, Near Term Transfer, and Far Term Transfer. Acquisition involves acquiring the basic data elements within a domain; Automaticity refers to the application of these elements to the point of performing actions automatically, without conscious, cognitive intervention; the two Transfer phases refer to generalizing the application of principles within a domain, Near Term and across domains, Far Term. Both of the latter phases require higher order cognitive and meta-cognitive development.

We then chose four domains, in which to instantiate the taxonomy: Cognitive, Psychomotor, Affective, and Interpersonal. We also included a chapter on the integration of technology to illustrate how the principles can be implemented with, and extended by, the use of computers in a real world context. Initially the domains were selected because traditionally they seem to have been treated as the primary, independent domains. It soon became obvious that interdependence and not independence was the rule. Perhaps the easiest way to illustrate the obviousness of the overlap amongst the dimensions is to share an anecdote with the reader. A number of years ago, the senior author was preparing for the psychologist licensing examination in the state of Virginia. The exam itself was a Cognitive examination; and in studying for it, he organized and studied all the materials, which would be useful for taking examination. His studying involved isolating himself from others for a period of two weeks prior to the exam in order to immerse himself in the relevant material and to avoid distractions. Two days before the examination he moved to a motel a few blocks from the building in which the testing was to take place. He then paced off the distance from the motel to the designated testing site in order to determine how long it would take so that he could review part of the test scheduled for the afternoon by walking back to the motel and studying during the lunch hour. Next, he walked into the testing site and into the testing room to familiarize himself with all of the stimuli pertinent to being in the examination room. All of these exercises taken together enabled him to lower the Affect level and focus his energy externally toward test mastery, to engage the Psychomotor domain relevant to preparing for the test, and to maximize the level of Cognitive preparation in order to actually take the test.

In Chapters 1 and 2, we elaborated on this interrelatedness, where we noted that over the years there seems to have been enough evidence accumulated from research (e.g., Bargh & Chartrand, 1999; Barkow, Cosmides, & Tooby, 1992; Broadbent, 1952a, 1952b; Mayer, 2002; Murphy & Martin, 2002), clinical observation (e.g., Grinder & Bandler, 1981), and anecdotal evidence to establish the fact that the domains of cognitive, psychomotor, affect, and interpersonal act pretty much together. Further, we assert that each experience may be characterized not as an isolated domain experience, but rather as a multi-domainal range of experience. Therefore, each experience carries with it multi-channel sensory inputs, affective involvement, cognitive transformation, kinesthetic feedback, and some form of organized motor output. Thus, we also readily agree with the inference by Rosenbaum, Carlson, and Gilmore (2001) that most abstract problem solving probably involves, even to the tiniest degree, some sort of real or imagined motor execution.

For ease of discussion, we nevertheless treated the domains in separate chapters, and developed models to illustrate and further clarify the overlaps among them. The following chart of the learning process requirements was modified from Table 1.1 in Chapter 1, which was developed as an advanced organizer and visual aid to help the reader maintain her or his focus while perusing the book. The relevant domain portion of the advanced organizer is repeated at the beginning of each chapter as a facilitator for the reader. As noted in Chapter 1, the chart was developed following an approach by Romiszowski (1999).

Table 6.1. Taxonomy (Modified from Chapter 1)

Process Requirements	Acquisition	Automaticity	Transfer: Near term	Transfer: Far term
	Learning domain elements	Integrating and applying elements through extensive repetition	Developing ability to apply principles and strategies within a domain	Learning to discover new principles and applying them across domains
Knowledge Domains: Cognitive, Psychomotor, Affective, Interpersonal				

For the format within each chapter we presented first a listing of the most relevant Descriptive Principles (from the psychological literature). Next, we followed this with an Introduction, a discussion of the general instructional class of tasks for the domain in question. Then, we parsed the bulk of each chapter into two sections: Section I, Recommended Instructional Strategies for the targeted, specific tasks (the guidance); and finally, Section II, the Supporting Research and the relevant theories.

COGNITIVE DOMAIN

In Chapter 2, to exemplify the Cognitive Domain, we chose reading since it is the epitome of learning for Far Term Transfer. Reading involves the learning of principles or schemas (schemata), which are applied to learning in all domains. We are always reading to do or act on something. Our instructional example concerned the tasks to be learned by the developing reader.

The highlighted learning heuristics listed include: operant principles of minimizing errors, using small steps, and providing immediate reinforcement for acquisition of initial elements of domain knowledge, advanced organizers to facilitate integrative skill acquisition and capitalize on prior knowledge, continual use of active learning, part-task training to break up complex tasks into manageable chunks, and providing multiple-context environments to facilitate positive transfer within and across domains. Following these highlights, we supply the reader with recommended instructional strategies to implement them. In the final section of the chapter, we then discuss the psychological literature relevant to Reading, as the chosen example of the cognitive domain.

PSYCHOMOTOR DOMAIN

We outlined a model in Chapter 3 illustrating the interdependence and potential overlap between the cognitive and motor components of psychomotor skill development as well as the changes in relative contribution made by these two components as the learner progresses from the beginning Acquisition phase through Automaticity. We also followed earlier frameworks, which distinguished between Open and Closed-end tasks as well as tasks demanding large muscle involvement vs. fine muscle usage. Instructional examples included learning sports tasks in basketball, tennis, and baseball, learning how to receive Morse code, and learning a military task of how to fire a rifle. It was important to emphasize also that, while the progression through all four phases appears linear, re-cycling can and does occur with Open tasks. For example, in learning tennis, one might achieve mastery of all techniques needed to play at a given level; and automaticity with almost total motor control might take over one's play. But, suddenly, a new opponent appears at a higher level and the cognitive processes are invoked to learn strategy elements for playing at this new, higher level of tennis. Presumably, this can occur repeatedly each time transfer of a skill to a new situation is required.

Heuristics noted relevant to psychomotor skill development include the following areas: task analysis within a consistent motor skill taxonomy, part-task learning with complex skills, use of imagery to prepare for overt practice, observational learning from modeled performances, systematic repetitive practice, knowledge of performance, transitioning from cognitive involvement to automatic movement, and designing instruction for transfer. Again, Section I provides recommended instructional guidance while Section II discusses the relevant psychological literature.

AFFECTIVE DOMAIN

Learning of Affect as discussed in Chapter 4, starts with learning who we are as an emoting and motivating self, and how to express our Affect. Here too, we presented a model for conceptualizing Affect, including the dimensions level of energy and focus of that energy, either on oneself, or, on the learning and performance of the task at hand. For example, a secure individual is able to focus her or his energy externally, and be motivated by learning and mastering the task at hand. The self-concerned individual, however, is emotionally involved with avoiding personal threat, comparing herself or himself to others, and therefore, diffuses her or his energy away from the task at hand and towards self-preservation.

This chapter discusses learning heuristics as they apply to the learning of Affect and the influence of Affect on other learning. The initial listing includes the following: Classical conditioning is the force behind much emotional and attitudinal development. When intelligence is treated as developmental and not a fixed entity, task-oriented, focused learning behavior is facilitated. Conversely, treating intelligence as a fixed entity, promotes an ego-involved, threatened approach to learning, and learning suffers. Establishing contingencies between actions and positive feedback results in a sense of control and self-competency in interacting with one's environment. Positive transfer is facilitated when meta-cognitive skill development, including self-regulation, is encouraged within a focused, task-oriented learning environment. Sections I and II follow the pattern noted above, of recommended guidance and research support.

INTERPERSONAL DOMAIN

Chapter 5 concerned the Interpersonal Domain, in which an individual learns how to interact with others and then how to learn from these people. The environment and, that which composes the environment, as well as the developed self (personal, cognitive and behavioral), are necessary to form new interactions and enjoy the capacity to learn new things. We learn how to acquire and maintain healthy social skills through the use of a variety of methods, such as modeling, role-playing, etc. Maintenance is achieved through reinforcement and the positive interactions one experiences.

Building upon our discussion of Affect development in Chapter 4, when a learner is asked to focus on the task at hand, he or she does so from a position of security or insecurity, which is in turn based upon appropriate or dysfunctional attachments developed since birth. The problem is that nothing is 100 percent. Therefore, cognitive goals and the motivation to master a learning task get mixed with ego needs, avoidance of failure, and attendant personal fears. Now, if the context of the task to be learned; e.g., the classroom, is not mastery-focused but performance-oriented; i.e., based upon student comparisons with others, etc., any insecurities in the learner's affective makeup can lead to a shift in focus away from the task and motivation to master it, toward personal threat, and energy governed by threat; i.e., emotion.

The point to emphasize is that the domains are interrelated. They may function in harmony to maximize, say, cognitive or psychomotor skill development. The degree of harmony, however, is contingent upon the "self" development (Affective Domain), the relational self (Interpersonal), and the context or environment within which learning is to take place.

Unique heuristics were highlighted in Chapter 5 on Interpersonal Development. Each was discussed within the chapter and strategies were suggested for implementation. The following heuristics were included in the chapter. Imitative learning (observational) and modeling of authority figures, starting with parents, influences the development of filters and templates, through which the child learns to see her or his world. In addition, developmental factors affect observational learning. Repeated exposures to modeled behaviors are necessary because of potential complexities and rates of presentation, both of which can decrease attention. Additionally, Whom one associates with (social networks), imposed or by preference, limit the observational patterns to which the individual is repeatedly exposed and therefore, those which will be learned more thoroughly than others. Finally, peer learning is a powerful influence in school learning and outside the school environment. The guidance in Section I provides suggestions for maximizing function and minimizing dysfunction for the relevant interpersonal development; this is followed in Section II by the research supporting such recommendations.

SUGGESTIONS FOR THE INTEGRATION OF TECHNOLOGY

In preparing our treatise, it became obvious that we needed to include a chapter, Chapter 6, on technology integration with instruction. Heuristics highlighted in this chapter on the integration of technology include: Be explicit about the purpose for which the technology is being used. Conduct appropriate evaluations: matching the purposes for using the technology with the appropriate methods and measurements. Manage the implementation process by incorporating empirically tested principles for successful integration of technology. Distinguish between developing instruction with technology and delivering instruction with technology. In developing instruction, choose the appropriate authoring system or language with systematic examination of the development requirements and the functions of the authoring system. For delivering instruction, apply the technology appropriate to the learning phase.

Indeed, the power of technology, as we noted, with its current and potential influence on techniques for development of instructional materials and on strategies for learning, can both implement and extend the heuristics discussed in the domain chapters. Since the development of programmed instruction some fifty years ago, technology has held out the promise for improving all facets of learning. Some remarkable technical developments in computing technology have occurred during this time, from simulation capabilities to electronic learning environments, and even to virtual reality. Software advances, enabling easy and efficient development of instructional materials, have been equally significant. These accomplishments are described briefly. Next, we discuss the ways in which technology has already benefited implementation of many heuristics in all phases of our model, from Acquisition through Far Term Transfer

We cautioned that the two kinds of technologies, instructional versus computing, should not be confused. We give analogies to clarify the distinctions. For example, we must keep in mind the distinction between the recipe and the ingredients and the decision-making, which goes into the creation of a cake for example, as opposed to the oven, the microwave, or the refrigerator, which can house the ingredients and the product. Similarly, we must distinguish between the vehicle that carries the vegetables from the vegetables themselves. And finally, in this day and age the analogy is made that we must certainly keep in mind the distinction between the pipes and the pumps, which can deliver the oil, from the oil itself. So too, must we as instructional developers distinguish between the course material, curriculum organization, and our systematic, instructional decision-making from the hardware and software including the Internet, which can provide tremendous capacities for developing and delivering this material to the learner. Also discussed is the fact that there has been some movement to capitalize on technology and shift towards learner-centered instruction. We therefore have described these developments. At the same time we note that the promise of wholesale reform of education is still a promise and close by discussing significant individual and organizational issues remaining to be resolved in order to make the promise a reality.

CONCLUSION

Finally, our intent from the outset was to be user-oriented and developer-friendly, which is why we incorporated a two-part format of each chapter, with suggested guidance presented first followed by a section on supporting research, for a more complete understanding of the rationale behind the recommended guidance. It has been the desire of the authors to provide in this treatise a broad, empirically supported platform based on principles from the literature of the psychology of learning and cognition, with which developer-practitioners could launch sound programs of instruction. At the very least, it is our fondest hope that the reader will find the information presented herein useful ingredients for organizing and developing the next set of education or training materials.

REFERENCES

Bargh, J. A. & Chartrand, T. L. (1999). The unbearable automaticity of being, *American Psychologist, 54*(7) 462-479.

Barkow, J. H., Cosmides, L., & Tooby, J. (Eds.) (1992). *The adapted mind: Evolutionary psychology and the generation of culture.* New York: Oxford University Press.

Broadbent, D. E. (1952a). Speaking and listening simultaneously. *Journal of Experimental Psychology, 43,* 267-273.

Broadbent, D. E. (1952b). Listening to one of two synchronous messages. *Journal of Experimental Psychology, 44,* 51-55.

Grinder, J. & Bandler, R. (1981). *Trans-formations: Neuro-linguistic programming and the structure of hypnosis.* Moab, Utah: Real People Press.

Mayer, R. E. (2002). *The promise of educational psychology: Volume 2, Teaching for meaningful learning.* Upper Saddle River, NJ: Prentice Hall.

Murphy, S. M. & Martin, K. A. (2002). The use of imagery in sport. In T. S. Horn (Ed.), *Advances in sport psychology* (2nd ed.) (pp. 405-439). Champaign, IL: Human Kinetics.

Romiszowski, A. (1999). The development of physical skills: Instruction in the psychomotor domain. In C. M. Reigeluth (Ed.), *Instructional-design theories and models, Volume II: A new paradigm of instructional theory* (pp. 457-481). Mahwah, NJ: Lawrence Erlbaum Associates, Publishers.

Rosenbaum, D. A., Carlson, R. A., & Gilmore, R. O. (2001). Acquisition of intellectual and perceptual-motor skills. *Annual Review of Psychology, 52,* 453-470.

ABOUT THE AUTHORS

Currently, Dr. Robert J. Seidel is Research Chief Emeritus at the Army Research Institute. He attained his Ph.D. in Experimental Psychology from the University of Pennsylvania and was a NIH Special Postdoctoral Fellow at Stanford University. He has taught full- time at Denison University, and part-time at, George Washington University, the University of Maryland, and Trinity College in Connecticut. He has a varied and rich experience base spanning over 36 years of research, development, and management in the areas of experimental design, individualized instruction, computer-administered instruction, technology transfer, distance learning, and evaluation. In these areas of expertise, he has given many talks, nationally and internationally, published numerous articles and seven books. He was principal investigator for a National Science Foundation grant, which resulted in his co-authoring, (with colleagues B. Hunter, C. Kastner, and M. Rubin) *Learning Alternatives in U.S. Education: Where student and computer meet.* Dr. Seidel organized, then conducted an educational technology conference, and subsequently edited (with M. Rubin) a book, *Computers and Communication,* based on the findings from the conference. The next book, *Computer Literacy,* was edited by Dr. Seidel, R. Anderson, and B. Hunter. He has also managed groups of research personnel in both the private sector and in government, and has served many years as an advisor to NATO for the implementation of advanced technologies. As part of his NATO work, Dr. Seidel served as senior editor and contributed chapters to four books dealing with the use of technology in education and training: *Computer-Based Instruction in Military Environments, Advanced Technologies Applied to Training Design, Learning without Boundaries, Virtual Reality: Training's Future?* Dr. Seidel is on the editorial advisory board of Instructional Science, is a Fellow of the American Psychological Association and is a Charter Member and Fellow of the American Psychological Society. His current interests continue to be facilitating change in individuals and organizations.

Kathy Cox-Perencevich is finishing up her dissertation towards obtaining her Ph.D. at the University of Maryland in educational psychology, while working full-time as a lead researcher at The National Reading Research Center. She attained a M.S. in educational psychology at the Pennsylvania State University and completed teacher certification programs in elementary education and in special education in Massachusetts. Ms. Cox-Perencevich has been pursuing research related to diagnosing and improving students engagement in literacy development. Her overall focus has been on cognition and motivation in classroom settings. In that regard, she has a number of recent publications in educational psychology journals, and book chapters, dealing with techniques for enhancing motivation and cognitive development in the field of Reading.

Allyson Kett is presently completing her work towards a Psy.D. in Clinical Psychology from the American School of Professional Psychology at Argosy University, Washington D.C., and is a National Consortium Research Fellow at the U.S. Army Research Institute in Arlington, VA. Prior to coming to D.C., she obtained her M.A. in Clinical Psychology with a specialization in Education at Teachers College of Columbia University in New York City and her B.A. in psychology from the College of William and Mary in Williamsburg, Virginia. Ms. Kett has a broad, verse background in developing and delivering instruction in the training and educational fields. She worked at the New York Bankers Association developing educational programs for bankers of all levels. In addition, she has experience working in the educational field, including developing instructional materials for, and assisting in the teaching of, children of all ages who are mentally challenged and/or have developmental disabilities. Ms. Kett also assisted in planning, organizing, and implementing seminars and leadership forums for a national, industry sponsored, college Scholars Program.

INDEX

Accommodation, 54, 171, 204, 206

Acquisition, xxi, 1-2, 5-7, 11-16, 19,
23-24, 26-28, 31, 34, 39, 47, 53,
58-59, 65, 75-80, 82-88, 90-92,
94, 96-105, 107, 109, 115-116,
119-121, 125, 127-128, 130, 132,
141, 151, 153-154, 157-159, 161-
163, 169-171, 174, 185, 189, 192,
194, 196, 203, 211, 213-214, 216

Advanced organizers, 3, 7, 18, 24,
102, 213

Affect, 8-9, 115-118, 121, 131-132,
134-135, 138-139, 141-143, 146,
153, 169-170, 212, 214-215

Affective Domain, xxi, 8, 10-11, 17,
25, 67, 92, 110, 115, 118, 130-
131, 141, 145, 152, 169-171, 176,
179, 211-215
acquisition, 119, 132
automaticity, 125, 134
far term transfer, 128, 135
learning, 116-117, 133, 214
near term transfer, 127, 135

Aggression, 125, 142, 158, 160, 169-
172, 174

Anger, 120-121-, 124-126, 131, 139,
160, 169-170, 174

Anxiety, 92, 94-95, 116, 120, 124,
126, 132, 139, 141, 143-144, 160
Management Program, 126
separation, 159
test, 116, 164

Assimilation, 47, 54, 57, 171, 204,
206

Attachment theory, 133, 171-172

Authenticity, 125

Authoring, 193, 199

languages, 185, 198-199, 216
systems, 185, 197-199, 216

Automaticity, xxi, 5, 10-15, 18-19,
23, 26-27, 31-32, 34, 39, 47, 49,
65-66, 75-76, 79, 82-91, 97-101,
103-106, 109-110, 115, 117, 120,
125, 127-128, 130, 134, 141, 151,
153-154, 158-159, 161-163, 170,
173, 178, 185-186, 190, 192, 194,
203, 211, 213-214

Chunking, 3

Coaching, 35, 165-168, 179
masterful, 166-167
remediational, 167

Cognitive Domain, xxi, xxiii, 2, 8-13,
19, 23-24, 47, 66, 76-77, 79, 81-
82, 86-87, 89, 92-94, 97, 100-
102, 105, 108-110, 116, 132-133,
137, 141, 144, 146, 153-153, 161,
171, 173, 177, 185, 192-193, 211-
215
abstractions, 4
acquisition, 26-27, 47
-affective, 142
automaticity, 26, 31, 47
-behavioral, 92
development, xix-xxi, 6, 211, 215
distractions, 116
far term transfer, 27, 39, 58
flexibility theory, 5, 13-14, 39,
41, 135
identification phase, 89
intelligence, 116
IQ tests, 138
learning, 9, 57, 88, 172
load, 5, 15-17, 35, 41, 56, 65-66

meta-, 14, 27. 39-40, 47, 52, 58,
91, 92, 115-116, 118, 120,
125, 127-128, 138-139, 211,
214
models, 5
near term transfer, 26, 34, 53
neo-association, 169
overload, xix, xxi, 41-43, 65
processes, xxi, 13-14, 24, 26, 42-
43, 52, 65, 77, 98, 102, 136,
176, 214
process model, 89-90
psychology, 1
rehearsal, 81, 98, 100
schemas, 26
self-guidance, 82, 98
skills, 12-13, 25, 43, 47, 61, 109,
115-116, 118, 120, 125, 127-
128, 138-139, 214-215
social-, 142
strategies, 25, 47, 53, 55, 58, 81,
91-92, 98, 101, 127, 136
task analysis, xxi
theorists/psychologists, 14, 17, 53
theory, xix, 65-66
theory, social-, 98, 100, 152, 154,
161, 168
Communication, 62, 120-121, 132,
167, 174, 176-178, 185, 188, 194-
195, 199, 205
Comprehension monitoring, 27, 40-
41, 58
Computer, xxi, 42, 62-63, 86, 106,
141, 185-194, 196, 198-199, 201-
205, 211
-assisted instruction (CAI), 189
-based drill and practice, 188
-based instruction (learning), 130,
138, 188, 193, 195, 198, 200-
201, 203
concept map, 193

literacy, 202
programming, 17, 196
science, xxii, 196
Supported Intentional Learning
Environments (CSILE), 62
technology, 185, 202
Computing opportunities, 202
Concept instruction, 44, 62-63
Conditioned habits, 11, 115, 119,
125, 127, 128
Conditioning, 117, 131, 133-136
classical, 115, 133, 214
instrumental, 133
operant, 12, 14-15, 19, 48
Consortium, 204
Context, xx, xxiii, 2-8, 10, 12, 14, 16,
18, 26, 30, 32, 37-41, 45-47, 50,
53-54, 56, 65, 78, 80-81, 91, 95,
98, 102, 106-107, 117-118, 121,
128, 130, 133, 135, 137-140, 146,
154, 161, 187-188, 194-195, 199-
200, 206, 211, 215
clues, 41, 47-48, 52
functional, xx, 3, 7-8, 14, 18-19,
24, 46, 106
learning, 16
multiple, 4-5, 7, 16-17, 24, 32,
39, 45, 51, 60, 88, 127-128,
135, 213
social, 142, 157, 174
Contiguity, xxi, 133
of events, 2, 133
Control, 9, 32, 44, 52, 54, 76, 82-83,
93-94, 97-98, 101, 109, 116, 125,
134, 136, 140, 152, 160, 167,
172, 174, 195, 199, 205, 214
cognitive, 107-108
interpersonal, 11, 151, 154, 158-
159, 161, 163
motor, 107-108, 214

self (personal)-, 11, 13, 82, 98,
        115, 119, 121, 125-128, 140,
        158, 205
    variables, 64-65, 99, 175
Cost-effectiveness, 196-197, 202-203
Culture, 161-163, 166, 169, 172,
        187-188, 200, 205-206
Curriculum enhancement, 202
Daycare, 154-156, 172-173
Developmental Factors, 150, 153,
        215
Developmental Learning Phases, 178
Developmental Level, 121-122
Developmental Stages, 132-133
Ecological validity, xx
Education, xix, xx, xxii, 25, 43, 59,
        80, 124, 130, 134, 142, 146, 152-
        153, 155, 164, 168, 172, 175,
        177, 179, 187-189, 199, 200-206,
        211
    developers, practitioners,
        designers, 1, 189, 199
    entertainment-, 176-177
    individualized, 188
    materials, 25, 217
    medical, 46
    physical, xxiii
    re-, 136
    reading, 46
    reform, 197, 216
    research, xxi, 3, 141
    software, 190
    special, 202
Ego-involved, 115, 118, 130, 134,
        214
Elaborative interrogation, 37, 40-41,
        55, 58
Emotion (al), 9, 24-25, 94, 116-118,
        120, 122-124, 129, 132-136, 138-
        146, 152-154, 160, 162, 164-165,
        169, 171-172, 177-178, 214-215

    arousal, 126
    attachments (bonds), 132, 171,
        173
    conditioning, 117, 131, 136
    development, 115, 132, 135, 152,
        159, 214
    experience of, 9, 116
    expression, 116, 120, 122-124
    intelligence, 116, 135, 146
    learning, 119, 124, 130-131, 152
    problems, 120
    state, 116, 120, 123-124, 134
    trait, 116
Environment, xx, xxiv, 2, 4, 10, 15,
        18, 28, 32, 44, 49, 56, 85, 95,
        107, 116, 120, 122, 124, 129,
        134, 136, 152-154, 156-157, 162,
        164, 168-172, 177, 186, 194-195,
        203-204, 214-215
    classroom (school), 46, 121, 135,
        152, 188, 215
    conditions, 97, 107, 109
    emotional, 120-122
    home, 124
    interpersonal, 120, 123
    learning, 16-17, 46, 62, 89, 101,
        116, 129-130, 135, 138-140,
        179, 188, 194-195, 198, 200,
        203-205, 216
    mastery, 120-121, 126
    military, 165
    Multi-Dimensional User
        (MUDS), 188
    multimedia, 9, 198, 192, 196, 200
    multiple text (context)-, 17, 24,
        27, 56, 60, 213
    performance, 95-96, 140
    social, 170-172
    variables, 94, 203

work, 77, 89
Envy, 125, 139
Evaluations, 131, 142, 167, 183, 201, 216
Expectations, 1-2, 46-48, 94, 121, 163, 204
Fear, 95, 116-117, 120, 124-125, 133, 138-139, 163, 169, 171, 215
Feedback, 2, 7, 35, 78, 86, 98, 102, 104, 137-138, 140, 168-169, 191, 195, 205
  expert, 195
  kinematic, 86-87, 104
  kinesthetic, 8, 212
  inconsistent, 140
  intermittent, 2
  -loops, 167
  negative, 178
  observational, 84, 87
  positive, 48, 116, 214
Feelings, 120-124, 129, 139, 142-143, 156-158, 162, 169-170, 185, 201
Framework, xxiii, 16, 18, 60, 76, 89, 118, 132-133, 141, 145, 176, 198-199
  conceptual, 108, 117-118, 146
  meta-theoretic, xxii
  organizing, 141
  theoretical, xxiii
Functional context, xx, 3, 7-8, 14, 18-19, 24, 46, 106
Graphic organizers (semantic organizers), 38, 41, 55, 57, 62, 193
Help-seeking, 126-128, 138-139
Heuristics, xxii, 1, 5, 7, 10-12, 15, 19, 23, 75-76, 115, 117, 128, 135, 151, 170, 185, 211, 213-216
Human concerns, 200

Imagery, 9, 76, 81, 85, 91-92, 129, 146, 214
  arousal, 146
  cognitive-specific, 85, 146
  guided, 9, 166
  kinesthetic, 99
  motivation general-mastery, 85, 146
  in sports, 9, 146
  visual, 99
Implementation process, 185, 216
Input, 4, 17, 102, 153
  auditory, 17
  sensory, 8, 17, 77, 88, 212
  visual, 17
Information processing, xxi, 17, 65, 76-78, 98, 102, 105, 116, 141, 170
Instructional technology, 186, 189, 194
Intelligence, 52, 64, 94, 115, 136, 142, 163, 171-172, 187, 203, 214
  artificial, xxiii, 186
  cognitive, 116
  emotional, 116, 135, 146
  interpersonal, 152
  intrapersonal, 152
  multiple, 7, 152
  social, 146, 152, 172
Interference, 65
  proactive, 6
  retroactive, 6
Interpersonal, xiii, 8, 11, 25, 110, 116, 120, 147, 151, 168, 179, 194, 211-213, 215
  acquisition, 154, 171
  automaticity, 159, 173
  communication, 176-177
  control skills, 11, 151, 154, 158-159, 161, 163

development, 151-152, 161-162, 165-168, 171, 176, 178, 215
environment, 120, 123
far term transfer, 163, 177
intelligence, 152
learning, 153, 168, 179, 195
near term transfer, 161, 174
relationships, 9, 165
schemes, 171-172
skills, 67, 164-168, 176, 178, 185
Institutionalization, 204
Instruction, xix-xxiii, 1, 3-4, 7-8, 10, 12-14, 16-19, 24, 26, 30, 33, 35, 38, 44, 46, 49-50, 53, 56-61, 63, 81, 83, 86, 92, 97-98, 104, 1118, 120-121, 124-126, 129-131, 135, 137, 139-141, 146, 152, 157, 162, 174, 183, 186-192, 194, 198, 200-204, 211, 213-214, 216-217
affective, 118
computer-assisted (CAI), 189
computer-based, 130, 138, 188, 194, 196, 198, 200-201
concept, 44, 61-63
Concept-Oriented Reading (CORI), 61
developer (designer), 7, 42, 117, 186, 198-199, 216
development, 145, 183, 199, 201, 216
design, xix, xxi, xxiii, 6-7, 16, 18, 66, 76, 87, 138, 188, 198-199, 201, 214
guidance, 27, 40, 47, 78, 118, 132, 140, 154, 187, 189-190, 202, 214
part-task, 83
reading, 13, 29, 34, 50, 65
social skills, 154, 156

strategies (techniques), xx-xiii, 8, 12, 32, 34-35, 43, 61, 91, 101, 139, 178, 196, 206, 211, 213
technology, 183, 186, 188-189, 194, 200, 206, 216
theorists, 7-8
theory, xxii-xxiii, 7
Knowledge, 1, 4, 7, 12, 14-18, 26, 30, 32, 34-35, 43-45, 48-49, 51, 53-64, 78-80, 86, 93, 97, 101-102, 105-107, 116, 122, 130, 137, 156, 164, 167, 170-171, 176, 178-179, 186, 188, 192-193, 195-196
activating background, 34-34, 47
application, 14
acquisition, 1, 5, 14, 18, 58-59, 97, 169, 211
conceptual, 5, 45, 51, 54-55
creation, 14
domains, xxiii, 5, 11-13, 23-24, 27, 31, 34, 39, 44-45, 63, 75, 115, 151, 213
explicit, 101
implicit, 101
organization, 15, 66
of Performance (results, KR), 2, 7, 76, 84, 86, 102, 104-105, 214
prior (existing), 2, 4-5, 13-14, 24, 32, 35, 40-41, 50-60, 65, 101, 213
strategic, 52
tacit, 179
text-based, 62
transfer of, 13, 51-52, 54, 136
Leadership, 161, 166-167, 172, 179, 189, 194
Development Program, 167
Institute, National (NLI), 167
Military, 166, 168, 178-179

skills, 11, 15, 154-155, 158-159,
    161, 163, 179
Learning,
    academic (school), 59, 131, 137,
        153, 215
    active, xxi, 24, 155, 213
    adult, xxiii
    affective, 115-117, 133, 214
    associative, 132-133
    authentic, xx, 3, 211
    to care, 156
    cognitive, 9, 57, 88, 172
    collaborative, 179, 188, 195
    Collaborative for Academic,
        Social, and Emotional
        (CASEL), 119, 130
    competitive, 140
    complex, 46
    comprehension, 56
    computer-based, 130, 138, 188,
        193, 195, 198, 200-201, 203
    conceptual, 7, 14, 26, 30, 41, 44-
        45, 50-51, 56-59, 61-65
    constructivist, xxi
    context-free, 128, 135
    cooperative, 11, 126, 140, 150,
        154, 156, 158-159, 161, 163-
        164
    definition of, 1, 76
    disabilities, xxiii
    discrimination, 133
    distance, 138, 188, 194, 198, 200-
        201, 204
    electronic, 205, 216
    emotional, 130-131, 152
    hyper-text, 46
    interactive, 155
    interpersonal, 153, 168, 179, 195
    language, 24
    modeled, 174
    motor, 77-78, 100, 104-105

    mulitmedia, 9, 42, 65-66
    multiple context, 60
    observational (imitative), 76,
        100-101, 151, 214-215
    operant, 12, 14, 48
    over-, 84, 86, 97
    part-task, 4, 11, 23, 27, 31, 34,
        39, 76, 82, 105, 214
    peer, 152, 175, 215
    perceptual, 18
    predictive, 133
    psychomotor, 6, 9, 76, 78, 86-87,
        93, 97, 105-106, 108-109
    re-, 80
    to read, 25, 30, 48, 52
    rote, 11-12, 18, 23, 26-27, 31, 34,
        39
    schematic, 45, 51, 135, 213
    situated, xx, 16, 53, 211
    social, xxii, 63, 130, 161, 164,
        169, 172, 174, 176-177
    stimulus-response, xxi
    strategic, 11, 13, 23, 26-27, 31,
        34-35, 39, 175
    strategy, deep, 130
    strategy, surface, 130
    task-oriented, 116, 214-215
    technology-based, 194
    theorists, xxii
    theory, xxii-xxiii, 5, 188
    transfer, 7, 13, 23, 25, 27, 31, 34,
        39, 213
    web-based, 135, 194
Mastery approach, 118, 126, 129,
    138, 143
Meaningfulness, 3, 7-8, 121
Mental rehearsal, 79-80
Media, 56, 155, 161, 169-170, 177,
    187, 194, 205
    hyper-, 193-194
    -logic, 199

multi-, 9, 42, 65-66, 130, 186-
187, 193-194, 198, 200
Meta-analysis, 57, 81-82, 98, 116
Meta-cognitive,
awareness, 39
development, 116, 128, 138, 211,
215
principles, 14
strategies, 27, 52, 91-92, 127-129
skill, 116, 118-119, 125, 127-128,
138-139, 215
Modeling, 35, 84, 88, 123, 151, 162,
164, 169, 172, 177, 179, 192, 215
Models, xix, 4, 8, 14, 45, 62, 93, 99-
101, 104, 108-110, 122, 161-162,
176, 194, 204, 206, 212
Morality, 118-119
Morse code, 13, 77-78, 85-86, 88-90,
95, 109, 214
Motivation, xxi-xxii, 7, 9, 11, 24, 39,
43, 47-48, 52, 54, 60-62, 78, 81,
85, 88, 92, 94, 98, 100, 115, 117-
120, 124-125, 127-129, 135-143,
146, 154, 172, 179, 185, 192,
198, 200-201, 215
process model, ARCS, 129, 138,
200
Non-examples, 30
Operant,
conditioning, 12, 14-15, 19, 48
learning, 12, 14, 48
principles, 18, 24, 213
Operationally defining, xxi, 1
Output, 4, 8, 17, 49, 77, 89, 102, 212
Peer, 41, 58, 60, 63, 110, 120, 122-
123, 126-127, 132, 152-156, 163-
165, 169, 172-176, 215
Persuasion, 11, 41, 151, 154, 159,
161, 163, 194
Play, 10-11, 25, 28-29, 52, 78, 77,
79, 84, 87, 91, 93, 95, 99, 104-

106, 109-110, 117, 122, 126, 155,
171, 214
cooperative, 11, 151, 154, 158-
159, 161-163
creative, 155
-er, 13, 92, 96-97, 107, 110, 187,
206
inactive, 155
pretend, 123
role-, 155, 157, 160, 162, 166,
215
unstructured, 154-155
Practice, 3, 7-8, 13, 15-16, 28, 30-31,
33, 35-36, 45, 47, 54, 79-86, 88, 93-
95, 97-98, 103-104, 106, 109, 152,
164, 169, 175, 190, 192
covert, 174
distributed, 42, 84, 103
drill and, 185, 188, 190, 203-204
guided, 101-102
massed, 103
mental, 81-82, 91-92, 98-99
overt, 76, 79, 214
physical (motor), 99, 109
reinforced, 1
repetitive, 11, 23, 27, 31, 34, 39,
76, 84, 86, 110, 214
whole-task, 102
Problem solving, xxii, 8-9, 11-14, 18,
23, 27, 31, 34, 39, 52, 54, 56, 60,
63, 66, 143-144, 158, 162, 186,
212
Process requirements, 12, 27, 31, 34,
39, 75, 79, 84, 87, 91, 109, 115,
119, 125, 127-128, 152, 154, 159,
161, 163, 168, 212-213
Project ACHIEVE, 159
Pro-social,
behavior, 153, 157, 172, 174, 177
skills, 11, 151, 154, 158-159,
161, 163, 169, 174, 176

Psychological factors, 78, 98
Psychomotor, xxiii, 8-9, 11, 25, 75-
    76, 92-93, 96, 100-101, 108, 110,
    116, 141, 152, 171, 192, 211-214
    acquisition, 79, 98
    automaticity, 84, 100
    far term transfer, 91, 105
    learning, 6, 9, 76, 78, 86-87, 93,
        97, 105-106, 108-109
    near term transfer, 87, 105
    skills, 67, 76, 78, 80, 92, 95, 97-
        98, 101, 109-110, 144, 214-
        215
Purposes, 196, 202
Questioning, 34, 36, 41, 45, 47, 49,
    51, 54-56, 58
    Self-, 35, 55
Reading, 5, 11-13, 15-16, 19, 23-25,
    47, 136-137, 158, 174, 189-193,
    213
    Activity Inventory (RAI), 64
    acquisition, 26-28, 47
    automaticity, 26, 31, 47, 190
    breadth of (amount of), 27, 63-65,
        190
    choral, 33
    comprehension, 34, 49, 51, 61,
        64-65, 192
    engagement, 27, 43, 60-61
    expressive, 31, 33, 49, 190
    far term transfer, 27, 39, 58, 192
    guided, 33
    independent, 64
    leisure, 64
    motivation, 60-62, 137
    near term transfer, 26, 34, 53, 192
    oral, 31, 33, 49, 190
    paired, 33
    Panel, National, 34, 47
    repeated, 33

    self-selected, 33
    skill, xxiii, 13, 28, 48, 58
    sight, 28, 190
    silent, 49, 65
    strategic, 13, 26, 51
    strategy instruction, 34
    storybook, 26, 28, 32, 65, 190
    for understanding, 19
    with technology, 41
Recognition, 14, 127, 152, 159
    auditory, 29
    character, 88-89
    error, 100
    letter, 12, 28-29
    -memory confidence, 178
    rote, 16
    sound, 28-29
    Tests, Author (ART), 64
    Tests, Title (TRT), 64
    word, 26, 28, 31-32, 47, 49, 190-
        191
Rehearsal, 7
    amount of, 3
    cognitive, 81, 98, 100
    imagery, 92
    mental, 79-80
    motor, 101
Reinforcement, 2, 7, 48, 133, 160-
    161, 215
    consistent, 6
    immediate, 24, 213
    inconsistent, 6
    positive, 140, 160-161
    self-, 58
    withdrawal of, 6
Relativism, xx
Repetition, 2-3, 7, 11-13, 23, 75, 107,
    109, 115, 151, 191, 213
Resources, 83, 172, 205
    community, 61

for parents, 120-121
technological, 187-188, 197
Retention, xxi, 2, 6, 19, 59, 78, 81,
    84-86, 88, 97-100, 201
Role models, 110, 161-162, 194
Schemas, xxi, 4-6, 11-16, 19, 23, 25-
    27, 31, 34, 39-41, 45-46, 51, 54-
    55, 59, 66, 88, 105-106, 128, 135,
    154, 165-166, 70, 172, 177-179,
    185-186, 192, 203, 213
Searching, 34, 36-37, 47
    for information, 54-56, 63
Self-, 8, 11, 34-35, 39, 54, 58-59, 61,
    63-64, 92, 110, 115-116, 119,
    121-122, 124-125, 127, 130, 134-
    136, 140, 143, 145, 153, 159,
    162, 171, 177-179, 185, 214-215
    awareness, 125, 136
    control, 11, 52, 82, 98, 115, 119,
        121, 125-128, 158
    competency, 116, 214
    determination, 11, 115, 119, 125,
        127-128
    efficacy, 61, 136, 162
    esteem, 116, 119-120, 122, 131,
        178
    fulfilling prophecy, 142
    -generating, 11, 13, 23, 27, 31,
        34, 39
    instructional guidance, 40
    monitoring, 5, 40, 47, 91-92, 101,
        129, 139
    questioning, 35, 55
    reflection, 11, 115, 118-19, 125,
        127-128
    regulatory (regulation), 11, 16,
        44, 47, 105, 115, 119, 125-
        130, 138, 140, 179, 214
    relational, 154, 174, 179
    social- (interpersonal), 168, 215

statements, coping (reinforcing),
    40
talk, 81, 91-92, 98, 102, 122, 129,
    160
Skills,
    adult interpersonal, 165, 178
    cognitive, 12-13, 25, 43, 47, 61,
        109, 115-116, 118, 120, 125,
        127-128, 138-139, 214-215
    distinguished from ability, 93
    interpersonal control, 11, 151,
        154, 158-159, 161, 163
    leadership, 11, 15, 154-155, 158-
        159, 161, 163, 179
    management, 11, 151, 154, 159,
        161, 163
    prerequisite, 4, 106
    pro-social, 11, 151, 154, 158-159,
        161, 163, 169, 174, 176
    psychomotor, 67, 76, 78, 80, 92,
        95, 97-98, 101, 109-110, 144,
        214-215
    self-regulatory, 11, 115, 119,
        125-128, 139
    social, 131, 153-161, 164-165,
        169, 172-175
    socialization, 11, 151, 154, 158-
        159, 161, 163
    word-decoding, 13, 26, 28-31, 47
Social,
    cognitive theory, 98, 100, 152,
        154, 161, 168
    competence, 154-155, 172-173
    cues, 146, 157
    experiences, early, 154
    habits, 11, 151, 159, 161, 163
    intelligence, 146, 152, 172
    interactionist theory, 170
    interactions, 28, 171
    learning, xxii, 63, 130, 161, 164,
        169, 172, 174, 176-177

learning theory, 172, 176
networks, 152, 176, 215
processing model, 170
psycho-, 132
self, 168, 215
skills, 131, 153-161, 164-165,
     169, 172-175
stories, 157
Socialization, 11, 151, 154, 158-159,
     161, 163, 172
Spiral curriculum, 16, 18-19, 50, 78,
     128, 135, 141
Spirituality, 118
Story grammar, 34, 38, 47
Summarizing, 34, 37, 40, 55, 57, 68
Task, xx, xxii-xxiii, 2, 12, 14-16, 19,
     30
analysis, xxii, 79, 101-102, 214
authentic, 8
closed, 85, 98, 109
continuous, 84, 96
discrete, 96
open, 25, 85, 109
part-, 4, 11, 22, 27
Taxonomy, 1, 6, 8, 10-19, 23, 74, 76,
     93, 95, 100, 108-110, 115, 151,
     211, 213-214
Teams, 8, 11, 44, 63, 151, 159, 164
Technology, 41, 119, 138, 185-187,
     193
instructional, 186, 189, 194
integration, 183
     developer guidance, 196
Templates, 151, 165, 170, 177, 179,
     198-199, 215
Text, 51
structure, 34, 41, 50
Training, xix, xxiv, 1-2, 4, 6, 25, 41-
     43, 58, 78, 81-90, 92, 96-98, 102,
     108-109, 164-165, 167-168, 175,

179, 187-190, 197, 202, 204, 213,
     217
Transfer, xi, xxiv, 1-4, 6, 18-20
and affective domain, 115
     near term, 127, 135
     far term, 128, 135
and cognitive domain, 23
     near term, 26, 34
     far term, 27, 39
and interpersonal domain, 151
     near term, 161, 174
     far term, 163, 177
and psychomotor domain, 75
     near term, 87, 105
     far term, 91, 105
taxonomy, definition of (near and
     far term), 11
and technology, 192-196
Transformation, 8-9, 17, 61-62, 167,
     188, 205, 212
Trust, 120-121, 132, 160, 170-171
Understanding, Teaching or Reading
     for, 25, 32, 58
Values, xxi, 119, 120, 122, 131, 134,
     145, 147, 165, 170, 172, 197
Varied examples, 106, 192
Visual demonstration, 80, 83, 99
Vocabulary, 31, 190
Word decoding, 26, 29-30